The Lives of the English Regicides: And Other Commissioners of the Pretended High Court of Justice, Appointed to Sit in Judgement Upon Their Sovereign, King Charles the First, Volume 1

Mark Noble

21621

2

THE
LIVES

OF THE

ENGLISH REGICIDES,

AND OTHER

COMMISSIONERS

OF THE PRETENDED

HIGH COURT OF JUSTICE,

Appointed to fit in Judgment upon their Sovereign,

KING CHARLES THE FIRST.

By the Reverend MARK NOBLE, F. A. S. of L. and E.

RECTOR OF BARMING, IN KENT, AND
DOMESTIC CHAPLAIN TO GEORGE EARL OF LEICESTER.

IN TWO VOLUMES.

VOL. I.

LONDON:

PRINTED FOR JOHN STOCKDALE, PICCADILLY.

1798.

DEDICATION.

TO THE

REGICIDES OF *FRANCE.*

GENTLEMEN,

It is ufual on this fide of the water to dedicate our volumes to thofe who, from fome peculiar circumftances, they are moft appropriate. None of my friends can have any claim upon me to fubfcribe this work to them—I crofs the channel, and give them to the world under your names; more tremendous ones cannot be found.

You have copied the worft tranfaction recorded in our annals; and have the fupreme infamy of having far exceeded thofe whofe lives are here given:

A 2

Preparatory to the murder of your own gracious fovereign, you printed the mock trial of our unhappy monarch. You will now alfo fee, as a prelude to your own fate, that of King Charles I.'s judges.

GENTLEMEN, you may learn, from perufing thefe volumes, that if any of you, actuated either by a fincere repentance, by a real wifh to ftop the farther effufion of Gallic blood, or defire to procure your pardon, the enjoyment of what you have obtained, you may, like fome of the Englifh Regicides, make your peace by tendering your influence in bringing back your KING. By doing which you can only efcape having your names loaded with all that deteftation which has attended fuch of thefe, your wicked preceptors, who neglected the only mean of averting fo dreadful a misfortune.

Wishing you the spirit of repentance, and that so sincere and effective as to obtain the pardon of God and man, of your exiled virtuous sovereign, and of the King of kings,——in doing thus, I cannot better evince to you, that, though I detest your crimes,

I am,

Gentlemen,

Your real Friend,

The AUTHOR.

5th Jan. 1798.

A 3

PREFACE.

EUROPE in the middle of the laft century faw one of the moft ancient and moft illuftrious thrones overturned, and the mighty monarch who had fat upon it ignominioufly led from a prifon, to a pretended tribunal, and from thence hurried to a premature grave. In thefe our days we have witneffed the fame deplorable tragedy, a cataftrophe that has ftained the annals of France, and its effects crimfoned the chriftian hemifphere; thefe two fad difafters

A 4

will be deplored as long as the hiftoric page remains.

In writing the memoirs of the Cromwells, I made many minutes of thofe men's lives, who dared to fteep their hands in their fovereign's blood; the prefent day demands of all men to hold up their crimes, and their punifhment, to fhew the deferved deteftation their contemporaries and pofterity did, and ftill do, entertain for them and their memories.

Their hiftories are an awful leffon to the regicides of France, and to an abandoned faction at home who are linked with them in intereft and affection. " There is a way that " feemeth good unto a man, but the end there- " of is death." Every true Briton in vindicating the juft prerogatives of his fovereign protects his own rights, for by fo doing he defends the conftitution.

In writing thefe lives I have feparated the man from the crime : I have traduced none, how guilty foever ; I have fpoken from the plaineft facts. I have written of them not from what their enemies have given us, but chiefly from the public records, from ftate papers, from fuch authorities that cannot be called in queftion. To give my authorities to every circumftance would have been ufelefs ; fuch who have read my memoirs of the Cromwells, will fee whence I have taken my materials ; and to what appears there may be added many topographical and other books. It may here however be remarked that the authority is often given in the body of the work.

Some of the commiffioners of the high court of juftice, as it was impioufly called, have been noticed in the Cromwell memoirs ; what is here given of them is mentioned only, to make the prefent volumes the more perfect, unlefs new information could be detailed, and which often is the cafe.

Thefe characters now offered to the public, include, with thefe in the work juft fpoken of, moft of the remarkable ones which occur amongft the republican party during the ufurpation.

Thefe kingdoms were ruined by religious fanaticifm, by hypocritical pretences to piety. France by an open contempt for all revelation.

Let us guard our religion, our laws, and our country, and then we may bid defiance to hofts of canting devotees, and legions of pretended philofophers.

Let us be content with enjoying the RIGHTS of the gofpel, and the juft and equal laws of the land, and never barter them for the tinfel de-

corations of the modern regicides, nor the fanctified profligacy of the former ones. Let us
be content with God's mercies to us, a favoured
people, and ftrive by holinefs and virtue, to
merit ftill greater.

CONTENTS.

VOL. I.

LIVES OF

CONTENTS.

LIVES OF

INTRODUCTION.

IT will be impossible for the reader to understand the subsequent pages without first giving him some idea of the circumstances which occasioned the crime of regicide. I shall, therefore, compendiously mention the facts which preceded that dreadful crime, and also what was chiefly done in the different days that the pretended High Court of Justice sat; subjoining also the names of those LEGAL Judges before whom the regicides were brought at the restoration, with some other matters relative to them.

The House of Commons, January 3, 1647-8, resolved, that no farther addresses should be made to the king by themselves, nor by any other, without leave of both Houses of Parliament, and those that did should incur the penalty of High Treason; and they declared they would receive no more messages from his majesty, and enjoined, that no person whatsoever should receive, or bring any message from him, to both or either of the Houses, or to any other person; and on January the fifteenth following, the Lords concurred in these votes.

VOL. I.   B

On the feventeenth of Auguft 1648, the Commons agreed with the Peers, that thefe votes for non-addreffes fhould be revoked.

On the twentieth of November 1648, the army prefented their remonftrance to the Parliament, for bringing delinquents to juftice.

On the twenty-fourth of the fame month, the treaty of the Ifle of Wight was voted to continue until the twenty-feventh.

On the firft of December Denzil Hollis, Efq., afterwards Lord Hollis, prefented an account of the treaty with the king.

On the fame day the Parliament received information of his majefty's being removed from Carifbrook Caftle to Hurft Caftle.

On the fifth of this month the king's anfwer to the propofitions furnifhed a ground for the Houfe to proceed upon, for the fettlement of the peace of the kingdom.

On the next day, the members who were known averfe to the intereft of the army, and would not affift in deftroying the king, were prevented from going to the Houfe of Commons, and many of them imprifoned.

On the feventh of this fame month the Houfe of Commons, garbled as it was, appointed a day of humiliation, preparatory to their infamous wickednefs, and felected Hugh Peters, Caryl, and Marfhal, to perform this hypocritical fervice.

The Commons voted, that the revoking their former votes " for non-addreffes to the king, for a treaty to be opened with his majefty, and that his anfwers to the propofitions were a ground for peace," were difhonourable and deftructive.

On the twenty-third a committee was appointed to confider how to proceed, in a way of juftice, againft the king, and other capital offenders.

On the twenty-eighth an ordinance for trial of the king was read.

On January the firft, 1648-9, it was declared and adjudged by the Commons, that by the fundamental laws of the land it is treafon in the king of England, for the time being, to levy war againft the Parliament and Kingdom.

On the following day, the Lords difagreed to this vote, and threw it out, and the ordinance for trial of the king, *nemine contradicente.*

On the next day, the fame vote was again put to the queftion in the garbled Houfe of Commons, and carried in the affirmative.

On the fourth of January, Mr. Gurland prefented a new ordinance for erecting an High Court of Juftice for trial of the king, which was read the firft, fecond, and third time, affented to, and paffed the fame day, and ordered that no copy fhould be delivered.

Same day it was refolved, that the People are, under God, the original of all juft powers.

That themfelves, being chofen by, and reprefenting, the People, have the fupreme power in the nation.

That whatever is enacted or declared for law by the Commons in Parliament, hath the face of a law, and the people concluded thereby, though

B 2

the confent of the King and the Peers be not had thereunto.

On the fixth of that month, the commiffioners for the trial of the king were ordered to meet upon Monday following, at two o'clock, in the Painted Chamber.

The days of fitting of the High Court of Juftice were the eighth, tenth, twelfth, thirteenth, fif-teenth, feventeenth, eighteenth, nineteenth, twen-tieth, twenty-fecond, twenty-third, twenty-fourth, twenty-fifth, twenty-fixth, twenty-fe-venth, and twenty-ninth of January.

They met in the Painted Chamber on Monday, January the eighth, when they chofe Mr. Afke, Dr. Doriflaus, Mr. Steel, and Mr. Cooke, coun-cellors; Meffrs. Greaves and John Phelps, clerks; Meffrs. Edward Walford, John Powel, John King, Phineas Payne, and — Hull, meffengers.

They alfo fent out their precept under their hands and feals for proclaiming their court in Weftminfter-Hall, to be held in the Painted Chamber on the tenth of that month: which precept is all in Mr. Ireton's hand-writing.

On Tuefday the ninth, the commiffioners or-dered that proclamation fhould be made in Cheap-fide and in the Old Exchange; and APPOINTED A COMMITTEE to confider of the matter of govern-ment, about making a new great feal; and refpec-ing the not ufing the name of a fingle perfon.

On Wednefday the tenth, they chofe Meffrs. Walford and Vowell, ufhers; and Mr. Litchman, a meffenger; Serjeant Bradfhaw, then abfent, was elected prefident; they alfo appointed Mr. Say, who was prefent, prefident, *pro tempore*, until Bradfhaw fhould attend. The commiffioners, at the fame time, thanked Mr. Garland for the great pains he had taken about the bufinefs of the court. Mr. Greaves was excufed from attending, becaufe engaged in other avocations for the public, and for that reafon Mr. Andrew Broughton was appointed in his room. Afke, Steel, Dorislaus, and Cooke, were named council for the Commonwealth; Steel to be attorney, and Cooke, folicitor. Meffrs. Love, L'Ifle, Millington, Garland, Marten, Thomas Challoner, Sir John Danvers, and Sir Henry Mildmay, or any two of them, were nominated to conduct the carrying on the bufinefs of preparation. Dendy, their ferjeant, certified to the commiffioners his having made due proclamation; who, in reward, appointed him their ferjeant at arms during the trial, and gave Mr. John King the office of cryer to the court. The doors were then thrown open, proclamations were thrice made, and the abfent commiffioners were ordered to be fummoned.

On Friday the twelfth, Serjeant Bradfhaw profeffed to decline being prefident, but his apology was not accepted: and Broughton and John Phelpes, gentlemen, were conftituted clerks, and ordered to attend. Leave was given to fearch all public offices for papers and books, with power to fend for, and command every perfon they judged neceffary, to attend. Sir Hardrefs Waller and Colonel Harrifon were ordered to defire the

Lord General to appoint fufficient guards. Cols.
Titchbourne and Rowe, aud Meffrs. Blackftone
and Fry were deputed to fee that the trial fhould
be performed in a folemn manner; and they were
permitted to appoint workmen. At this time
Mr. Love made his report from the fecret com-
mitee, and, in confequence, fome regulations
were agreed upon. Sir Hardrefs Waller, Colonel
Whaley, Mr. Scot, Colonel Titchbourne, Colonel
Harrifon, Lieutenant-General Cromwell, and
Colonel Deane, were appointed to confider of the
place of trial, and make their report the next day.
The charge againft the king was ordered to be
brought in on Monday.

On Saturday the thirteenth, the court fat privately, when the Serjeant at Arms was ordered to
appoint other meffengers, he giving in their
names. The vaults under the Painted Chamber
were directed to be fearched for fear of any fecret
treachery towards the commiffioners. Upon Mr.
Garland's report, it was decreed that the trial of
the king fhould be where the courts of King's
Bench and Chancery Courts were in Weftminfter-
Hall.

On Monday the fifteenth, the council brought
in a draught of the charge againft the king; when
power was given to Commiffary-General Ireton,
Meffrs. Millington and Marten, Colonel Harvey,
Mr. Challoner, Colonel Harrifon, Meffrs. Miles,
Corbet, Scot, Love, L'Ifle, and Say, or any
three of them, to advife, and compare evidence,

and to meet the next morning at eight o'clock in the queen's court.

Also ordered, that Colonels Ludlow, Purefoy, Hutchinson, Scroop, Deane, Whalley, Huson, Pride, Sir Hardress Waller, and Sir William Constable, together with the committee for making preparations for the trial, or any three of them, should be a committee to consider of the place where the king should be kept during his trial, with other things relative to it, and they were directed to meet the next day, at eight o'clock in the morning, in the Inner Star Chamber. Mr. L'Isle was at this time ordered to move the House of Commons to adjourn the term for a fortnight.

On Thursday the sixteenth, Titchbourne delivered a petition to the Commons, in the name of the Commons of London, in common council, differing from the Lord Mayor and Aldermen: the substance of which was, a wish that the king might be brought to justice, which was ordered to be registered in the books of the common council.

On Wednesday the seventeenth, the charge against his majesty was re-committed to the committee. The absent members of the court were summoned to attend, who resided within twenty miles of the capital. Upon the report of the committee, appointed to consider of the manner of the trial, it was concluded upon, amongst a variety of other circumstances, that the king should be lodged at the house of Sir Robert Cotton, and the Lord President at Sir Abraham Williams's houfe, in the New-Palace Yard ; that Sir Henry Mildmay, and Mr. Holland, and Mr. Edwards, fhould provide every thing neceffary for both the king and the prefident. It was obfervable that it was alfo ordered, that "all back doors from the Houfe, called HELL, fhould be fhut up during the king's trial." John Humphreys, Efq. was ordered to bear the fword before the Lord Prefident.

Afterwards the court fat private, when they ordered that their committee fhould meet the next morning at eight o'clock, in the Exchequer Chamber.

On January the eighteenth, Colonel Titchbourne excufed the abfence of Mr. Steel, who pleaded indifpofition, which was, he fent word " a great affliction to him, as he wifhed to manifeft his affection to the caufe."

On Friday the nineteenth, Colonel Hutchinfon from the committee, reported refpecting the habits of the officers, when three gowns were ordered for the three ufhers, and three cloaks for the three meffengers. Mr. Millington reported the charge and form of words for exhibiting it, which the attorney, or, in his abfence, the folicitor fhould do. The fergeant at arms was at this time ordered to fecure Mr. Squibb's gallery.

On Saturday the twentieth, in the forenoon, the court ordered that Sir Henry Mildmay fhould deliver the fword of ftate to Mr. Humphreys, that it might be borne before the Prefident. The folicitor prefented the charge, engroffed, which

being read and figned by him, was returned to
him to be exhibited, and the commiffioners then
adjourned to Weftminfter Hall.

The court fat private, when it was ordered
amongft other things, that if the prifoner fhould,
in language or carriage towards the court, be in-
folent, outrageous, or contemptuous, that the
Lord Prefident fhould have power to reprehend
him; but it was decreed, that the prifoner might
be excufed for putting off his hat that day.
Mr. L'Ifle and Mr. Say, by the Lord Prefident's
defire, were to affift him, and for that purpofe
were ordered to fit near his perfon.

Weftminfter Hall. On Saturday the twentieth,
in the afternoon, the king was brought in to this
mock court by Colonel Tomlinfon, attended by
Captain Hacker, and thirty-two partizans, when
Cooke exhibited the charge; but his majefty, not
owning their authority, he was remanded, and
the court adjourned until Monday. As the unhappy monarch returned, it was remarked that
the people cried out GOD SAVE THE KING.

Painted chamber. On Monday the twenty-fecond, in the forenoon, the commiffioners paffed
a vote, approving what their prefident had done
on Saturday, and they refolved, that the king
fhould not be fuffered to queftion their jurifdiction.

Weftminfter Hall. The fame day, in the afternoon, Cooke prayed that the king be directed to
anfwer, and if he refufed, that the matter of the

charge be taken *pro confeſſio*. His majeſty this day, not owning their authority, was remanded.

Weſtminſter Hall. On Tueſday the twenty-third, in the afternoon, his majeſty, when brought before the commiſſioners, not owning their authority, was again remanded, and the court was adjourned to the Painted Chamber, and it was then reſolved that witneſſes againſt the king ſhould be examined.

Painted Chamber. On Wedneſday the twenty-fourth, the court ſpent their time in examining witneſſes.

Thoſe who were produced againſt their ſovereign were,

Henry Hartford, of Stratford upon Avon, in Warwickſhire.

Edward Roberts, of Biſhop's Caſtle, Shropſhire, ironmonger.

William Braynes, of Wixhall, in Shropſhire, gentleman.

Robert Lucy, of the town and county of Nottingham, painter.

Robert Loades, of Cottam, in Nottinghamſhire, tailor.

Samuel Morgan, of Wellington, in Shropſhire, felt maker.

James Williams, of Roſs, in Herefordſhire, ſhoemaker.

Michael Potts, of Sharpereton, in Northumber-land, vintner.

Giles Gryce, of Wellington, in Shropſhire, gent.

William Arnop, not examined.

John Vinſon, of Damerham, in Wiltſhire, gent.

George Seely, of London, cordwainer.

Thomas Ives, of Boyſel, in Northamptonſhire, huſbandman.

James Croſby, of Dublin, in Ireland, barber.

Thomas Rawlins, of Hanſlop, in Buckinghamſhire, gentleman.

Richard Bloomfield, citizen and weaver of London, aged 35.

John Thomas, of Llangollen, in Denbighſhire, huſbandman, aged 25.

Samuel Lawſon, of Nottingham, maltſter, aged 30.

John Pyneger, of the pariſh of Fainer, in Derbyſhire, yeoman.

George Cornwal, of Aſton, in Herefordſhire, ferryman, aged about 50.

Thomas Whittington, of the town and county of Nottingham, ſhoemaker, aged 22.

William Jones, of Uſke, in Monmouthſhire, huſbandman, aged 22.

Humphrey Browne, of Whitſondine, in Rutlandſhire, huſbandman, aged 22.

Arthur Young, citzen and barber, chirurgeon of London, aged 29.

David Evans, of Abergavenny, in Monmouthſhire, ſmith, aged 23.

Diogenes Edwards, of Carſton, in Shropſhire, butcher, aged 21.

Robert Williams, of the pariſh of St. Martin, in Cornwall, huſbandman, aged 23.

John Bennett, of Harwood, in Yorkſhire, glover.

Samuel Burden, of Lyneham, in Wiltſhire, gent.

William Cuthert, of Patrington, in Holdernefs,
    Yorkfhire, gentleman, aged 42.

John Moore, of the city of Cork, in Ireland,
    gentleman.

Thomas Read, of Maidftone, in Kent, gent.

Henry Gooche, of Gray's Inn, in Middlefex,
    gentleman *.

At the fame time Meffrs. Millington and Thomas Challoner were ordered to go to John Brown,
Efq. clerk of the Houfe of Peers, to fearch for
papers in his cuftody.

Painted Chamber. On Thurfday the twenty-
fourth, in the afternoon, the court examined another witnefs,

Richard Price, of London, Scrivener.

Mr. Thomas Challoner at this time produced
fome of the king's letters. After which, the
court fat private; when it was refolved to proceed
to fentence of condemnation againft their fovereign, and that this fhould be decreed for his being " a tyrant, traitor, murderer, and public
enemy to the commonwealth," and alfo that this
condemnation fhould be extended to death.

And it was ordered that a fentence, grounded
upon thefe votes, be prepared by Meffrs. Scot,
Marten, Colonel Harrifon, Mr. L'Ifle, Mr. Say,
Commiffary-general Ireton, and Mr. Love, or
any three of them; but a blank was ordered

---

* Thefe witneffes were generally royalifts, who had ferved in
the army of his majefty, but were now compelled to appear at his
pretended trial.

to be left for the manner of the royal fufferer's death.

It was decreed at this court that fummonfes fhould be iffued to fuch members as were abfent.

Painted Chamber. On Saturday the twenty-feventh, in the forenoon, the fentence having been ingroffed, the court refolved, that the fame fhould be what was to be read and publifhed in Weftminfter Hall the fame day.

That the prefident fhould not permit the king to fpeak after fentence.

That after the fentence fhould be read, he fhould declare it to be the fenfe and judgment of the court.

That the commiffioners fhould, to fhew their confent, all ftand up.

The fame day the Commons ordered the clerk to bring in the records of that judgement to the Houfe.

Weftminfter Hall. The fame day, in the afternoon, the king being brought in, and not owning their authority, the fentence was read.

Upon the declaration of the prefident that it was the judgement of the court, the commiffioners ftood up and owned it, and adjourned to the Painted Chamber.

Whilft there, they appointed Sir Hardrefs Waller, Colonel Harrifon, Commiffary-general Ireton, and Colonels Dean and Okey, to confider of the time and place for execution.

This day the king, by the procurement of the officers, was grofsly infulted by the foldiers and

rabble in coming to, and in returning from, Weſtminſter Hall, but ſilently pitied and lamented by
the people.

Painted Chamber. On Monday the twenty-
ninth, upon the report of the committee, it was
ordered that a warrant ſhould be drawn for executing the king, in the open ſtreet, before Whitehall, the next day, and the court directed it ; Colonel Francis Hacker, Colonel Hunks, and Lieutenant-colonel Phayre, which was done accordingly.

It was alſo ordered, that Colonel John White,
or any other officer in the Tower, in whoſe poſſeſ-
ſion it was, ſhould deliver " the bright execution
axe for the executing malefactors."

Painted Chamber. On January the thirtieth,
in the forenoon, it was ordered that Meſſrs. Mar-
ſhall, Nye, Caryl, Salway, and Dell, be deſired
to attend the king, to adminiſter to him thoſe
ſpiritual helps which were ſuitable to his condition, and Lieutenant-colonel Goffe was directed
to give them notice.

The king told them, that as they had often ſo
needleſsly preached againſt him, they ſhould not
now, in his agony, pray with him, but if they
pleaſed, they might pray for him, and he would
be obliged to them. Biſhop Juxon gave the royal
ſufferer the conſolations of religion.

It was ordered that the ſcaffold ſhould be cove-
red with black. This, not having been before
thought of, made a delay, and kept the unhappy
ſovereign at Whitehall, where he heard the noiſe

of the hammers in completing the fad preparations.

Thus was a mighty monarch of three nations publicly murdered in his own capital before one of his own palaces, at two o'clock in the afternoon.

Painted Chamber. The fame day in the afternoon Colonel Harrifon, Colonel Okey, Mr. Carey, (Carew) Colonel Deane, Mr. Allen, Mr. Scott, Colonel Titchbourne, Mr. Holland, Colonel Wanton, Colonel James Temple, Colonel Ludlow, Mr. Mayne, Colonel Rowe, or any five of them, were authorifed to give warrants for the payment of fuch fums of money as fhould be adjudged neceffary, through the hands of Captain John Blackwell; and Colonel Titchbourne was directed to take particular care of it.

On January the thirty-firft it was ordered by the Commons, that Lord Grey, out of Haberdafhers' Hall, fhould difpofe of the fum of one hundred pounds for the fervice of the Commonwealth.

Painted Chamber. On February the firft it was ordered, that Lieutenant-Colonel Goffe, Colonel Ewers, Colonel Pride, Sir Hardrefs Waller, together with the reft of the committee of accounts, fhould be appointed to take the examination of William Evans, gentleman, and of all others, for words, or actions done, or fpoken againft the court, with power to examine papers, letters, or writings.

Painted Chamber. On the fecond it was ordered, that Captain Blackwell pay fuch fums as were ftill owing for expences relative to the court, and that the next morning he fhould deliver in an exact account to the committee at Whitehall.

John Hall, upon the evidence of Thomas Maurice, William Hitch, and Thomas Baxter, were committed to the cuftody of the Marfhal-General of the army, for having been in a defign againft the court.

As were Mr. Nelfon and Mr. Evans, upon the evidence of John Minfhaw, Mary Minfhaw, John White, and John Haydon, clerk; and Colonel Moore was appointed to acquaint the Houfe therewith.

The Lord Prefident moved that the guards be paid for their careful fidelity, and their cheerfulnefs in attending.

Colonel Titchbourne reported, that the committee had confidered of what gratuity fhould be given to every officer and attendant of the court; which being approved of, Colonel Harrifon was ordered to move the Houfe to fatisfy the fame.

Mr. Garland, Mr. L'Ifle, Sir Hardrefs Waller, Mr. Say, Commiffary-general Ireton, Mr. Marten, and Mr. Scott, or any three of them, were ordered to perufe and confider of the fubftance of the court's proceedings, and prepare them to be prefented to the Houfe of Commons; and Mr. Say was ordered to prefent it.

By the expiration of the month, the time, in the act of parliament, limited for the commiffion to hold the High Court of Juſtice, it became a non-entity, after completing the nefarious purpoſes for which it was inſtituted.

On the ſame day the Houſe of Commons ordered that, in the firſt place, ſhould be taken into conſideration, and debate of the Houſe of Lords, for a ſettlement of the government.

On the ſixth, the Houſe, containing only ſeventy-three members, had this queſtion argued, "Whether that Houſe ſhould take the advice of the Houſe of Lords in the exerciſe of the legiſlative power?" when the Houſe dividing, it was carried in the negative by fifteen voices.

And it was then reſolved, that "the Houſe of Peers was uſeleſs and dangerous, and ought to be aboliſhed;" and they ordered that an act ſhould be brought in for that purpoſe.

On the ſeventh, the Commons declared that "the office of a king in a nation, and to have power thereof in a ſingle perſon, was unneceſſary, burdenſome, and dangerous to the liberty, ſafety, and public intereſt of the people, and therefore ought to be aboliſhed."

On the ninth, it was ordered, that the narrative of the proceeding, and records for trial of the king, be forthwith brought into the houſe.

On the ſixteenth, it was ordered, that the clerk of the High Court of Juſtice ſhould be deſired to bring in thoſe proceedings to their houſe the next day.

On March the ——— Sir Arthur Heſelrigge reported from the committee, that Charles and

James Stuart, fons of the late king, fhould die without mercy, wherefoever they fhould be found.

On December the twelfth, 1650, Mr. Say reported to the Houfe of Commons the proceedings of the High Court againft the king, contained in a book entituled, " A Journal," &c., which was read at large by their clerk.

He likewife prefented from that court the act for trial of the king, and the precept for holding the court. The charge was exhibited the twentieth, and the fentence read the twenty-feventh of January 1648 ; and thereupon the Houfe declared,

" That the perfons inftructed in that great fervice had difcharged their truft with great courage and fidelity :

" That the Parliament was well fatisfied in that account of the particulars and proceedings."

And the Houfe ordered, that " the fame records do remain amongft the records of Parliament ; that thofe proceedings be engroffed in a roll, and recorded amongft the parliament rolls, for tranfmitting the memory thereof to pofterity."

And the Houfe refolved, that " their commiffioners for the great feal iffue a certiorari to their clerk to tranfmit thofe proceedings into the Chancery, there to be on record.

" And that the fame be fent by mittamus from thence to other courts at Weftminfter, and the cuftos rotulorum of the counties, to be recorded."

I have now ftated the whole of this moft criminal proceeding againft the fovereign : I fhall next as concifely fhew how, when the kingdoms were reftored to their legitimate government, thofe chiefly implicated in the crime of murdering the king were brought to juftice, at leaft fuch of them as could be feized.

On February the twenty-firft, one thoufand feven hundred and fifty-nine-fixty, General Monk came to Whitehall attended by the fecluded members, to whom he gave a guard to introduce them again into the Parliament; upon which the chief of the independent faction withdrew.

On the fixteenth of March, the long parliament, in derifion called the Rump, releafed all the royalifts; repealed the oath of abjuration of Charles Stuart, and all the royal family; appointed a new council of ftate; made great changes in the London militia; abrogated the engagement to be true and faithful to the commonwealth without a king, or houfe of peers; and then diffolved themfelves, fummoning in their room a free parliament, compofed of a Houfe of Peers, and a Houfe of Commons.

On the twenty-fifth of April both Houfes of Parliament met in Weftminfter Abbey; and after hearing a fermon went to their refpective Houfes, and each chofe their fpeaker.

On the firft of May Sir John Granville prefented his Majefty's gracious letters and declarations to the two Houfes of Parliament, and others to the General and Admiral; upon which the Houfes voted, that the government ought to be by King, Lords, and Commons; at the fame time the Houfe of Commons voted the fum of fifty thoufand pounds for his Majefty's immediate ufe.

On the third, the city of London and the fleet declared for the king.

On the feventh, the late fovereign's ftatue was fet up again in Guildhall, and the Commonwealth's arms were taken down.

On the eighth, the king was folemnly proclaimed, at which both Houfes of Parliament affifted, both in London, and at Weftminfter : this was accompanied with a univerfal joy, fuch as had never been known; and it fpread through every part of the kingdom, each perfon congratulating his friend and his neighbour in the hope of fpeedily being relieved from anarchy, confufion, flavery, and every kind of impiety, which had been practifed under the mafk of a fanctified hypocrify.

On the twenty-fifth, the king and his brothers landed at Dover, and his majefty was met by General Monk, whom he raifed and embraced.

On the twenty-ninth, the monarch made his triumphal entry into London; and it being his majefty's birth day the rejoicings were doubly great.

On the thirty-firft, both Houfes of Parliament accepted the pardon offered by the king in his declaration, dated at Breda.

On June the firft an act paffed conftituting the convention a parliament.

On the fixth a proclamation was iffued to command the Regicides to furrender themfelves within

fourteen days, under the penalty of being excluded out of the act of indemnity.

Some of the chief republicans demanded the
king's particular letters of pardon, which were
granted to all of them who were not immediately
concerned in the murder of his royal father.

On the twenty-ninth of Auguſt his majeſty in
perſon paſſed the Bill of Indemnity, out of which
were excepted for life and eſtate theſe perſons :
Thomas Challoner, Eſq. Colonel Owen Rowe,
Auguſtine Garland, Eſq. Colonel Harvey, Henry
Smith, Eſq. Henry Marten, Eſq. Sir Hardreſs
Waller, Knt. Colonel Adrian Scroop, John Carew,
Eſq. Robert Titchbourne, Alderman, Colonel
James Temple, Colonel Peter Temple, Colonel
Thomas Wayte, Simon Mayne, Eſq. William
Haveningham, Eſq. Colonel George Fleetwood,
Alderman Iſaac Pennington, Colonel Robert Lil-
burne, Gilbert Millington, Eſq. Vincent Potter,
Eſq. and John Downes, Eſq. Theſe had ſur-
rendered themſelves. Colonel Scroop and Mr.
Carew were excluded the benefit of the act, by
which, in caſe they were attainted, execution
ſhould be ſuſpended, till the king, and the par-
liament ſhould order it.

Theſe were excepted abſolutely as to life and
eſtate, Sir Michael Liveſey, John L'Iſle, Eſq.
Lieutenant General Edmund Ludlow, William
Say, Eſq. Commiſſary General Edward Whalley,
Major General Thomas Harriſon, William Cawley, Eſq. Daniel Blagrave, Eſq. Cornelius Holland, Eſq. Gregory Clement, Eſq. Thomas Scot,

Efq. Miles Corbet, Efq. Nicholas Love, Efq. Colonel Valentine Wanton, Colonel John Okey, Colonel John Hewfon, Colonel William Goffe, Colonel John Jones, Colonel John Dixwell, and Thomas Wogan, Efq.

And thefe who had not been Judges, but officers in the Court. John Cooke, Efq. Edward Dendy, Efq. Serjeant at Arms, Andrew Broughton, William Hewlet, and Mr. Hugh Peters; who was the moft infamous reptile that ever pretended to be a preacher of the gofpel.

The following Judges were attainted, though dead : Oliver Cromwell, Efq. Henry Ireton, Efq. Colonel Ifaac Ewer, Colonel William Purefoy, Colonel John Alured, Colonel Richard Deane, Colonel Thomas Horton, Major-General Philip Skippon, John Bradfhaw, Efq. Prefident, Colonel Thomas Hammond, Colonel Thomas Pride, Sir John D'Anvers, Sir Thomas Mauleverer, Sir William Conftable, Sir John Bourchier, Sir Gregory Norton, John Blakefton, Efq. Francis Allen, Efq. Peregrine Pelham, Efq. John Venn, Efq. Thomas Andrews, Efq. Anthony Stapley, Efq. and John Fry, Efq. All their eftates, goods, rights, and trufts were forfeited.

The following were excepted from receiving any benefit from their eftates, and fubjected to fuch farther punifhments, as fhould be inflicted upon them. Sir Henry Mildmay, Sir James Harrington, Robert Wallop, Efq. Lord Monfon, James Challoner, Efq. and Mr. John Phelps.

Sir Henry Vane, Sir Arthur Heſelrigge, and Major-General Lambert, were, as very dangerous and obnoxious characters, alſo excepted out of the act.

John Hutchiſon and Francis Laſſels were made incapable of exerciſing any office, and condemned to one year's forfeiture of the income of their eſtates.

October the ninth, the Regicides were indicted at Hicks's Hall.

On October the tenth, Sir John Robinſon, Knt. Lieutenant of the Tower, in compliance to the warrant directed to him, delivered to the Sheriffs the priſoners, who were in ſeveral coaches, with a ſtrong guard of horſe and foot, conveyed to Newgate, and about nine o'clock in the morning they were delivered to the keepers of that priſon, and thence brought to the Seſſions Houſe in the Old Bailey, London, where the Commiſſioners of Oyer and Terminer were in the Court aſſembled, and where their indictment was publicly read, by Edward Sheldon, Eſq. Clerk of the Crown.

The Commiſſioners were,

Sir Thomas Allen, Knt. and Bart. Lord Mayor of London; Sir Edward Hyde, afterwards Earl of Clarendon, Lord High Chancellor of England; the Earl of Southampton, Lord Treaſurer of England; the Dukes of Somerſet and Albemarle; the Marquis of Ormond, Steward of his Majeſty's Houſehold; the Earls of Dorſet, Berkſhire, and Sandwich; Viſcounts Say and Sele; Lords Robartes and Finch; Denzil Hollis, Eſq.

(afterwards Lord Hollis); Sir Frederic Cornwallis, Knt. and Bart. Treasurer of his Majesty's Household; Sir Charles Berkley, Knt. Comptroller of his Majesty's Household; Mr. Secretary Nichols, Mr. Secretary Morris; Sir Anthony Ashley Cooper, (afterwards Earl of Shaftesbury), Sir Orlando Bridgeman, Lord Chief Baron; Justices, Sir Robert Foster, Knt. Sir Thomas Mallet, Knt. Chief Justice of the King's Bench, Sir Robert Hyde, Knt. Edward Atkins, as Baron of the Exchequer; Thomas Twisden, Justice of the King's Bench; Thomas Tyrrel, a Justice of the Common Pleas; Christopher Turner, a Baron of the Exchequer; Sir Harbottle Grimstone, Knt. and Bart. Sir William Wild, Knt. and Bart. Recorder of London; Mr. Serjeant Brown, Mr. Serjeant Hale; John Howel, Esq. Sir Jeffery Salmer, his Majesty's Attorney-General; Sir Heneage Finch, his Majesty's Solicitor-General; Sir Edward Turner, Attorney to his Highness the Duke of York; and Wadham Windham, Esq. Edward Shelton, Esq. Clerk of the Crown.

The Grand Jury were, Sir William Darcy, Bart. Sir Edward Bowles, Bart. Sir Edward Ford, Knt. Sir Thomas Prestwick, Sir William Coney, Knts. Sir Charles Sidley, Bart. Sir Lewis Kirk, Knt. Sir Henry Littleton, Bart. Sir Ralph Bovey, Bart. Edward Chard, Esq. Robert Giddon, Esq. John Fotherly, Esq. Charles Gibbon, Esq. Thomas Geree, Esq. Richard Cox, Esq. Robert Bladwell, Esq. Henry Mustian, Esq. John Markham, Esq. Edward Buckley, Gent. Francis Bourchier, Gent.

Edward Loleand; and—Hart was Crier of the Court.

The witneſſes were William Clark, Eſq. James Nutley, Eſq. Mr. George Maſterſon, Clerk, George Farringdon, Hercules Hunks, Dr. William King, Martin Foſter, John Baker, Stephen Kirk, Richard Nunnelly, John Powel, John Throgmorton, John Blackwel, Ralph Hardwick, Thomas Walkley, Gent. Holland Simpſon, Benjamin Francis, Colonel Matthew Tomlinſon, Mr. Lee, Robert Ewer, John King, Griffith Bodurdo, Eſq. Samuel Boardman, Robert Carr, Eſq. Richard Young, Sir Purbeck Temple, John Ruſhworth, Eſq. John Gerrard, John Hearn, Mr. Coitmore, Mr. Cunningham, Mr. Clench, William Jeſſop, Eſq. Edward Auſtin,——Darnel, Eſq. Mr. Brown, Thomas Tongue, John Bowler, Mr. Sharp, Edward Trolley, Mr. Gouge, and Anthony Mildmay, Eſq.

This day Sir Hardreſs Waller, Thomas Harriſon, William Haveningham, Iſaac Pennington, Henry Marten, Eſqrs. Gilbert Millington, Gent. Robert Titchbourne, Owen Rowe, Robert Lilburne, Adrian Scroop, John Carew, John Jones, Thomas Scot, Gregory Clement, John Cooke, Edmund Harvey, Henry Smith, John Downes, Vincent Potter, Auguſtine Garland, George Fleetwood, Simon Mayne, James Temple, Thomas Waite, Eſqrs, Hugh Peters, Francis Hacker, Eſq, and Daniel Axtel, Eſq. were arraigned.

On the eleventh, being the following day, Thomas Harriſon, Adrian Scroop, John Carew, John

Jones, Gregory Clement, and Thomas Scot, challenging their jury, were tried feparately. Harrifon was this day found guilty, and fentence was paffed upon him.

On the twelfth, Meffrs. Jones, Scroop, Scot, Clement, and Carew, were again brought to the bar, but challenging their jury, only Mr. Scroop and Mr. Carew were tried and convicted. Mr. Clement confeffed the fact, and Mr. Jones was convicted.

On the fourteenth, Meffrs. Cooke, Peters, Hacker, and Axtel, were fet to the bar, and the two former convicted.

On the fifteenth, Major-general Harrifon and Mr. John Carew, were executed at Charing Crofs, fronting the Banquetting Houfe, where the late King had been inhumanly and traitoroufly murdered.

On the fame day, Meffrs. Axtel, Hewlet, alias Howlet, againft whom an indictment had been found, October 12, at Hicks's Hall, were tried, as was Colonel Francis Hacker.

On the fixteenth, Meffrs. Pennington, Marten, Millington, Titchbourne, Rowe, Lilburne, Smith, Harvey, Downes, Potter, Garland, Mayne, J. Temple, P. Temple, and Wayte, were tried, all of whom were found guilty.

Meffrs. Cooke and Peters were executed this day.

On the feventeenth, Meffrs. Scot, Clement, Scroop, and Jones, were put to death.

On the nineteenth, Mr. Haveningham received sentence of death.

And on the same day, Meffrs. Axtel and Hacker were executed at Tyburn.

On the eighth of December, both Houfes of Parliament ordered that the bodies of Cromwell, Bradfhaw, Ireton, and Pride, fhould be hung upon the gallows at Tyburn, and afterwards buried under it.

On the thirtieth of January, 1660-1, this was carried into execution, except the omiffion of dragging the corpfe of Pride out of his refting place; the heads of the others were fet upon Weft-minfter Hall.

On the eleventh of May, the remains of the loyal and heroic Marquis of Montrofe, were buried with uncommon folemnity in Scotland.

On the twenty-fecond, the folemn League and Covenant was burnt in London and Weftminfter by the common hangman, and afterwards in every part of England.

On the twenty-eighth, the writing called the Acts for the trial of his late Majefty King Charles I. the Engagement againft a King and Houfe of Peers; the Declaration publifhing that England was erected into a Commonwealth; the renunciation of the title of Charles Stuart, and the bill for the fecurity of the Lord Protector's perfon, were all burnt by order of the Parliament in Weftminfter Hall, by the public executioner, whilft the courts were fitting.

On the feventh of June, the funerals of Sir Charles Lucas, and Sir George L'Ifle, were folemnly celebrated at Colchefter; thefe gentlemen had been publicly fhot for their heroic loyalty.

On July the twelfth, the eftates of the deceafed regicides were by Parliament confifcated. Lord Monfon, Sir Henry Mildmay, and Mr. Wallop, were ordered to be led to the gallows at Tyburn, and confined in the Tower for life; but they were firft to confefs their crimes at the bar of the Houfe of Commons.

On the twentieth of November, the Spiritual Lords took their feats in the Houfe of Peers.

On the twenty-fifth of that month, the regicides who came in upon the proclamation were brought to the bar of the Houfe of Lords to anfwer what they could fay for themfelves, why judgement fhould not be executed againft them, upon which they feverally alledged, that " upon his majefty's gracious declaration from Breda, and the votes of Parliament, and his majefty's proclamation, publifhed by the advice of the Lords and Commons then affembled in Parliament, they did render themfelves, being advifed that they fhould thereby fecure their lives; and humbly craved the benefit thereof, and the mercy of the Houfes, and their mediation to his majefty in their behalves."— Harry Marten brifkly fubjoined to this fubmiffion, that " he had never obeyed any proclamation before this, and he hoped he fhould not be hanged for taking the king's word now."

Great oppofition was made to their having a pardon, a bill for their execution having been read twice; but at length it was dropped, and they were fent to feveral prifons, and but very little more heard of.

On the nineteenth of April, 1662, Meffrs. Miles Corbet, John Okey, and John Barkftead, three of the regicides, were executed at Tyburn, having been brought up to the King's-Bench bar, and their perfons fworn to.

On the fixth of June Sir Henry Vane was convicted.

On the ninth of June General Lambert was convicted, but reprieved.

On the twenty-fourth of that month Sir Henry Vane was beheaded.

On the twenty-fourth of January, 1662-3, Archibald Johnfon, Lord Warrefton, was brought to England, and on the thirty-firft fent to the Tower, and thence tranfmitted to Edinburgh, where he was executed according to the fentence of Parliament on a gibbet twenty-two feet high, as having been the chief incendiary of that kingdom.

Such is the journal of thefe proceedings of the king's violent death, and the punifhment of fuch of his judges who furvived the reftoration, fhortly taken from their rife until their clofe.

The monarchy fuffered a total overthrow by thefe violent men, chiefly perfons in the army ; and as no nation can for any length of time be governed by the military without total ruin, fo thefe kingdoms at length faw their imminent danger, and threw off a yoke which was become intolerable, and were reinftated in the bleffings of peace and order, by the reftoration of that happy conftitution, which is the pride, the glory, and the only fecurity of Britons.

I fhall only add, that fo extremely infamous was the very name of the High Commiffion become, that the Parliament wifhed to put every perfon to death who had fat in one; but this fanguinary meafure was defeated chiefly through the mercy of King Charles II., and it was only enacted that fuch who had given fentence of death in any of them fhould be difabled from being members in any Parliament, or bearing any office in England or Wales. Colonel Ingoldfby and Colonel Tomlinfon, two of the regicides, for their particular merits, were, however, excepted out of this bill of penalties and difabilities.

THE

LIVES

OF THE

ENGLISH REGICIDES,

&c.

The Life of JOHN BRADSHAW, *Efq.*

Lord Prefident of the High Court of Juftice.

JOHN BRADSHAW, Efq. was a gentleman of
a very antient and refpectable family in the county
of Lancafter, but of a branch that was feated in,
or near Namptwich, in Chefhire. Of his parents
much has been written, but I am not certain they
have been identified.

He was a ftudent of the law in Gray's Inn, but
he had not been much noticed in Weftminfter
Hall, though he had confiderable chamber practice, efpecially from the partizans of the Parliament, to whofe intereft he was extremely devoted;
he was not, fays Lord Clarendon, without parts,
but of great infolence and ambition: he had re-

ceived little patrimonial inheritance, but he had acquired some fortune by his own reputation and prudence.

The first public duty I find him employed in, was in October 1644, when he was appointed by the Parliament to prosecute Lord Macquire and Macmahon, the Irish Rebels; he was joined in this business, of which the Parliament was extremely solicitous, with Mr. Prynne and Mr. Nudigate. Lord Macquire was condemned and executed.

We hear nothing more of him until October 8, 1646, when he was joined with Sir Rowland Wandesford, and Sir Thomas Beddingfield as Commissioners of the Great Seal for six months, by a vote of the House of Commons, in which the Peers were desired to acquiesce; we must suppose that this employment was procured him through the influence of some of his great clients in the House of Commons, and it led him to still farther promotion; for February 22, 1646-7, both Houses voted that he should be Chief Justice of Chester, an office no doubt peculiarly agreeable to him, as he was a native of a place so near that city. Mr. Chute became Commissioner of the Great Seal at the expiration of the time for which he had been named in one of the Parliament ordinances; but he was appointed instead of it, one of the Welch Judges, which I believe he held with his post at Chester.

He was named by the Parliament, June 27, 1647, of the Council to prosecute the loyal and virtuous

Judge Jenkins, a perfon held in univerfal efteem with all good men; he did not decline this odious office, any more than St. John, Jermyn, or Prynne.

At a call of Serjeants October 12, 1648, by order of the Parliament, he was voted to receive the coif, together with Sir Thomas Weddrington, Sir Thomas Beddingfield, Mr. Keble, and Mr. Thorp, from Gray's Inn. At the fame time five gentlemen of Lincoln's Inn, three of the Middle Temple, and three of the Inner Temple, had the fame degree conferred upon them.

When the army had decided in their private meetings to deftroy the king, that they might give all the little fanction they could to it, to make it appear a legal act, their Committee, who were in-tirely under the influence of the military commanders, appointed that the Serjeants Bradfhaw and Nichols, with Mr. Steel, fhould be affiftants; this was fo determined on the third of January, 1648-9, fo that at this time Mr. Bradfhaw was only intended to take an inferior part in this ne-farious bufinefs; but the Judges, though of their own appointment, too well knew the fpirit of the Conftitution to dare to act; neither could they prevail upon Serjeant Nichols to give attendance.

It was for this reafon that the Commiffioners in their fitting held in the Painted Chamber, January the tenth, chofe Serjeant Bradfhaw, who was one of their number, to be Lord Prefident; but he not being prefent, they appointed Mr. Say to that of-fice pro tempore, and until he fhould attend the fervice.

VOL. I.   D

At this diftant period it is not poffible to deter-
mine whether Mr. Bradfhaw had afpired to this
pre-eminence in wickednefs, or even knew that
there was any idea of electing him to it ; but
there is moft reafon to fuppofe that he was neither
ignorant of their intentions, nor averfe to the
office, becaufe had he declined it, as there were
none more daring, it might have been refufed by
every other gentleman of the profeffion.

Upon fpecial fummons he attended the Court
January the twelfth, and according to the former
order, called to take his place of Prefident, when
he made an earneft, though probably an hypocritical, apology to be excufed ; but not prevailing,
in obedience to the commands and defires of the
Court he fubmitted to their order, and took his
place as fuch.   The Court thereupon ordered,
" that John Bradfhaw, Serjeant at Law, who is
" appointed Prefident of this Court, fhould be
" called by the name, and have the title of Lord
" Prefident, and that as well without as within
" the faid Court, during the Commiffion and
" fitting of the faid Court." He then and every
fucceeding day took the chair as prefident.

Lord Clarendon tells us " that when he was
" firft nominated he feemed much furprized, and
" very refolute to refufe it ; which he did in fuch
" a manner, and fo much enlarging upon his own
" want of abilities to undergo fo important a
" charge, that it was very evident he had expected
" to be put to that apology.   And when he was
" preffed with more importunity than could have

" been ufed by chance, he required time to con-
" fider of it," and faid ' he would then give
" his final anfwer,' which he did the next day;
" and with great humility accepted the office,
" which he adminiftered with all the pride, im-
" pudence, and fupercilioufnefs imaginable."

If this ftatement of his Lordfhip's is accurate
Mr. Bradfhaw had been previoufly fpoken to
about the place he was to fill; but the Journals
of the Court do not notice it.

Never was an individual raifed in a moment to
fuch a fituation as this man; who was inftantly
from a private gentleman, elevated to a moft unufual
pre-eminence; twenty officers or other gentlemen
were appointed to attend him, going and returning from Weftminfter Hall. He had lodgings
provided for him in Sir Abraham Williams' houfe,
in the New Palace-yard during the fitting of the
Court; and Sir Henry Mildmay, Mr. Holland,
and Mr. Edwards had the office to fee that every
thing that was neceffary was provided for him, as
they were alfo for the Royal Prifoner; he was preceded by a fword and a mace, carried by two gentlemen, with all other officers of an inferior nature around him, and the twenty-one gentlemen
that were near him, carried each a partizan; and
he had in the Court two hundred foldiers for a
farther guard. He had a chair of crimfon velvet
in the middle of the Court, with a defk, upon
which was laid a velvet cufhion: he wore his hat
when his majefty appeared, and was highly of-
fended that his fovereign fhould not be uncovered

in his prefence. The " offence" was pardoned
the firft day of the King's appearance, but order
was taken refpecting it in future ; but the daunt-
lefs monarch conducting himfelf with real dignity, did not condefcend to the infolence of his
fubject, though his pretended judge.

Overcome with vanity, he behaved to fallen majefty with a rudenefs that thofe who prefide in our
criminal courts never ufe to the loweft culprit.
It is not my defign to follow him through a mock
trial which is difgraceful to our annals : it is fufficient to obferve that the King would not own
what the Commiffioners had no pretence to, any
jurifdiction over him, their Sovereign, and that he
as Prefident had the audacity to pafs fentence of
death upon the king as a traitor, tyrant, murderer,
and public enemy to his country, and ordered him
to be executed by decapitation, and by a warrant,
which he as Prefident, figned firft ; this was carried into effect to the regret of the whole kingdom, if we except the army and a very few others.

The Lord Prefident was not gratified only by
the fplendour which furrounded him during the
trial ; he obtained a fortune which the longeft fervices of his profeffion would not have gained
him ; the Deanery Houfe in Weftminfter was
given him as a refidence for himfelf and his pofterity, and the fum of five thoufand pounds allowed him to procure a fuitable equipage, pro-
portionate to his new fphere of life, and fuch as
the dignity of his office demanded ; " and now,"
fays Lord Clarendon, " the Lord Prefident of

" the High Court of Juftice feemed to be the
" greateft Magiftrate in England. And it was
" not thought feafonable to make any fuch de-
" claration, yet fome of thofe whofe opinion grew
" quickly into ordinances, upon feveral occa-
" fions, declared that they believed that office
" was not to be looked upon as neceffary pro hac
" vice only, but for continuance; and that he
" who executed it, deferved to have an ample and
" liberal eftate conferred upon him for ever.
" Which fudden mutation and exaltation of for-
" tune could not but make a great impreffion
" upon a vulgar fpirit, accuftomed to no exceffes,
" and acquainted only with a very moderate
" fortune.".

This gentleman, now become tremendous from
his office, was regarded with univerfal terror, alike
courted and dreaded by all; even Archbifhop Williams, the late Lord Keeper, ftooped to folicit his
protection. His compliances demanded all he was
pleafed to afk, or wifh, and as his new office did
not expire with the king's trial, the parliament,
February the fixth, permitted him to make a deputy in Guildhall where he fat as a Judge; and he
was elected on the fourteenth of that month one
of the thirty-eight members of the Council of
State, amongft whom were the Earls of Denbigh,
Mulgrave, Pembroke, and Salifbury; and Lords
Gray, Fairfax, General Lord Grey of Groby, and
L'Ifle, the heirs apparent to the Earls of Stamford and Pembroke, who all degraded their per-

fons and nobility by joining in the ufurpation; and raifed to be Lord Prefident in the High Court of Juftice, it is not to be wondered at that Brad-fhaw fhould afpire to, or that he fhould be in-dulged in, the fame poft in the Council; and this " new man" took precedency of thefe ancient and potent peers.

His firft attendance upon this Council was March 10, 1648-9, where he feemed, fays Mr. Whitlock " but little verfed in fuch bufinefs," and fpent much of the Members' time by his own long fpeeches.

Upon the twelfth of that month he was made Chief Juftice of Wales; but he did not go thither immediately, for on the twentieth he fat again in the Council as Lord Prefident, and here again Mr. Whitlock remarks, he " fpent much of their time in urging his own long arguments, which are inconvenient in ftate matters;" " his part," fays that gentleman, " was only to have gathered the fenfe of the Council, and to ftate the queftion, not to deliver his own opinion." Thefe circum-ftances evince that Lord Clarendon well knew, though not perfonally, the character of this ex-traordinary man.

The parliament ordered that the fum of one thoufand pounds fhould be paid to him June 19, 1649, and the fame day referred it to a committee to confider how lands of inheritance of the yearly value of four thoufand pounds fhould be fettled upon him, and his heirs.

On July the 20th he was appointed Chief Juſtice of Cheſter, and Mr. Hull the ſecond judge of that city.

The parliament paſſed a bill, July the 15th, ſettling two thouſand pounds a year upon him and his heirs; and, on the 24th following, granted him another two thouſand pounds per annum, to him and them, probably the ſum formerly voted to him; theſe were eſtates belonging to the Earl of St. Alban's and Lord Cottington; and an exact ſurvey was ordered to be made of theſe lands.

On the 28th of the ſame month, an act paſſed, conſtituting him Chancellor of the Duchy of Lancaſter; and when ſeveral places were aboliſhed, this was retained merely on his account, and, April 2, 1652, they ſecured it to him.

Few royal favourites have been ſo much enriched, and ſo ſuddenly: Republicans can be as prodigal of the public purſe to their friends, as the moſt laviſh monarch could to his chief and moſt valued courtier.

He was again named of the Council of State, in the years 1650 and 1651; and in both he retained the Preſidency.

Hitherto he had proceeded in a career of power and ſplendour, wealth and conſequence, that aſtoniſhed all, and probably ſurpriſed none more than himſelf; but, when Cromwell ſeized the government, a very different ſcene preſented itſelf. None could be more obnoxious to Oliver, than the man who had ſat in judgment upon his liege Lord, to whom, on every account, he owed alle-

giance. What was a usurper to expect from such
a character? Bradshaw, who had violated the most
sacred duties, to cut off his lawful sovereign, and
change the government, could ill brook the idea
of having a superior placed over him, who, by
birth, was little more than his equal. He was sensible too, that he must appear odious in the eyes
of a supreme magistrate, who would always sus-
pect him ; nor could he be pleased to see another
eclipse him in pomp and splendour, the glare of
which had greatly attracted his attention, and of
which he was not a little vain.

Proscribed as he was by the exiled King, as the
most obnoxious of all his subjects, he could the less
be satisfied to have another master near him, to
whom he would be nearly as odious. He was conscious he was not, nor ever would be, trusted by
the Protector.

Therefore he resolved to counteract the dissolu-
tion of the republican government all he could ;
and when General Cromwell had in so furious a
manner dissolved the Long Parliament, in the
morning of April 20, 1653, he determined to take
his place at the Council of State, with many other
members, in the afternoon, thinking, perhaps,
that his person would overawe the farther designs
of Cromwell.

But he who had gone such lengths was not to
stop short in his aim for the sovereignty. Taking
Lambert and Harrison with him, he went to the
Council, and, at his entrance, addressing them,
said, " Gentlemen, if you are met here as private

" perfons, you fhall not be difturbed; but if as a
" Council of State, this is no place for you ; and,
" fince you cannot but know what was done at
" the Houfe in the morning, fo take notice that
" the parliament is diffolved."

To which the haughty and ferocious Judge of
a King, full of indignation, replied, " Sir, we
" have heard what you did at the Houfe in the
" morning, and before many hours all England
" will hear it : But, Sir, you are miftaken to
" think that the parliament is diffolved, for no
" power under heaven can diffolve them but
" themfelves ; therefore, take you notice of
" that."

He already thought he had Oliver before the
murderous tribunal, at which he had prefided;
but the ftern General had to back his authority
what the monarch, at his fad hour, wanted, a victorious army. Therefore, after fome faint fpeeches
of Sir Arthur Hefelrigge, Mr. Love, and Mr.
Scot, the Council, like the Parliament, were obliged to quit their fituation and retire.

Cromwell paid fo much attention to him as to
continue all outward marks of refpect; but he
knew, that though his name was put in the Affembly that was to meet relative to a fettlement of
the government, it was only a compliment; and
he therefore did all he could to obftruct the defigns of this artful man; efpecially by fhewing
his ambitious aim to the younger members.

Oliver, until he had fecured the fovereignty,
continued to pay him the moft flattering refpect

and attention; that done, they feparated with mutual coolnefs.

The Protector expected every homage and attention from the higheft as well as the loweft, and infifted upon every one taking out a commiffion from himfelf, if they chofe to retain their places under his government; but, when the Lord Prefident appeared, he abfolutely refufed, alledging, that he had received his commiffion, as Chief Juftice of Chefter, to continue *qumdiu fe bene gefferit*, and he fhould retain it without any other, unlefs he could be proved to have juftly forfeited it by want of integrity; and if there were any doubts upon it, he would fubmit it to trial, by twelve Englifhmen; and foon after fet out on the circuit without waiting farther orders; nor did Oliver think it prudent to prevent or recall him, as he had faid, nothing but force fhould make him defift from his duty. This highly exafperated the Protector, who fent a letter to Chefter, to requeft that the Lord Prefident might be oppofed by every mean, in the enfuing election for that city. This he did that it might put a particular difgrace upon him; but it had not the effect intended; the letter by fome means came into the hands of his friends, who publicly read it at Chefter; and he had there fo many, whom he had an influence over, that he was returned a Member for the county by the Sheriff; but others, in the Cromwellian intereft, returning another, neither fat, becaufe it had been fo decided in cafe of double returns.

What indignation muft the man who had dared to adjudge his fovereign feel ; he boiled with vengeance ; he entered into a confpiracy againft the author of his difgrace ; the plan of which was to feize General Monk, then Major-General ; Overton was to have drawn three thoufand foot, with fome horfe, into the field, and foon after to have marched for England, where he and Sir Arthur Hefelrigge were to have joined them, with very confiderable forces ; and Vice-Admiral Lawfon was to have declared in their favour, with a fquadron of the fleet ; Colonels Pride, Cobbit, Afhfield, Lieutenant-colonels Mafon, Michel, and Wilkes, with feveral others, were engaged in the plot ; and there were declarations printing to fpirit up the people, who were to affift in reftoring the commonwealth.

This fcheme blew over, and no notice was taken of it by the Protector, who, to keep up fome fhew of regard to him, on September 16, 1653, had it enacted by Parliament, that the continuance of the palatinate power of Lancafter fhould be vefted in him, and this was but the year fucceeding that in which he had engaged in this defign. Each watched the other with the moft fedulous attention : in the arts of policy and hypocrify Cromwell had no fuperior.

The Lord Prefident, defeated, yet not defpairing of his revenge, purfued his aim, and to accomplifh it the better, united himfelf, in 1656, to the violent deteftable faction of thofe who called themfelves Fifth Monarchy-men, but not openly ;

thefe fanatics fuppofed, that "now was the time "for deftroying and pulling down Babylon and "its adherents, and the faints muft do it, who "were to bind kings in chains; and it was to be "done by the fword." With thefe defpicable men did he hold correfpondence, telling Okey and Goodgroom, two of them, that "the Long "Parliament, though under a force, were the fu- "preme authority of England;" and he carried on his projects in the city, which, as well as the other defign, were known to his Highnefs; who, not daring to feize this great incendiary, continued to watch and defeat his defigns. A new parliament was to be fummoned, and he could not think of having him in it; for the Republicans looked up to his opinion as a law to them, and nothing could have reftrained them in parliament. Major-general Bridge was therefore ordered to prevent his return for Chefhire. This was done, however, with great difficulty, for he had a decided intereft in the county, and even amongft thofe whom the Protector had appointed his commiffioners. He loft his election in London, which he had aimed at; and, to crown all his mortifications, he was deprived of his favourite office of Chief Juftice of Chefter.

Thefe mutual difgufts muft have been fatal to one of them, if either durft openly have avowed themfelves a decided enemy to the other; but each waited for the exact moment to ruin the other, which, however, never took place, from the caution of both. Their hatred was vifible to all;

Mutual Hatred of Cromwell Bradshaw + Cromwell.

and Mr. Whitlock fays, that in November, 1657, " the diflike between them was perceived to in- " creafe."

· We may fuppofe, that whenever Oliver faw him, it recalled to his mind the worft action of his life; and he well knew the pleafure Bradfhaw would have in paffing the fame fentence upon him as he had upon the king; and Bradfhaw never faw him, we may prefume, but he fighed for an oppor- tunity to convince the world that he was no re- fpecter of perfons, nor regarded names, but to publicly evince, that a fingle perfon, by whatever title known, was inimical to him.

Fortunately for him, the Protector died the fol- lowing year, and his fucceffor was too weak and feeble to injure him. Richard being laid afide, and the Long Parliament reftored to the fo- vereignty, he obtained a feat in the Council of State, was elected Lord Prefident, and appointed, with Serjeants Fountain and Tyrrel, Commiffioner of the Great Seal. This was on June 3, 1659; and on the following day, the two latter took the oaths, and received the feals; but, on the 21ft of that month, he was ordered by the Parliament to take them. He now feemed to be regaining all his former dignity; but his health, which had been fome time declining, became fo precarious, that he wrote to obtain leave to decline the duties of that important office, and in confequence of it, they excufed his attendance as a commiffioner during his indifpofition.

The army had again put a force upon the House of Commons, by feizing the Speaker, Lenthal, as he was going thither, and by it fufpended all farther proceedings of the then exifting government. Bradfhaw felt the infult; and, ill as he was, knowing that the Council of State fat that day, he repaired to it, that he might do all he could to ferve the caufe of the Republic; and, when Colonel Sydenham, one of the members of the Council, endeavoured to juftify the army in what they had juft done, and concluded his fpeech, by faying, according to the cant of the day, that they were neceffitated to make ufe of this laft remedy by " a particular call of the Divine Providence;" " weak and extenuated as he was, yet animated," fays Ludlow, " by his ardent zeal, " and conftant affection to the common caufe, he " ftood up, and interrupting him, declared his ab- " horrence of that deteftable action; and telling " the Council, that being now going to his God, " he had not patience to fit there to hear his great " name fo openly blafphemed." He then abruptly left them, retired to his lodgings, and withdrew from public employment.

He furvived this but a few days, dying November 22, 1659, of a quartan ague, which had held him a year. " A ftout man," fays Whitlock, " and learned in his profeffion: no friend to mo- " narchy;" and, fo little did he repent of the wickednefs of his conduct towards his fovereign, that, " he declared, a little before he left

" the world, that if the king were to be tried and
" condemned again, he would be the firſt man
" that ſhould do it."

Notwithſtanding the diſtractions of the times,
he was buried with great funeral pomp, in Weſt-
·minſter-Abbey, from whence his body was dragged, at the reſtoration, putrid as it was, to be ex-
poſed upon a gibbet, with thoſe of Cromwell and
Ireton. Had he ſurvived a little longer, he would
have paid the forfeiture of his life for his then unparalleled wickedneſs. It was ſingular, that Mr.
Row, who preached his funeral ſermon, took his
text from Iſaiah, ", *The righteous man periſheth,*
" *and no man layeth it to heart; and merciful men*
" *are taken away,*" &c.

In the life of this perſon, we ſee no one prominent
feature to intereſt, much leſs to pleaſe us; a bold
and daring ſpirit, that was unawed by divine or human juſtice, or at leaſt a miſtaken unbounded zeal
for liberty, is all that we find in his character; but,
that one bred to the law, and confeſſedly conver-
·ſant in it, ſhould ſo far miſtake, as to think he
could arraign and condemn his ſovereign, and
thoſe illuſtrious unfortunates who had fought to
reſtore him, is not to be believed; riches, honours,
·falſe ambition, all came in, and drowned his reaſon. As to his calling upon the name of the Lord,
relative to the army's laſt violence, or his declaration at his death, it little ſignifies. He was a
friend to the army when they laid their ſword
upon the parliament, which led to his exaltation;
and had he been in health, and that act could again

have reinftated, or augmented his power, he would
have been equally lavifh in his praifes, as he had
been on the former account. His laft declaration
only evinces, that riches and honours, power and
confequence, were more valuable in his eye, than
all the rewards of righteoufnefs in another world ;
and that he had dreaded even mediocrity with a
good confcience, more than eternal torments,
though thefe torments were juft commencing. If
he was fincere in thinking he had done right,
which might be thought abfolutely impoffible, it
is no excufe ; for falfe principles will carry a man
as far as the moft juft and holy. The moft impious blafphemer may die with as much courage
and zeal as the moft pious martyr. To tena-
cioufly hold a wicked principle, is not true conftancy, nor to die for it, heroifm.

There is an engraved portrait of him, by M.
Vandergucht, 8vo. from an original painting;
large hat, which he wore at the King's trial,
which is in Afhmole's Mufeum at Oxford; it
fhews what dangers he apprehended, as it is well
guarded within with iron. There is another,
partly fcraped, partly ftipped; large 4to. He is
fuppofed to have communicated fome old evi-
dences to Marchimont Nedham, to be inferted in
his tranflation of Selden's Mare Claufum.

His marriage I have never been able to know.
His kinfman and heir, juft before the reftoration, was driven from Founthill-houfe by the
heir of Lord Cottington, it having been part
of what the parliament had given the regi-

cide. It was, I prefume, Richard Bradfhaw, Efq. who was fent by the Protector Oliver to Hamborough, and afterwards Ruffia, and other Northern courts; and this I think very evidently to keep him as a pledge, in cafe it was neceffary; he let him conftantly be in want of money, and the government greatly indebted to him, that he might be obliged to remain whitherfoever he placed him. This gentleman poffeffed great abilities, and his letters in Thurloe's State Papers give us fome of the beft information we can obtain during the time he was employed in thofe Northern regions. In a letter to Secretary Thurloe, dated from Axe-yard, Nov. 1, 1658, being then juft returned to this kingdom, he requefted that the fum of 2188l. 0s. 9d. fhould be paid him, as due from the government; in his letter he ftates fome curious circumftances relative to himfelf.

He tells Mr. Thurloe, that in 1648, he was receiver of the crown revenue in North Wales and Chefhire for the ftate, and that coming to pafs his accounts, and pay in fome money to Mr. Fauconberg, the Receiver General, he had the misfortune to have his lodgings in King-ftreet, Weftminfter, broke open, the fame day that the apprentices rofe in London, and came down to Whitehall; and 430l. was taken out of his trunk, in the chamber where he lay. And though it was a time of great diftraction, yet by means of the warrants, and the affiftance of Mr. Fauconberg, he apprehended the culprits, and they were condemned at the Old Bailey, as Mr. Compton

knew, they being fons of perfons of note in Co-
vent Garden; that it was a bufinefs of the greateft
trouble he ever experienced, and with the lofs of
100l. and that before he could get his accounts
paffed in the Exchequer, where he expected this
money would have been allowed, he was commanded to Hamburg; and in his petition to the
Council of State, praying to be paid the full fum
of 2188l. 11s. 4d. he fays, that he had fuffered
the lofs of above 5000l. in the late wars of this
nation, without any reparation for the fame, and
had for above feventeen years freely expofed his
life at home and abroad in the fervice of the State;
that the fum was difburfed out of his affection to
his country, whilft he refided a public minifter in
foreign parts, and if not paid, he fhould be now
at his return rent from his fmall eftate, it being
more than he hath got in the fervice of the Commonwealth. The Council, March 9, 1659-60,
directed it to be paid, and on the twelfth his accounts were ordered for that purpofe to be laid
before the Parliament. He urged his petition
again to Thurloe, in letters dated the 23d and
31ft, but probably it was never paid, and from
the Prefident's attainder, it is moft likely he was
ruined. Catherine his wife wrote once to Thurloe, whilft he was abroad to thank him, for in-
troducing her to the Protector. The Refident
every where was treated with contempt and fcorn
by the Englifh, and often by foreigners, becaufe
he was the Lord Prefident's relation.

The Life of Sir WILLIAM AIRMINE, Bart.

SIR WILLIAM AIRMINE, of Ofgodby, in the county of Lincoln, was created a Baronet by King James I. November 28, 1619, in the life-time of his father, Sir William Airmine, of that place, Knight.

He early declared for the caufe of the Parlia-ment, who placed the greateft confidence in him, naming him one of their Commiffioners to attend the King, when his Majefty went towards the Scots; but his real office was that of a fpy upon the actions of his fovereign, whilft the royal army lay before Newark in 1645; and upon the news of Lord Fairfax having been defeated in the North, the Parliament in great fear fent him, with Sir Henry Vane, junior, and two others, with Mr. Marfhall and Mr. Nye, puritan divines, to defire the brethren of Scotland would inftantly come to their affiftance. It was an office that the Earl of Rutland avoided fharing, by pleading indifpofi-tion, and Lord Grey of Wark refolutely declined, though he was imprifoned in the Tower for his difobedience to their mandate.

He alfo affifted at fome of the conferences for peace as one of the Parliament Commiffioners; he was appointed, with others, in 1646, to receive the King at Holdingby, but this he declined. He was alfo named of the Committee for the parts about Kefteven, the fouth-weft divifion of Lin-colnfhire.

Obedient as he had been to the Parliament, and though he had taken the Proteſtation, yet he avoided committing himſelf in the King's death, never attending any of the ſittings in the High Court of Juſtice, though named one of the Judges. This however did not make him forfeit the good opinion of the uſurping powers, who knew his conſequence with all around him, and his ſincere averſion to the royal cauſe. For theſe reaſons he was elected a Member of the Council of State in the years 1649-1650 and 1651. I have not ſeen the time of his death.

By Elizabeth, daughter of Sir Michael Hickes, of Beverſton, in the county of Glouceſter, Knight, and ſiſter cf Sir William Hickes, created a Baronet, he had Colonel William Airmine, a Parliament officer, and equally averſe to the royal cauſe as his father; he ſucceeded to the title, but leaving only daughters, it became extinct.

The Life of FRANCIS ALLEN, Esq.

MR. FRANCIS ALLEN was a citizen and gold-smith of London, refiding near St. Dunftan's Church, in Fleet-ftreet. Probably he was very opulent, for at that time thofe of his trade were the principal bankers in the city.

He was elected a Member for the Borough of Cockermouth, in Cumberland, in the Long Parliament, and his declaring in favour of that intereft, in oppofition to that of the Sovereign, they in 1646 appointed him a Commiffioner for conferving the peace between England and Scotland, and gave him the lucrative poft of a Treafurer of the Army; to retain which he fcrupled at nothing which the fuperior officers ordered him to do; his love of money naturally led him to conftantly declare in favour of the army, and to oppofe by every means a fettlement of the kingdom; it was this policy that urged him to keep back the fum of 49,000l. which the Parliament had placed in his hands to prevent the military coming up, and overawing the Parliament and city; and when they did march to the capital, the government became their own.

Grateful for the part he had taken, the army junto named him one of the Commiffioners of the High Court of Juftice, as they were pleafed to term it, and he fhowed his devotion to the will of his employers; for he fat in the Court held in the Painted Chamber on the 17th, 22d, 23d, 24th,

25th, 26th, 27th, and 29th; and in Weftminfter.
Hall on the 20th, 22d, 23d, and 27th of January,
and figned the warrant to put the unhappy monarch to a public death.

He obtained under the Republic many lucrative
offices; and his emoluments muft have been
great, for befides the place of Treafurer of the
Army, he had that of Cuftomer of London, with
others, and he knew how to obtain money by receiving compliments under the name of acknow-
ledgments of attention; and he was by all thefe
various means enabled to purchafe the property
of the Church. My author fays, the Bifhop's
houfes at Winchefter and Waltham. I prefume
he has not ftated it right; it is however evident
that he laid out his money in epifcopal eftates,
and his intereft was fuch, that he gained what he
purchafed at a very low rate.

He was extremely warm in his attachment to
the Republican form of government, and for that
reafon very obnoxious to General Cromwell, who
perfonally alluded to him when he, by force,
diffolved the Parliament, telling them that the
public was cheated by one of them, looking at
Mr. Allen at the time he faid it; his conduct
upon this occafion fhewed a courage that was the
very oppofite to the pufillanimous behaviour of
the other members who difgracefully flunk out of
the Houfe, as if Oliver had been their legal mafter, and not their fervant; for when the General
faid, " It's you that have forced me to this; for
" I have fought the Lord night and day, that he

" would rather flay me, than put me upon the
" doing of this work;" he anfwered, " It is not
" yet gone fo far, but that all things may be re-
" ftored again, and if the foldiers were com-
" manded out of the Houfe, and the mace re-
" turned, the public affairs might go on in their
" former courfe." Enraged at this boldnefs,
Oliver charged him openly with a deficiency in
his accounts of fome hundred thoufand pounds,
and for which he threatened to queftion him, and
then ordered his mufqueteers to take him into
cuftody; but no ways intimidated, he replied,
that " it was well known the fault was not his;
" that his accounts had not long fince been made
" up,—having tendered them to the Houfe,"
concluding, " I afk no man any favour in that
" matter."

As we hear of no profecution after the affump-
tion of power by Oliver, we muft fuppofe that
the charge was ill founded, or that he made his
peace with the Protector, or that his Highnefs
found it not convenient to meddle with fo daring
a fpirit. It is evident that Oliver had no ill opinion of him, or thought it prudent to gain him
over to his intereft, for his name appears in 1655
in the commiffion for the county of Berks for
raifing the affeffments for Government.

He lived long enough to fee the folly of truft-
ing to a military force, which though at firft it
is made the inftrument of fetting afide fome fuppofed grievances, in the end is fure to eftablifh

a real tyranny, whatever form, or under whatever name, it affumes.

Happily for himfelf he died before the return of King Charles II. but his name occurs in the act of attainder and confifcation, fo that what eſtates he had obtained of a lay nature, were loft to the crown, whilft thofe he had procured from the church returned to their legitimate owners, leaving his family probably deftitute of every kind of provifion.

The Life of Sir WILLIAM ALLENSON, Knt.

SIR WILLIAM ALLENSON was an alderman of the city of York, and joined with the Parliament in oppofition to King Charles I. He was in the confidence of the army, who named him one of the commiffioners to try the unhappy monarch; but he had the virtue, as well as prudence, to decline having any concern whatever with that nefarious tranfaction.

Though he did not go all the lengths that the army wifhed, yet he was not difcarded; for obtaining a feat in Parliament, like the other Members, he gained a very lucrative appointment, being nominated Clerk of the Hanaper, then worth 1000l. per annum, which with other means, too well underftood by the perfons then in power, he acquired fo much money, that he was enabled to purchafe Crable Caftle, belonging to the archiepifcopal fee of York, worth 600l. a year, befides much more epifcopal lands, upon very eafy terms.

He furvived the reftoration, and as he had no concern in the death of the late Sovereign he was permitted to end his days in peace, but probably in much poverty, for all his money having been laid out upon the fpoils of the church, and they returning to their legitimate proprietors, left him, we muft fuppofe, poorer than when he firft embarked in the Parliament intereft.

The return therefore of his Royal Master must have been extremely disagreeable to him, on all accounts. He appears to have possessed no splendid abilities, nor to have distinguished himself much either in the cabinet or the field.

The Life of JOHN ALURED, *Esq.*

JOHN ALURED, Efq. was a native of Yorkfhire, and was returned a member of parliament
for the borough of Heydon in that county in
1640. He took the Proteftation in the following
year, and upon the fword being drawn, entered
into the army with the greateft alacrity, and rofe
to be a Colonel of Horfe.

The Parliament placed great confidence in him,
his name conftantly appears in their committees
for the Eaft Riding of Yorkfhire, and notwithftanding the felf-denying ordinance, his commiffion was continued to him. The deaths of Sir
John Hotham and his fon were greatly owing to
his ungenerous conduct, in fhewing papers entrufted to him in fecrecy.

He was extremely active in procuring the murder of his fovereign, accepting the office of one
of his judges, and attended in the Painted
Chamber January 8, 1648-9, and again the 15th,
and in Weftminfter Hall the 20th, and in both the
22d and 23d; in the Painted Chamber the two
following days; and in both upon the 27th when
fentence was given, and he figned the warrant
for execution.

I have not feen when he died, but it was fome
time before the reftoration, when his name was
put in the act of attainder, that his property of
every defcription might be forfeited. As there
were two of his brothers in the army, Colonel

Matthew Alured, and Lancelot Alured, I am not certain whether it was the Regicide or Matthew who in 1651 diftinguifhed himfelf in fo gallant a manner by retaking the towns in the county of Fife, which had revolted from the Englifh, from a fuppofition that they had left the kingdom; he obtained them by ftorm, and gained prifoners, colours, artillery, and arms; but by furprizing old General Lefley, Earl of Leven, near Dundee, with feveral Noblemen with him, who were raifing forces, he performed ftill more effectual fervice, as it prevented the Scotch from putting themfelves under a commander of great reputation and experience, who might have at leaft prolonged the war for a confiderable time. If this was John, probably he died in Scotland.

Colonel Matthew Alured made a great figure; the Protector had fent him to Ireland, and defigned to have given him a command in the Highlands of Scotland, but his great diflike to the government of a fingle perfon made him averfe to Oliver, and he was at little pains to conceal his difaffection. Cromwell having " difcovered his evil intentions," wrote May 16, 1654 to Lieutenant-General Fleetwood, his fon-in-law, requefting him to fend for the Colonel to Dublin, and take away his commiffion, and to difcover what might be learnt againft him, and fend him and the information immediately over. The apprehenfion of the Protector muft have been great, for he orders that not a day may be loft in performing what he had written relative to Alured,

to whom alfo he wrote the fame day, by the hand
of Secretary Thurloe, but figned by himfelf.

SIR,

I defire you to deliver up into the hands of
Lieutenant-general Fleetwood fuch authorities
and inftructions, as you had for the profecution of
the bufinefs of the Highlands in Scotland, and
you doe forthwith repaire to me to London; the
reafon whereof you fhall knowe, when you come
hither, which I would have you doe with all fpeed.
I would have you allfoe give an account to the
Lieutenant General, before you come away, how
farre you have proceeded in this fervice, and
what money you have in your hands, which you
are to leave with hym.   I reft
                   Your loveinge freind,
16 May, 1654.   OLIVER P.

The judgment formed of him was well
grounded; for Fleetwood, in a letter written upon
the 18th, only two days after, fays, that he had betrayed his thoughts to two perfons whom he fuppofed diffatisfied, and that thefe fentiments were
fuch that it was improper to truft him with any
employment; for fays the General, he looks upon
himfelf, as fent out of the way, and openly fpoke
his diffatisfaction to fuch who had gone over
into Scotland, fo that he could not truft him,
though he had not faid any thing to him, that
the fervice might not fuffer; and Mr. Thomas
Sandford on the 24th confirms this, and farther

added, that he had been "tampering with some of the Anabaptifts' judgment," then a moft pernicious fect of men, who difliked all regular government.

Upon his return to England, he with two other Colonels drew up a dangerous petition of a very inflammatory nature; and it being difcovered in his houfe, he was committed a prifoner November 13, 1654 to the Mewes; it was thought his life was in danger, and therefore Fleetwood, Lord Deputy of Ireland, whofe fecret fentiments were much the fame as his, wrote to Secretary Thurloe, " I can- " not but fuppofe that the bufinefs of Colonel " Alured may reach his life: if any thing of that " nature fhould be done, it would fadly wound " me ; and therefore I earneftly beg, that if any " fuch thing be, you will endeavour the preven- " tion thereof, otherwife it will weaken my hands " in my worke: therefore I hope you will ef- " fectually mind it." Perhaps this might fave his life, but it did not do more, for he remained long a prifoner; he and Colonel Overton, though a prifoner at Dundee, united in a petition to the Protector, in which they faid they " hoped his " Highnefs would no longer exercife their patient " expectations with delays, for they were tender " of that reputation which he might, as to men, " both give and take away;" but though this was in January 1654-5, yet in a letter addreffed to Thurloe to intreat for permiffion to have an audience of the Protector, whom he had obtained leave to fpeak with a fortnight before, and who

had ordered him to come on Monday following;
but though he had attended that day, and almost
every other in that week, he could not get an audience, becaufe of his Highnefs's more weighty
concerns; and he complained of his more than
ten months imprifonment. December 25 following he wrote from his prifon to the Protector,
ftating, that " he had importuned my Lord
" Lambert to mediate with his Highnefs for his
" enlargement, and receiving fome hope, he took
" the 'freedom to affure him that he would not,
" either directly nor indirectly, act any thing pre-
" judicial to his Highnefs, or the prefent Govern-
" ment, or the peace of the Commonwealth;
" but by God's affiftance would live peaceably
" and quietly following his lawful occafions, and
" would be always ready, when he fhould be by
" his Highnefs thereto called, to fhew himfelf as
" formerly againft the cavalier party."

We hear nothing farther of him until the re-
fignation of the Protector Richard, when he was
appointed Captain of the Life-guard to the Parliament and Council, July 9, 1659; and, February
11th, following, he was, by an act of parliament,
named a commiffioner, with Heflerigge, Walton,
and Morley, for the government of the army,
jointly with Monk the General; but this greatly
difpleafed the latter, as they were known to be
men of violent fpirits, and firmly attached to the
republican form. It was a meafure judged neither wife nor politic by any, efpecially as Heflerigge was fo furious in his whole conduct. The

reftoration reduced him to lefs, perhaps, than his original outfet. He was married; for his wife prefented a petition to Oliver. A perfon of his name, feated at Burton upon Trent, married a daughter of Sir Henry Every, of Egginton, in Derbyfhire, Bart. He, and his brother Lancelot, are mentioned in the Committees of the Eaft Riding of Yorkfhire, in 1657. I perhaps ought to apologize for faying fo much of Colonel Matthew Alured; but the brothers are fo often miftaken for each other, that I thought it might be ufeful to future inquirers.

The Life of THOMAS ANDREWS, *Esq.*

MR. THOMAS ANDREWS was an Alderman of the city of London, and, from the firſt, a violent oppoſer of the King; and, having been nominated one of his Majeſty's Judges, to pleaſe the Army, attended in Weſtminſter Hall, January 22d, 23d, and 27th, when ſentence was pronounced, and ſigned the death-warrant. For theſe compliances, he became very dear to the republican party, who made him, not only Treaſurer of the money and plate ſent to Guildhall, where he and Lord Say and Sele obtained very large ſums, but appointed him Treaſurer at War, with three-pence in the pound ſalary, and a Commiſſioner for the ground belonging to St. Paul's church.

In the year 1651, he was made Lord Mayor of London, an important time, as the Scots had advanced into England, to ſet King Charles II. upon the throne of his anceſtors. Andrews, however, kept the capital very quiet, whilſt the Engliſh General advanced againſt him, and, by giving the unfortunate young Prince a defeat, ruined for a time all the hopes of the loyal part of the kingdom.

By preſenting a petition, of a dangerous nature, he fell under the diſpleaſure of the Protector Oliver. To the Royaliſts he was peculiarly obnoxious, as one of the High Court of Juſtice, where he had aſſiſted in the condemnation of other illuſtrious characters, beſides the unhappy mo-

narch. His fentiments were, no doubt, entirely
for a commonwealth; fo that a fingle perfon was
odious to him, whether he bore the title of King,
or Protector. Had he lived to have feen the return of his banifhed Sovereign, he would either
have expiated his crime by an ignominious and
painful death, or fpent the remainder of his life
in poverty and imprifonment. That property,
which he had purchafed by fo many crimes, was
loft at the reftoration by the act of attainder.

The Life of JOHN ANLABY, Esq.

JOHN ANLABY, of Elton, in the county of York, was named one of the Commissioners for trying his Sovereign, but he never sat a single day, nor took the least part in the lamentable tragedy. He was so private a person, that his name does not occur during the busy scene that England displayed while he lived; nor would he have been thought of, for this base purpose, if it had not been for his having married Dorothy, the daughter of Sir Matthew Boynton, of Barmston, in Yorkshire, Baronet; so created by King Charles I. which he basely returned with the blackest ingratitude, by injuring his Majesty in the House of Commons, where he sat as a Member of Parliament for Heydon, in that county; and by preventing the Hothams delivering up Hull to the King.

The Life of THOMAS ATKINS, Esq.

MR. ATKINS was returned one of the members to represent Norwich, in the Parliament called in 1640, and continued such until the restoration, having survived Mr. John Tooley, who are both described as citizens of that place, of which the latter was an alderman; but Atkins outshone the other in becoming an alderman, and, in 1644, Lord Mayor of London.

Though a strenuous republican to the last, he took no part in the King's death; but it did not lose him the confidence of his party, who made him one of their Treasurers at War, in which employment he acquired a very considerable fortune. Mr. Paul Wright gives him the same arms as the Baronet Family of Atkins, of Clapham, in Surrey.

The Life of Sir EDWARD BAINTON, *Knt.*

SIR EDWARD BAINTON was of a knightly family, feated at Brumhall, in the county of Wilts; he was fon of Sir Henry Bainton, of that place, Knt. Diffatisfied with his Majefty's government, he refufed to contribute to the Scotch War; and, upon the calling of the memorable Parliament in 1640, he was elected one of the Members to reprefent the Borough of Chippenham, and diftinguifhed himfelf againft the Court; being the firft perfon, after the Speaker, Mr. Lenthal, that took the Proteftation*. The Parliament named him one of their Committee for his county; but, like feveral other Members, feeing that the Parliament were proceeding to dangerous lengths, he was difgufted, and going into the Ifle of Wight, he fpoke very opprobrioufly againft them, for which he was fent to prifon; but in the following year, upon his prefenting a fubmiffive petition to the Houfe, he was reftored; though they had, for the fame fort of offence, put Mr. Alexander Carew, one of their members, to death, and paffed a vote to difable Sir John Harrifon, Sir Henry Anderfon, and Mr. Conftantine, other members, and new writs were iffued out in the room of thofe gentlemen.

* I have not mentioned any of thofe whofe Lives are here given, after this time as taking the Proteftation; fuffice it to fay, they all took it, and the Covenant.

He was named as one of the Commiffioners to try the King, but perhaps both without his knowledge and confent, for he never attended, nor took the leaft concern in it, and probably he was hurt at the lengths of his party, for he declined taking any part in the government after the King's violent death, until the reftoration, which he lived to fee.

He married Elizabeth, daughter of Sir Henry Maynard, of Walthamftow, in Effex, Knt. fecretary to Lord Burleigh, Queen Elizabeth's great Minifter, by Sufan, daughter and co-heir of William Pierfon, Efq. Gentleman Ufher of the Star Chamber. By this Lady he had Edward Bainton, Efq. his heir, who, in 1640 was returned to ferve in Parliament for the borough of Devizes. He feems no more attached to the fpirit of the times than his father; for in 1647 he was accufed in the Houfe of Commons of figning a warrant for raifing horfe in the city, to further the late tumults, meaning the attempt to reftore the King to his liberty. For this offence he was fufpended the Houfe.

The Life of JOHN BARKSTEAD, *Efq.*

M<small>R.</small> J<small>OHN</small> B<small>ARKSTEAD</small> was a goldfmith, in London, and, from the commencement of the un-happy quarrel between the King and his Parlia-ment, fided with the moft vehement ; and perhaps nothing was more acceptable to him than having permiffion to fit in judgment upon his Sovereign. He attended every day during the whole trial, ex-cept on the 13th of January, and figned the war-rant to complete the cataftrophe.

Though a thorough republican, he joined every government during the ufurpation. Cromwell knighted him, made him one of his lords, and confided the cuftody of the Tower to him, ori-ginally given to him by the Parliament, and ap-pointed him Major-general of London. He feems well adapted to the office of chief jailor.

There are many of his letters in Thurloe's State Papers. He was undoubtedly a man of abilities, but of very little, or no eftimation any other way, than that in which he was continued by the elder Protector, who always gave to each his appro-priate office.

The feverities he had exercifed againft the un-fortunate loyalifts, made him the moft odious and deteftable character in the kingdom, Bradfhaw excepted.

Knowing his danger, he fled to the continent at the reftoration ; but, unhappily for himfelf, that money which he had obtained by the bafeft

means, he employed in purchasing episcopal estates, so that he could not use any, in judiciously
warding off the keenness of the pursuit made
against him.

He first settled at Hanau, in Germany, where
he was elected a burgess; but imprudently leaving that free city, and venturing into Holland, he
was seized upon, and sent into England, by Sir
George Downing, the British Resident, who had
been his former companion and friend. With
him were also conveyed, Mr. Corbet and Mr.
Okey, both implicated in the same crime as himself. He, with them, was brought up to the
King's Bench Bar, condemned, and executed at
Tyburn, April 19, 1662. He died meanly, say
the Royalists, having, it was supposed, taken some
stupifying drug previous to his leaving the prison. But Ludlow tells us, on the contrary, that
" he died with chearfulness and courage, no way
" derogating from the soldier, and a true Eng-
" lishman;" but he was not in England, and
probably he was misinformed. He once was extremely brave, displaying the truest courage, whilst
captain of foot, under Colonel Venn, and whilst
governor of Reading; but guilt and detection
make heroes cowards.

His head was set upon a pole, and placed upon
Traitor's Gate, in the Tower, of which he had
been governor. His wife, I believe, survived
him.

The Life of Sir JOHN BARRINGTON, *Bart.*

SIR JOHN BARRINGTON, of Barrington-Hall, in Herts, Knight and Baronet, was one of the heads of that famous confederacy of relationſhip that met in the Houſe of Commons in 1640, all of whom were extremely diſſatisfied with the Court. But Sir John does not appear to have had any perſonal diſlike to the Sovereign, and much leſs to a monarchical form of government. His alliance with the Cromwell family made him much attached to that intereſt, whilſt it kept the adminiſtration; but, as he had never puſhed his power more than prudence and honour dictated, he was ſaved all unpleaſant circumſtances at the reſtoration, and he was ſuffered to live and die in peace and retirement. He was near ſeeing the revolution, dying ſo late as March 24, 1682.

No doubt he was greatly hurt at having his name inſerted in the commiſſion, and we muſt ſuppoſe, that Cromwell looked upon it certain that he ſhould have prevailed upon him to have taken an active part in this nefarious buſineſs; but moderation and caution guided all Sir John's actions; beſides, the honour of having ſome of the blood-royal flowing in his veins, would make him more averſe to this ſhocking office to which he was invited. The deſcendants of Sir John ſtill reſide at their family manſion, in great reſpect.

The Life of JOSIAS BERNERS, *Esq.*

JOSIAS BERNERS, Esq. was so very private a person that I have never once, that I recollect, seen his name in all the busy scenes that passed before him, prior to this, and he had the prudence to avoid every open concern with the shocking transaction, as also in that against Dr. Hewit, though it was well known he greatly promoted both; but he was prevented sitting in either of these high courts of justice by the continual prayers and intreaties of his wife. He resided at Clerkenwell, and was supposed to have been originally " a serving man;" and at the restoration was thought to be so dangerous a person that government would not pardon him, but from the lenity of a good-natured monarch he received no injury, nor, I believe, any trouble. He had been one of the Council of State in 1659; it is difficult to say how he acquired his consequence.

I have never discovered whether he had any family. It was the part of prudence at the restoration for these busy spirits to seclude themselves in the closest retirement, which may account for the little we know of him, and many other characters after the return of the King and the constitution.

The Life of JOSEPH BLACKISTON, Esq.

JOSEPH BLACKISTON, Esq. was originally a tradesman, generally, though erroniously, said, a shopkeeper in the town of Newcastle upon Tyne, in the county of Northumberland. He was not originally a member of the Long Parliament, but was returned, through the influence of the Scotch, for one of the members of the borough in which he resided. This he was desirous of, to screen himself from paying 6000l. which came into his hands as the executor of the executor of Sir Thomas Farmer, who had bequeathed it to charitable uses; and a bill in Chancery had been filed against him for the performance of the trust, which, by his obtaining a seat he hoped to evade; and he did defeat every attempt to bring him to account by the friends he formed at Westminster, who protected their own party however unjustly.

The Parliament made him quite their tool; they appointed him one of their committee in Newcastle, and named him a commissioner for the observance of the treaty made with the Scotch nation; and when the Scots made such high demands for money upon England, and the Parliament wished to bring their claims to a greater shew of justice, Denzil Lord Hollis says, they " thrust on some of their little Northern Beagles, " as Mr. Blackiston, and others, to inform them " what high sums they had raised on the country;" who reported they had taken as much, or more, as they had demanded; but in the end a very large fum was given, to prevent blood between the nations, though neither was fatisfied; for the Scotch army had reckoned upon poffeffing vaft wealth, and the Englifh who had called them in, at once feared, and defpifed them.

This man raifed by the circumftances of the times, went every criminal length of that faction, who fecured to him the enjoyment of his ill-acquired wealth, and for this purpofe he not only accepted the office of one of the King's judges, but was in every fitting in the Painted Chamber and Weftminfter Hall, and wrote his name to the fatal warrant. He furvived this wickednefs only a few months, dying in 1649.

Perhaps few at that period obtained more than this perfon by his compliances, having gained from the Parliament at one time 14,000l. befides 560l. given to his brother, Mr. John Blackifton, under pretence of fatisfying him for the loffes he had experienced from the Scotch, I fuppofe, and which he was allowed by Mr. Sandis of the Temple, chairman of the committee, appointed to examine the claim. There was alfo 3,500l. voted in June, 1649, to his wife and children, and which was directed to be paid out of the eftates of the Marquis of Newcaftle and Lord Witherington. He alfo had held the place of coal meter, worth 200l. per annum, and had obtained the Caftle of Durham belonging to the epifcopal prelatines of that fee.

It is fingular that in Nalfon's trial of King

Charles I. his baptifmal name is invariably given John, but it was Jofeph; his brother John was one of Oliver's committee for the county of Northumberland fo late as 1657.

It has been ufually faid, that Mr. Blackifton was a mean perfon of low origin; but that does not appear; for though he was in trade, at a period when perfons in that line of life were not regarded, as they very properly now are, yet his family was very confiderable, one branch of them having been created Baronets by King James I. and John Blackifton, of Blackifton, Efq. was his grandfather, and his father was a very highly beneficed clergyman, being Marmaduke Blackifton, A. M. prebendary of the feventh ftall in Durham cathedral, vicar of Woodhoufe, and treafurer of that cathedral; he had alfo the churches of Redmarfhall and Sedgfield, archdeacon of the Eaft Riding of Yorkfhire, and prebend of Wiftow in the cathedral of York.

The Regicide had three younger brothers and a fifter. Thomas, the eldeft of them, was a clergyman, to whom his father refigned the prebendal ftall of Wiftow: Robert, another, was likewife in the church, to whom his father furrendered up his ftall in Durham cathedral, and his living of Sedgfield: he died January 17, 1634, having married a daughter of Dr. John Howfon, bifhop of Durham. John, the other brother, has been noticed. The fifter was married to Dr. Cofin, alfo bifhop of Durham.

This refpectable genealogy is not given as any

softening, but aggravating, his demerits. Little did King Charles I. think when Mr. Robert Blackifton was, with other prebendaries, supporting the canopy over his head, that his brother Jofeph fhould fentence it to be cut off. Marmaduke Blackifton, Efq. the Regicide's fon, fold the family feat of Newton Hall, near Durham, to Sir Henry Liddell's anceftor; a proof that though the father was attainted when dead, yet the fon had a grant of the eftate.

The Life of DANIEL BLAGRAVE, *Esq.*

DANIEL BLAGRAVE, Efq. was defcended from a genteel family feated in the county of Berks, and bred to the Bar. He obtained a feat in the Long Parliament for the borough of Reading. As his fentiments were fo very different from thofe of his refpectable parents, it is generally fuppofed, that imagining which would be the victorious fide, he embarked in the Parliament quarrel with the expectation of enriching himfelf.

He went into the army firft at Reading, of which he was not only a reprefentative in Parliament, but fteward. The Parliament named him of their committee for Berks, and treafurer of that county. He diftinguifhed himfelf by his perfecutions of the orthodox clergy. He was therefore a proper perfon to be chofen for the black crime of putting the King to death : he attended the High Court of Juftice in the Painted Chamber, January the 8th, 10th, 13th, 15th, 17th, 20th, 22d, 23d, 24th, 25th, 26th, 27th, and 29th, and in Weftminfter Hall the 20th, 22d, 23d, 27th, and 29th, and he figned the warrant to put the King to death.

As a farther reward for this bafe compliance, which his knowledge of the law muft have inftructed him was the higheft crime that could be committed, he received the office of Exegenter in the Court of Common Pleas, then worth 500l, and became one of the Mafters in Chancery, which was of much greater value to him. By the emoluments of his offices, and other means, he was enabled to purchafe the King's fee farm of the great manor of Sunning, in Berkfhire, and other eftates, which he did upon very eafy terms.

Whatever were his fentiments, he kept in with every form of government during the interregnum, and he had the whole time great influence in the town of Reading.

If we may judge from one of his friend's fentiments, he was by no means attached to the Prefbyterians; for Barkftead, Lieutenant of the Tower, writes to Secretary Thurloe, Aug. 15, 1656,

" Sir, I am informed from very good hands,
" that one Coates, the poft-mafter of Reading,
" who appeared very active for Mr. Blagrave's
" party at the elections there, did rantingly ufe
" thefe fpeeches, that he had drawn his fword
" thefe thirteen years againft the Prefbyterians,
" and would not fheath it yet;" and no doubt he fpoke the paffions of Mr. Blagrave, whofe tool probably he was.

He was one of the few of the Rump who could obtain a feat in the Convention Parliament; but finding the danger of remaining longer in the kingdom, he effected his efcape to the Continent, or America, and fo well concealed himfelf, that he never more was heard of.

George Blagrave, of Surcott, and of Reading, Efq. and Alexander Blagrave, of Surcott, Efq. were no doubt his near relations; as were Colo-

nel William Blagrave, Efq. feated in Northumberland, and John Blagrave, of Arborfield, in Berks,
Efq. both of whom were fet down in the lift of
the knights of the royal oak, an order of knighthood intended to have been eftablifhed by King
Charles II. after his reftoration, to commemorate
his efcape in an oak after the battle of Worcefter;
the former of thefe gentlemen's eftate was valued
at 600l. the other at 2000l. per annum. George
and John were committee-men in 1657, and therefore trufted by, and employed in, Oliver's protectorate.

The Life of THOMAS BLUNT, *Esq.*

Thomas Blunt, Esq. was so obscure a person, that I am not able to ascertain who he was, or any thing whatever relative to him, and the common name he had tends to obscure him; but it is to his honour that he wholly avoided any participation in this act that disgraces our annals.

The Life of DENNIS BOND, Efq.

DENNIS BOND, Efq. was of a good family in Dorfetfhire whofe anceftors removed thither in the ninth year of King Henry VI.'s reign from the county of Somerfet, but he was brought up to trade, being a woollen-draper at Dorchefter, and an alderman of that town. He was returned in the fifteenth and fixteenth years of the reign of King Charles I. a member of parliament for the borough of Dorchefter, with Denzil Hollis, Efq. afterwards created Lord Hollis.

He foon rofe fuperior to his ftation, acquiring great power and confequence with the republican party; but though he had a real and fixed averfion to King Charles I.'s government, and probably to his perfon, yet he could not be prevailed upon perfonally to contribute to his death.

Mr. Bond was greatly trufted both by the long parliament and by the protector Oliver; from the commencement of the civil war he was of the committee for his own county, was one of the Council of State in 1649 and 1651, and proved on every occafion, that he was a perfon of great capacity, and much policy, which was evinced in nothing more than in the provifion he procured for his family; obtaining the government of Portland, and the office of receiver of his majefty's rents in the counties of Somerfet and Southampton for himfelf. For John, one of his fons, the mafterfhip of the Savoy, and afterwards of Trinity-Hall in Cambridge, which he held with the Law Profeſſors of Greſham-College, and for another the place of Auditor of the Exciſe, then worth 500l per annum.

He died Auguſt 30, 1658, the day of the extreme high wind, when it being ſo near the time of the protector's death, the loyaliſts jeſtingly ſaid " the Devil took Bond for Oliver's appearance."

I apprehend he had four ſons ; 1, Nathaniel, a councellor, a member of Parliament for Corfe Caſtle 31 King Charles II. and for Dorcheſter 7 King William III. whoſe ſon and heir was Dennis Bond, Eſq. a repreſentative alſo for Corfe Caſtle, who married a daughter of Edmund Dummer, Eſq. and widow of Valentine Knightley of Fawſley in Northamptonſhire, Eſq. This lady's mother was Sophia, daughter of Sir William Dutton Colt, Knt. born whilſt her father was reſident at the court of Hanover, and who received her baptiſmal name from her godmother the Princeſs Sophia, mother of King George I. 2, John Bond, LL. D. a divine, a civilian, and a legiſlator, having been a member of Parliament for Melcombe Regis ; loſing his profeſſor's place, and his maſterſhip at the reſtoration, he retired into Dorſetſhire, and died at Sandwich in the Iſle of Purbeck, a few miles from Steeple, to which his corpſe was conveyed, and interred in the church-yard July 30, 1676. He was one of the many who wrote political tracts under religious titles, and in ſcripture language, to ſerve the party he engaged with. 3, Elias Bond, of Warham in Dorfetſhire, who was buried at Steeple, November 15, 1680; and, 4, William Bond, who had a feat at Blackington near Lutton, in Dorfetſhire; he died September 7, 1669, and was buried at Wareham.

There were few perſons more diſliked by the violent partizans of King Charles I. than Mr. Dennis Bond; and the great ſhare of the elder protector's confidence which he poſſeſſed did not leſſen their hatred; numerous are the reflections caſt upon him; but as there has no particular circumſtance of tyranny or peculation been ſubſtantiated againſt him, we muſt attribute it only to party ſpirit. Poſſeſſing very ſuperior abilities, he directed his conduct ſo as to obtain what he could for his own and his family's aggrandizement without doing any private injury; and he contributed all he could to render the public ſuch ſervices as the times were capable of, conſiſtently with the bias of his political ſentiments. I am induced from theſe ideas which I have formed of him, to vindicate a character often vehemently traduced, and whom, had he ſurvived the return of his ſovereign, might, from the odium he experienced as the favourite of Cromwell, have experienced great hardſhips, unleſs his good ſenſe had diſcovered how to take off the edge of popular reſentment.

The Life of Sir JOHN BOURCHIER, *Knt.*

Sir John Bourchier was of a knightly family, feated at Benningborough, defcended from James Bourchier, natural fon of John Bourchier Lord Berners, a family which had given Earls of Ewe in Normandy, and of Effex in England, and from whom had fprung a Cardinal, Archbifhop of Canterbury, Barons Cromwell and Fitzwarren.

James Bourchier, mentioned above, married Mary, daughter of Sir Humphry Banifter, by whom he had his oldeft fon and heir, Sir Ralph Bourchier, Knt. who married Elizabeth, daughter of Francis Hall, Efq. and Chriftian, daughter of Rowland Shakerley; by the latter he had no iffue; by the former, William Bourchier, Efq. who died in 1584; who left, by the daughter of Sir Thomas Barrington, of Hatfield Broad Oak, in Effex, Bart. Robert, who died unmarried; Sir John, who became his heir; Thomas; and three daughters.

Sir John Bourchier was of great confequence in the reign of King James I. and had been one of the adventurers to Virginia, who fubfcribed to eftablifh a colony there in the year 1620. He took a very decided part in deftroying the King, attending in the Painted Chamber each day, except the 10th, 13th, 15th, 18th, and 26th, and every fitting in Weftminfter Hall, and alfo figned the warrant.

After that great national misfortune, the violent death of the King, he became one of the chief rulers of the nation; and, in 1650-1, he was elected a member of the council of state. Being a rigid independent and republican, he was very diffatisfied with Cromwell's ufurpation, who, to keep him quiet, made him one of his committee for the Weft Riding of Yorkfhire.

He juft furvived the reftoration, but on account of his age and infirmities, obtained permiffion to remain a prifoner in the houfe of his daughter. Had he lived, his life would have been forfeited; but happily he died where he was, in a fort of energy to defend the action, which his relations faw in its proper and odious light; and, whilft they were perfuading him to repent, though he had not moved fome days before, he got up, and having faid " it was a juft act, and all good " men will own it," he calmly fat down, and expired. He therefore efcaped the pain and fhame of a public trial, and perhaps execution; but as his name was inferted in the act of parliament attainting him with the other regicides, his fortune, whatever it was, became loft to his family.

He married Ann, daughter and heir of William Rolf, of Hadley, in the county of Suffolk, by whom he had three fons, Barrington, William, and John, both of whom died unmarried; and a daughter, Bridget, married to William Bethall, D. D.

Barrington Bourchier, Efq. his heir, was aged

thirty-eight in 1665; he married Frances, eldeft daughter of Sir William Strickland, of Boynton, Knt. and Bart. by whom he left

Sir Barrington Bourchier, Knt. born in 1654, and feated at Benningborough, and fet down as poffeffing 1000l. per annum, amongft fuch who were defigned to have been Knights of the Royal Oak, a ftrange circumftance for the grandfon of a regicide to be fo diftinguifhed; and proves, that King Charles II., who, with all his ill qualities, poffeffed mercy in an eminent degree, had rein-ftated the family in their paternal eftates, and perhaps very properly, for Sir Barrington might be loyal though defcended from a traitor. He married thrice; firft, Judith, daughter of Mark Milbanke, Efq. alderman, and twice Mayor of Newcaftle upon Tyne, and fheriff of Northumberland, who, after contributing to the purfe of the exiled king, greatly exerted himfelf to promote his reftoration to the throne of his anceftors; fecondly, Margaret, daughter and coheir of Thomas Hardwick, Efq. and his third wife was the daughter of Sir —— Dalfton, Knt. By the firft, he had Sir Barrington Bourchier, who died, leaving no child by his lady, a daughter of Sir Francis Compton, fon of Spencer, Earl of Northampton; and Mark, who alfo left no iffue; by the fecond marriage he had John, who became his heir, who, by Mary, daughter of —— Belwood, Efq. ferjeant at law, left two children, John and Mary.

The Life of THOMAS BOON, *Esq.*

THOMAS BOON, Esq. was, I suppose, one of the many adventurers, in these times of distraction, when some sensible active men, by a pretended zeal for the popular cause, took an opportunity of enriching themselves out of the estates of the persecuted loyalists. Such appears to have been Mr. Boon, who did not come into play until the civil war was over, but time enough to reap the benefit of it. Upon a vacancy in the long parliament, he was returned a member for the borough of Clifton-Dartmouth-Hardness, in Devonshire.

He was too wise, at least, to accept a place in the high court of justice, which sat upon his unhappy sovereign, though he was extremely active as one of Cromwell's committee for the county of Dorset.

Mr. Boon was employed in various public departments, and in 1659, he was one of the parliament's plenipotentiaries in the Sound; by his places he greatly improved the small stock he set out with, receiving, it is said, 6000 l. in the scandalous employment of sequestrator, which, with other such ways, he raised a vast estate, and, though extremely disliked, he met security and protection at the restoration, at which time he is mentioned by Blome, in his Britannia, amongst the gentry, where he is called Thomas Boone, of Mount-Boon; and, as a mean the better to hide his original obscurity, he pretended to be defcended from the great Bohun family, who were earls of Hereford, and that his name, Boon or Boone, was only a corruption of Bohun; though the Myftery of the Good Old Caufe fays, that he was originally an humble tapfter.

He left two daughters and coheirs; Mary, married to John Oldbury of London, merchant; and Ann, who became the lady of Sir Francis Drake, Bart. by whom fhe had no iffue. But the blood of Mr. Boon flows in the veins of feveral ennobled families, by the great alliances the defcendants of his daughter Mary made; Mr. Oldbury, like him, having only coheirs, who married extremely fortunately.

The Life of Sir WILLIAM BRERETON, Bart.

SIR WILLIAM BRERETON, of Hanford, in the county of Chefter, created a baronet by king Charles I. March 10, 1626, was defcended of a long line of anceftry; was returned a member of parliament for Chefhire in 1640, and immediately diftinguifhed himfelf againft the court, from his confirmed diflike to the ecclefiaftical eftablifh-ment; and took the Proteftation; immediately as a war was determined, he went into the army, and by his fkill and bravery he was one of the greateft friends the parliament had: his military career was wonderful.

He left London in 1643, with a troop of horfe and a regiment of dragoons, with which he marched into Chefhire, and fortified Namptwich, as a check upon the King's friends, who had done the fame to the city of Chefter; at firft he was defpifed by Lord Capel, his majefty's lieute-nant-general of Shropfhire, Chefhire, and North Wales; but his extreme attention to his forces, his popularity, the fobriety he eftablifhed in his army, and the punctuality with which he was en-abled by the parliament to pay them, foon gave him the moft decided fuperiority. When the Earl of Northampton had driven the parliament garrifon out of Litchfield, he, with Sir John Gell, marched thither with three thoufand horfe and foot, and attacked that nobleman; but though they were repulfed from the Clofe, yet it greatly injured the king, by having the loyal and brave Northampton fall in the engagement, at Hopton Heath, near Stafford, whither they had followed his Lordfhip, and had again been driven from the field of battle; but taking with them the corpfe of fo great a man, they feemed to themfelves victorious, for they demanded, when the young Earl afked, with filial piety, the body to convey to the family fepulchre, that they would have in exchange for it all the ammunition, cannon, and prifoners they had loft; and when the extravagant propofition was refufed, they would not give up the body, nor fuffer a furgeon to come and embalm it.

In this fame year he took Ecclefhall Caftle, the feat of the Bifhop of Litchfield and Coventry, defeated a party of forces of Lord Capel, under Colonel Haftings, and fjointly with Sir Thomas Middleton, took Holt Caftle, in Shropfhire, and other places in that county, for which important fervices the parliament gave him and Sir Thomas power to fequeftrate the property of the loyalifts, and levy money in Wales, in the fame manner as they had authorized the Earl of Manchefter in the affociated counties.

Soon after he fell upon the rear of Lord Byron's forces, and defeated them when they had furprized and routed a party of forces of Colonel Afhton, of Lancafhire, who was marching to join him; he then uniting his army with that of Sir Thomas Fairfax, marched to relieve Namptwich,

and obtained one of the greateſt and moſt important victories that was won during the whole war,
and with as little loſs to themſelves ; amongſt the
great number of officers taken priſoners, was Colonel Monk, who afterwards made ſo very conſpicuous a figure in our hiſtory.

His fame and importance was ſo well eſta-
bliſhed, that the parliament took every method
to gratify him, making him, in 1644, Major General of Cheſhire, and the adjacent parts, with
the ſame powers as in other aſſociations. He
was ſoon after ordered to join Sir William Waller
by the parliament, who placed Sir William at the
head of thoſe forces commanded by him, Lord
Denbigh, and Colonels Maſſey, Mitton, and
Rigby; but he was preſently ſent with Middleton to aſſault the garriſon of Cheſter ; and killed
Colonel Mitton, who made a ſortie againſt them;
and when Prince Rupert the next morning attacked them with two of his beſt regiments of
horſe, and a party of foot, they beat him back
again into the city, with the loſs, in killed and
wounded, of at leaſt four hundred.

He then ſeparating from Middleton, who was
ordered elſewhere, conducted the war with equal
prudence, ſending Colonel Jones againſt a party
of Prince Rupert's horſe, conſiſting of two thouſand ; of theſe, in the action fought near Malpas,
in Cheſhire, he took one hundred and forty, two
Majors, with many inferior officers and ſoldiers,
killed Colonels Baines and Conniers, with three
Majors, and one hundred of the common men ;

wounded the gallant Sir Marmaduke Langdale, and forced the defeated brigade to haften with the utmoft difpatch back again to Chefter.

Sir William foon after in perfon attacked and defeated the Earl of Derby in his way to relieve Liverpool, killing and taking five hundred of the loyalifts, and putting the remainder to the rout; and affifted in retaking Montgomery Caftle, with a moft decided defeat of the royal army, fo that it turned the fcale in favour of the parliament in Wales. They were fo pleafed with his conduct, that they fent him their thanks, and, what was more acceptable, gave him the fupplies he wanted.

Continuing his career, he defeated another party of the royalifts in Chefhire, and then marching to Chefter, blocked it up, and from thence went to Liverpool; the Irifh foldiers in garrifon there betrayed it to Sir John Meldrum, who was with Sir William; fecuring this place, he hafted to Stafford, and prevented its being delivered up into the hands of the King; and when a large force fell upon his quarters at Beefton Caftle, which he was befieging, he fent Lieutenant-colonel Jones, at the head of a body of horfe, and Major Lothian, who commanded the foot, who completely defeated the brigade, killing many, and took Colonels Worden and Ware, with many others of inferior rank. He was equally fuccefsful in gaining Patteſhall Houfe, which was a ftrong garrifon, and very obnoxious, as kept chiefly by the Roman Catholic gentry; this he obtained by furprifal, fending Captain Stone thither with a fmall but gallant force. Another party he fent againſt Holtbridge, where he was as fortunate; he put garriſons in each.

Himſelf attended to the ſiege of thoſe two important places, Beeſton Caſtle and Cheſter, but theſe he ſoon after left to the care of his officers, whilſt he marched out with ſome additional forces to watch the motions of Prince Maurice, who durſt not attack him; whilſt the forces he commanded took Apſley-Houſe in Shropſhire; and ſoon after Shrewſbury fell, having long reſiſted every attempt to take it, and the caſtle; but in a little while Prince Rupert, his brother Maurice, and Sir Marmaduke Langdale, having united their ſtrength, the committee at Namptwich informed the parliament, that Sir William would be in great danger if not ſpeedily relieved; who immediately ordered the letter to be ſent to the committee of both kingdoms, requeſting that a party of Scotch horſe, and dragoons might advance towards him, with a ſuitable ſupply for the troops under his command.

Sir William ſoon after ſent to inform the parliament that he was enabled to keep the field, and that the enemy had performed nothing againſt him, but had been guilty of plundering the country, committing many hundred rapes and cruelties, and that the Scotch horſe were advanced as far as Mancheſter to join him. It was a melancholy truth that there was no diſcipline in the royal armies, who being ill paid, took very great liberties, which it was impoſſible their officers

could check, as they ought, and wifhed to do; but
it is equally true that the parliament party conftantly exaggerated all their foibles into crimes;
for few fuch enormities as are here complained of
were committed during the war; but it is the nature of men who are fighting againft their lawful
governors, to make every excufe they can to
fanction their conduct.

Receiving fupplies, he again, in 1645 acted
upon the offenfive, fapping Hawarden Caftle,
and taking Goozanna Houfe, and in it a captain,
twenty-feven prifoners, and fome officers, and from
thence blocked up Chefter on the Welch fide,
gained Manley Houfe, killed fome, and took
prifoner a captain, and others, and then threw a
bridge over the River Dee to fupply his forces on
both fides of Chefter. The Earl of Leven foon
after fent him a detachment from his army.

When the Self-denying Ordinance paffed, his
fervices in the field were too great for the parliament to recall his commiffion, they therefore
paffed a vote to retain him ftill in the army for
forty days longer, and at the expiration of that
period it was ftill prolonged.

It was no fmall mortification to him to retire
from Chefter and give his majefty the power of
relieving it, but he was not able longer to remain
before it; he therefore ftruck his tents and
marched into Lancafhire to join the Scottifh forces,
and gaining affiftance, he was enabled immediately, almoft, to return into Chefhire, and retake
Beefton Caftle, and from thence to march to

Chefter, Colonel Booth, by order of parliament, joining him with the Lancafhire forces: he carried on the fiege with great vigour, but he could not prevail upon Lord Byron, the governor, to furrender it, but upon very high terms, and therefore the parliament again enlarged the time of his command another forty days.

Sir William renewed his fummons; but obtaining no anfwer to his demand, and five days having elapfed, he fent a letter infifting upon knowing the determination of the governor, who promifed to treat with him, if the king did not relieve them within twelve days, requefting permiffion to fend a pafs to his majefty; but this he refufed, and the treaty was on' that account fufpended. By his vigilance he took a letter that they had written to Oxford, in which Lord Byron informed the King " that if they had not relief by the laft of " January, then of neceffity they muft furrender " Chefter."

Sir William foon after wrote to Lenthal, fpeaker of the Houfe of Commons, that he had wifhed to preferve Chefter from ruin, and had therefore invited the befieged to a treaty, but that they had delayed to end it, though it had been continued for ten days, becaufe they thought of relief being given them by Afhley, Vaughan, the Irifh, and Welch, and by a new force lately come from Ireland, whom he had in vain endeavoured to furprife upon their landing in Anglefey; but, though he had not been able to effect that, he had, by fending Colonel Milton againft them, prevented a junction, which had so difpirited the garrifon, that at length they opened a treaty; and, to fhew that he was defirous to give them every fatisfaction, he was willing to have more commiffioners, judging that this conduct would make the officers in the garrifon better pleafed, and by it enable them to oblige the foldiers under their command to fulfil their engagements with punctuality: the garrifon, he farther related, wanted more time; but it being abfolutely denied, a treaty was concluded, by which all the ammunition, arms, ordnance, provifions, the feal of the county palatine, fwords, and all the records, were preferved. Thus did he procure Chefter, far the moft valuable place in that part of the kingdom, which the parliament confided to the care of Alderman Edwards, of that city, appointing him colonel of the regiment ftationed there.

Having fecured Chefhire, he hafted to Lichfield, which he obtained with the lofs of only three men killed, and a few wounded; and almoft as few flain of the royalifts, whom, though more than a thoufand horfe and foot, he drove before him into the Clofe.

He then joining with Colonel Morgan, governor of Gloucefter, marched againft Sir Jacob Aftley, who was conducting a large force into Oxfordfhire; he overtook Sir Jacob at Stow, on the Woold, on the borders of Gloucefterfhire; the conteft was as obftinate as the matter was momentous; the attack was extremely violent; the royalifts' word was, "Patrick and George;" the parliamentarians, " God be our guide;" but at laſt the former were obliged to ſubmit, and the victory was as complete as it was conſequential ; Sir Jacob was wounded, and taken priſoner, with about ſixteen hundred others, many of them of the higher gentry, and they loſt their carriages, arms, baggage, and every thing elſe ; ſo that, as it was almoſt the laſt hope of the king, Sir Jacob Aſtley emphatically ſaid to ſome of the parliament officers, " now you have done your work, " and may go and play, unleſs you fall out amongſt " yourſelves."

This indefatigable commander, joining Colonels Morgan and Birch, marched to Worceſter, and ſummoned it to ſurrender, aſſuring the inhabitants that his majeſty was unable, for want of forces, to relieve it: to which they anſwered, that " if it " had been ſo, they ſuppoſed they ſhould have " known the king's pleaſure therein; until when, " they would not ſurrender the place." The beſiegers knowing how impoſſible it was for them to hold out, and to convince the garriſon of the truth of what they had told them, retired a little; but, not to be idle, they fell ſuddenly upon Bridgenorth, took the town by ſtorm, and drove the ſoldiers into the caſtle, which they cloſely beſieged.

Leaving troops to act againſt both the city and town, he haſtened with great rapidity to Lichfield, to ſummon the royal garriſon who were in the Cloſe, telling them the danger and folly of holding out, by ſhewing them the various ſucceſſes which had attended the parliament arms at

Stow, by the victory over Sir Jacob Aftley, the capture of Exeter, Barnftaple, and other places ; and having obtained this, July 16 he went to, and took Tutbury Caftle, in Staffordfhire, and foon after Bridgenorth, by thofe he had left there ; he next attacked Dudley Caftle, which agreed to furrender upon articles, which, the parliament approving of, were accepted.

Having now done his ample fhare in the complete ruin of the royal caufe, he came to attend his duty in parliament, where he was received by them as his fkill, valour, and activity, deferved; the fpeaker, by the order of the Houfe, giving him their thanks for his important fervices, but more particularly for taking Chefter ; this was June 22, and the 8th of the following month they paffed an order for ftating the accounts of Sir William as major-general, and for giving 500l. for the forces which were before Lichfield, and that he fhould go down to that ill-fated city, which again was befieged ; thither he repaired, and foon obtained a furrender of it upon articles, by which he gained all their ordnance, arms, and ammunition. This I think was Sir William's laft military exploit, and in which he was exceeded by few, of the many, who commanded in this unhappy war, and there was little to do in arms after this time ; for the parliament had every where conquered, and the crown lay proftrate at the feet of the two Houfes, which if they had then taken the advantage of, a legal, and fomewhat temperate, fettlement might have been made ; but deferring it until the army became all powerful, they made the imperious Commons the tools of their lawlefs tyranny and impious crimes.

Sir William, however, feems more to have wifhed to injure the church, than ruin the monarch, for he could not be prevailed upon to take any part in the violent death of the king. He had no other merit, but that of a military nature, we may prefume; for except in 1646 his being named as a commiffioner for conferving the peace between the Englifh and Scotch, I do not fee him noticed until 1656, ten years afterwards, when he put up for a member for his county to fit in Oliver's parliament; but it appears by a letter of Major-general Tobias Bridge to the protector, dated from Middlewiche, that Sir William " had " been beflirring himfelf what he can by himfelf " and agents, to procure voices; but I find," fays the major-general, " his intereft amongft " the gentlemen very little; only fome of the " rigid clergy cry him up," meaning no doubt the prefbyterian ones; and as Bridge propofed to his highnefs Colonel Croxton, Meffrs. Marbury, Hide, and Manning, it fhews that he had no wifh to have him returned. It is feen from this, that he had loft his popularity in his native county; and probably he lived to repent of his own victories. He died before the reftoration, and was fucceeded in his title by Sir Thomas Brereton, Bart.; the male line failing, it is now extinct. He had a relation alfo named William, created by King Charles I. Baron Brereton of the kingdom of Ireland, who was as eminently loyal as he was otherwife : he fell into the hands of the parliament, whom in 1644 his lordfhip petitioned to exchange him for Sir John Northeft, but which they refufed, alledging as their reafon for denying his fuit, that he muft firft give fatisfaction for his having killed feveral of their friends in cold blood at Namptwich ; but in the following year they accepted Sir John Harcourt, one of their members, for him ; his lordfhip furviving the reftoration was returned a member for Chefhire in King Charles II's. fecond parliament, and died whilft it was fitting. There is a fmall engraved portrait of Sir William Brereton in Rycraft's book.

The Life of GODFREY BOSVILE, Esq.

GODFREY BOSVILE, Efq. was defcended of a knightly family, feated at Gunthwaite, in the county of York. He was returned one of the reprefentatives for the borough of Warwick in 1640; and thus obtaining a feat in the long parliament, and having a prodigious prejudice againft the court, he became extremely popular in the Houfe. He took the proteftation, and in return for his earneftnefs in their caufe, they appointed him one of their committee for his native county, for that of Warwick, and for the city of Coventry.

When the fword was unhappily drawn in the fatal quarrel between the king and the parliament, he obtained a commiffion in the army of the latter, and he rofe to the rank of colonel. He diftinguifhed himfelf, in 1643, by marching from Coventry with eight hundred horfe, and taking with them the garrifoned houfe of Sir Thomas Holt by ftorm, and in it eighty prifoners, and much property of various kinds, befides money and plate to a confiderable amount. In 1644 he affifted Colonel Purefoy, of Warwickfhire, at the fiege of Banbury.

The garbled parliament put his name as one of the commiffioners of the high court of juftice to try the king, but he prudently declined taking any part whatever in the blackeft tranfactions

that ftains our hiftoric pages.   After the death of
his fovereign, he probably retired very much from
public concerns.   In the protectorate of Oliver,
his name is omitted in all the committees he had
been of; yet he was living at the reftoration, for
he is mentioned as an obnoxious character in the
Myftery of the Good Old Caufe.   His family ftill
retain their feat, which is now the property of
Godfrey Bofvile, Efq.

The Life of JOHN BROWN, *Efq.*

JOHN BROWN, Efq. was returned a member of parliament in 1640 for the county of Dorfet, and, joining againſt the king, was made a committee-man for his own county, where his family, from their wealth, was of much confequence ; and he continued with his party in all their extravagant exceſſes, which occaſioned, we may ſuppofe, his being named one of the commiſſioners appointed to try the fovereign ; and he fat in the Painted Chamber upon the 8th of January, the 12th, 13th, 17th, 18th, 19th, 20th, 25th, and 27th, and in Weſtminſter Hall the 20th ; but, fortunately for himfelf, not upon the laſt day, when fentence was given, nor figned the warrant for execution.

He was continued, by the Protector Oliver, in his odious office of a committee-man, and is accufed of having feized ſtock and goods, to the amount of one thouſand pounds, belonging to a farmer of the name of Wades, in Portland, whom, though the committee acquitted of malignancy, by which they meant loyalty, yet he could not recover the property, nor the value of it, he being a member of the Houfe. He furvived the reſtoration ; but, as he was not fo immediately guilty in the king's death, not having appeared at the laſt part of the trial, nor figned the warrant, he was not profe-cuted for it, fo humane were Charles and his council to men who were become odious beyond belief at that time.

He married a fifter of Sir Richard Trenchard. The name, being fo very common, it is difficult, if not impoffible, to diftinguifh his actions from fome of the many others who were engaged in the quarrel on the parliament fide; I have, therefore, faid the lefs of him, that I might not give erroneous information.

The Life of ABRAHAM BURRELL, Esq.

MR. ABRAHAM BURRELL was a gentleman of the county of Huntingdon, and had a landed property alſo in that of Somerſet, and is noticed only for his refuſal to contribute to the carrying on of the war with the Scotch in 1639, which endeared him to the parliament, ſoon after aſſembled. Whatever might have been his ſentiments relative to government, he was prudent enough to refuſe ſitting as a commiſſioner to try his ſovereign, or to have any other concern in the dreadful ſcene. He was one of the committee for the county of Huntingdon, and, probably, perſonally known to the Protector Oliver, before the long parliament was called. He was living in 1657, ſo that he might have ſurvived the reſtoration.

The Life of JOHN CAREW, *Esq.*

JOHN CAREW, Efq. was defcended of the ancient and very refpectable family of Carew of Anthony, in Cornwall; he was the fecond of three
fons of Sir Richard Carew, created a baronet by
King Charles I., Auguft 9, 1641; his eldeft brother, Sir Alexander Carew, Bart., who was one of
the knights for the county of Cornwall in 1640,
and who, from being a partizan of the parliament,
"deferted" to the king, as the former termed it,
which, as he had received a commiffion in their
army, and was governor of St. Nicholas' Ifland,
near Plymouth, fubjected him to be tried by a
court martial, which fentenced him to die, and he
was executed for it, by beheading, on Tower-hill,
December 23, 1644: he was unfteady and waver-
ing; his eftate was large, and he feared lofing
it, as the king's fucceffes were great near him;
thefe circumftances made him willing to defert
an intereft he did not difavow at his death, where
he acted very inconfiftently, though he affected
great religion and humility. Sir Thomas Carew,
the third brother, was knighted by King Charles I.
and was feated at Barley, in the county of Devon,
and left feveral children.

It was neceffary to fay fo much of this gentleman's family, as it was confpicuous in the unhappy tranfactions of the laft century.

John Carew, Efq., the fubject of this hiftory,
was returned to ferve in the long parliament, as

one of the members for the borough of Tregony, in Cornwall; and, in 1646, he was one of the commiffioners to receive the king at Holdenby. His conftant affection to the caufe of the parliament, though they had ufed fuch extreme feverity againft his brother, occafioned his being named in the commiffion to try the king, and they were not miftaken in their fentiments refpecting him, for he fat every day, both in the Painted Chamber and in Weftminfter Hall, in which they met, and figned the warrant for the execution.

He appears altogether to have been a tool to the republican and fanatical party, who laid him afide as foon as he had performed what they wifhed; for neither the parliament nor the protectors ever employed him in any manner; nor was he, until his friends obtained the reigns of government again, in 1659. Indeed he became fo wild a vifionary, as a fifth monarchy-man, that he looked upon human government as an encroachment upon the Meffiah's kingdom, which he flattered himfelf with foon feeing eftablifhed upon earth, fo that he was utterly incapable of any fober judgment or difcretion. He viewed King Charles I. and the Protector Oliver as equally ufurpers againft Chrift; and he had been fo idle in his conduct, that he, with Harrifon and others, had been imprifoned by Cromwell, firft at Pendennis, in Cornwall, but afterwards confined only in his own houfe.

At the reftoration he publicly fet out to come to London, in obedience to the order of parlia-

ment for all the king's judges to surrender themselves in that city within fourteen days; being
known, he was apprehended by a warrant from a
justice of the peace; but though his name was
mistaken in the warrant, and the officer refused
to detain him until the error was rectified, he
took no advantage of it, but told him he was the
person meant, he believed, acquainting him whither, and for what purpose, he was going; and
though this was within the fourteen days, yet
when application was made to the parliament to
adjudge it a surrender in obedience to their proclamation, they would not admit it, excepting him
both as to life and estate absolutely, without any
farther delay of execution, if he should be found
guilty.

He was brought to his trial before judge Foster,
October 12, 1660; he was set at the bar with Scot,
Jones, and Clement, but on account of their several challenges he was tried alone. It was with
great difficulty he could be prevailed upon to say,
" not guilty," and when he complied, he sub-
joined to the next usual answer, by God and his
country, " saving to our Lord Jesus Christ's right
" to the government of these kingdoms."

He then challenged twenty-three of the jury,
and being told by the lord chief baron, that he
might have pen, ink, and paper, he declined it,
having, as he said, no occasion for them. It was
proved that he was in the court the last day, when
sentence was passed upon the king, and that he
signed the warrant of execution. When called

upon for his defence, he launched out into a wild extravagant vindication of what he had done; but faying that " he had not done it becaufe he " had not the fear of God before his eyes, nor been " moved thereto by the devil, but in the fear of " God, and in obedience to his holy and righteous " laws," the people were fo fhocked, that they interrupted him; the judge, however, very properly obferved he ftood for his life, and defired them to let him have liberty; and when he had permiffion to proceed, he again fet out in fo extravagant and criminal a manner, vindicating it as a fact which the Lord had given anfwer to upon folemn appeals, that he was interrupted by the judge, who told him of the imprudence of his conduct, in making fo much of his prelude, to a confeffion of the facts ftated againft him, telling him, that to hear him making difcourfes and debates, which are a juftification of a horrid and notorious treafon, was not to be fuffered, it was treafon of itfelf; concluding that he, and thofe who fat with him, were upon their confciences, and muft appear before God for what they fhould do; and fo, fays the judge, are you too; but " remember " the devil fometimes appears in the habit of " an angel of light;" and then gave him permiffion to fpeak what he wifhed in a few words, though it was beyond the ftrict rules of the law; but he ftill perfifting to juftify what was done, as having been appointed under an act of parliament, and vindicating it upon that ground, he was, after various interruptions, ftopped from proceeding.

until he had pleaded to the fact, upon which he confeſſed giving ſentence and ſigning the warrant, when leave was given him to ſpeak to the matter of law ; but here again he launched out to ſtate the grounds of the quarrel between the late king and his parliament ; and when prevented from proceeding, by being told that the Houſe of Commons could not of themſelves make an act of parliament, nor was it the Houſe of Commons that had made it, for only 46 were permitted at that time to ſit, and of thoſe only 26 voted it. He ſeemed to urge the expediency of it, by ſaying, " neither was there ever ſuch a war, or ſuch a " preſident ;" and when the court abſolutely refuſed to hear any more of ſuch vindications, he replied, " I deſire I may be heard. I have not " compaſſed the death of the late king, contrived " the death of the king ; what I did I did by au- " thority."

Lord Anſley then acquainted him, that he was preſent in the Houſe of Commons when the vote paſſed for the agreement with the king in the treaty of the Iſle of Wight ; that his majeſty had condeſcended to moſt of the deſires of the parliament, who agreed that they were ſufficient for the grounds of a peace ; but that what he urged as an authority for acting under, was no parliament, and could give no ſuch authority, and therefore it was no juſtification for him, he being indicted under a clear act of parliament of 25 Edward III. though he defended himſelf under what was not an act of parliament.

Mr. Carew replied, " I am a ftranger to many " of thefe things which you have offered; and " this is ftrange; you give evidence fitting as a " judge." To whom the chief baron faid " you " are miftaken, it is not evidence, he fhews " you what authority that was, an authority of " twenty-fix members : how is this evidence? " Mr. Carew, if you have any thing more of fact, " go on; if you have nothing, but according to " this kind of difcourfe, I am commanded to di- " rect the jury."

He then faid, " I am very willing to leave it " with the Lord, if you will ftop me, that I can- " not open the true nature of thofe things that " did give me ground of fatisfaction in my con- " fcience, that I did it from the Lord." The fo- licitor-general with vehemence applied to have him ftopped in his fhocking extravagance, tel- ling him, " you have been fuffered to fpeak, you " have faid but little, only fedition; you pre- " tend a confcience, and the fear of the Lord, " when all the world knows you did it againft the " law of the Lord, your own confcience, the " light of nature, and the laws of the land, againft " the oath you have taken of allegiance and fu- " premacy."

Seeing all his defence was to no purpofe, when given to his judges, he addreffing the " gentle- " men of the jury," faid, " I fay I fhall leave it " with you. This authority I fpeak of is right, " which was the fupreme power; it is well known " what they were;" the counfel faid, " it is fo in-

" deed, many have known what they were;" and the lord chief baron addreſſed him thus: " You " have been heard what, and beyond what, was fit " to ſay in your defence; that which you have " ſaid, the heads of it you ſee the court hath " over-ruled. To ſuffer you to expatiate againſt " God and the king by blaſphemy, is not to be " endured; it is ſuffering poiſon to go about to " infect people; but they know now too well the " old ſaying, *in nomine Domine,* in the name of " the Lord, all miſchiefs have been done; that " hath been an old rule. I muſt now give di- " rections to the jury; but the priſoner inter- rupting, ſaid, " I have deſired to ſpeak the words " of truth and ſoberneſs, but have been hin- " dered;" the judge however proceeded in the charge to the jury, who after a very ſmall time of conſultation, returned their verdict Guilty; and being aſked what goods or chattels he had, ſaid none that they knew of; and though all the others arraigned with him, when aſked why ſentence ſhould not be given, threw themſelves upon the king's mercy, he ſaid, " I commit my cauſe unto " the Lord."

Ludlow, who was himſelf equally guilty, ſeems to think he had not ſtrict juſtice ſhewn him; but it is wonderful, that when he would not permit his ſovereign to ſpeak or argue upon the legality of a court, ſuch as the world had never before ſeen, and which never can be lawful, he ſhould doubt the validity of that which tried him. It was extraordinary too that he ſhould think God owned their caufe, becaufe they were fuccefsful in their projects, when it was an argument againft himfelf, going to fuffer for it, by a turn of the tide; befides, if fuccefs made actions virtuous, the vileft acts may be reconciled to religion, and faid to be effected with the approbation of God; it is fo monftrous a propofition, that murderers, and every other the moft infamous of men, may go on and triumph in their wickednefs, as chofen veffels, who are encouraged and protected by the Deity.

During the time of his fubfequent imprifonment, and until his execution at Charing Crofs, Nov. 15, 1660, he had all the raptures and extafies of enthufiafm; he gloried in his death, faying to his friends, " I die not in the Lord only, " but for the Lord;" he prayed " the Lord to " preferve them all from the portion of this ge- " neration." Of his extraordinary merit and fanctification he had not the fmalleft doubt; " the " Lord, faid he, " will bring my blood to cry " with the reft of the martyrs;" a martyr he deluded himfelf with thinking he was for Chrift, whom he thought would foon vifibly appear; and he told the Lord's people to wait patiently, " and " he that fhall come, will come, and will not " tarry." To fome of his friends he fent word, " that this was the laft beaft, and his rage was " great, becaufe his time was fhort." When he was told that Major-general Harrifon was put to death, he faid, " Well! my turn will be next, " and as we have gone along in our lives, fo we

" muſt be one, in our deaths." Harriſon was
alſo a Millenarian. When his relations ſhed tears
at taking their leave of him, he rebuked them,
glorifying that he was " counted worthy to be a
" witneſs of this cauſe." At the gallows his language was blaſphemouſly enthuſiaſtical; evincing
the wildneſs of his religious opinions. Amongſt
the number of his uncommon ſentences in his
long harangue to the people, he told them,
" there are many things laid upon many of thoſe
" that profeſs the kingdom, and glorious appear-
" ance of Jeſus Chriſt, as if they were enemies to
" magiſtracy and miniſtry; and, as if we were for
" the deſtruction of the laws and properties of
" mankind, therefore I ſhall ſpeak a few words
" unto that. And, if indeed we were ſuch, we
" were fit to be turned out of the world; as
" ſome now think they ſhould do good ſervice
" in ſending ſuch poor creatures quickly from
" hence. There is no ſuch thing; I deſire to
" bear witneſs to the true magiſtracy, that ma-
" giſtracy that is in the word of the Lord. -And
" that true miniſtry, which miniſtry is a miniſtry
" from the anointing; that doth bear witneſs to
" the Lord Jeſus, and hath his holy ſpirit. That
" teſtimony I deſire to bear; and that teſtimony
" I deſire to ſtand faithful in, with integrity to
" the Lord Jeſus, as king of ſaints and king of
" nations. And therefore it is, I ſay, to have a
" magiſtracy as at the firſt, and counſellors as at
" the beginning, men fearing God, and hating

" covetoufnefs. And that miniſtry as doth preach
" the everlaſting gofpel."

His prayer was equally extravagant ; he appears
by it to think himſelf a perſon of great confequence in the eye of his Creator ; for he ſays,
" O bleſſed Father, it is not that I do expect any
" thing from thee upon any account, below the
" account of the Lord Jefus ; and wherein *thou*
" *haſt been glorified by thy poor ſervant*, it hath
" been by thine own power, and thine own
" working."

. When the executioner had done his office, the
king, in reſpect for his elder brother's memory,
and for the fake of his ſurviving friends, gave his
quarters to be buried. It was greatly to be lamented, that a gentleman of family, of fortune, and
whoſe education was liberal, having been ſent to
one of the univerſities, and afterwards ſtudied
the law at the inns of court, fhould ſuffer himfelf to be fo far deluded by a lying ſpirit, as to
be not able to diſtinguiſh between good and evil ;
not to know that an unlawful aſſembly could not
make legal what they appointed ; not to know
that deſtroying the ſovereign was treaſon.

Mr. Ludlow ſays, that he was elected into the
council of ſtate, and employed in many important affairs, in which he fhewed great ability ;
but it is difficult to give credit to this. I can
better believe that, faint as he was, and waiting
for Chriſt to be king upon earth, he was very
anxious to make a fplendid appearance to his heavenly maſter ; for, though a younger brother, he

had at his imprifonment " a plentiful eftate."
By the book intituled " Regicides no Saints," it
is evident that thefe felf-fanctified men were by
no means neglectful of earthly things.

The people were beyond meafure exafperated
againft him, except fome of his enthufiaftic dif-
ciples; for it appears he was a preacher to the
brethren in the weft; this was evident by the conftant ufage he received from the time of his
feizure in Cornwall; for in moft towns that he
paffed through, the generality of the people reviled him with fuch words as thefe; " hang him,
" rogue; piftol him," faid others; " hang him
" up," faid fome at Salifbury, " at the next fign
" poft, without any farther trouble;" and when
he bore all this with calm compofure, with a face
unchanged, they faid, " they fuppofed he would
" alter his countenance and tremble when he
" came to the ladder." As this is the account
which his friends give, it proves how much King
Charles I.'s death was lamented by the people, and
how wonderfully far gone in fanaticifm he muft
have been; indeed it had been eafy for him to have
efcaped to the continent; but no, faid he, to fuch
who propofed it to him, " I have committed both
" my life and eftate to the Lord, to fave or de-
" ftroy as he thinks meet; I therefore will not
" by any means go out of the way."

In times of peace and domeftic harmony fuch
a character would have been judged religioufly
mad, and fhut up in a place proper for the reception of fuch unhappy creatures, and with due

care he might have been reftored to reafon; if not, he would have been prevented outraging the deareft rights of fociety.

If he left defcendants, they have, like his other relatives, been afhamed of owning him, or at leaft had the modefty not to glory in his crimes.

The diflike expreffed againft this regicide was extremely great by the parliament, who, when the act of indemnity paffed, excluded him and Colonel Scroop from every benefit of it; this was probably to prevent any infurrection being raifed by the mad enthufiaftical fifth monarchy men, who by delays might have gathered, to refcue fuch fuper-eminent faints from becoming martyrs.

The Life of WILLIAM CAWLEY, Esq.

WILLIAM CAWLEY, Esq. was originally a brewer in Chichester, in the county of Suffex; he was a member of the long parliament and when the war broke out, he obtained a commiffion in the army.

He was named a commiffioner in the pretended high court of juftice, which he attended as one of the judges on the 17th, and every fubfequent day, both in their fittings in the Painted Chamber, and in Weftminfter Hall, and he figned the warrant to put the king to death.

When a commonwealth was erected he was much trufted; in 1650-1 he was appointed one of the council of ftate; yet he acquiefced in Oliver's taking upon him the fovereign power, who made him one of his committee for the county of Suffex.

He was one of the very few of the king's judges who were able to obtain a feat in the convention parliament; but perceiving how much the popular tide was turned againft him, he concealed himfelf; and the parliament foon convinced him he had acted prudently, for he was abfolutely excepted from pardon both as to life and eftate.

Leaving the kingdom, he paffed through France, and ftrove to procure an affylum at Geneva, but finding it impoffible, he removed to Laufanne in Switzerland, where the lords of Berne granted him their protection; but he was ftill in fome meafure at the mercy of the royal family, who had devoted him to deftruction.

His fituation in banifhment muft have been extremely painful ; the fear of detection, the lofs of all fociety with thofe he loved, and compelled to refide in a foreign land upon a fcanty income, with the knowledge that he had called all this upon himfelf, and, we muft hope, fincere forrow for the dreadful crime which brought all this upon him. He, and fome others implicated with him, lived as if they wifhed to be forgotten, even whilft upon earth, and were fpectators, as it were, of being cut off from the land of the living. A more melancholy fituation cannot be conceived by the mind of man. It is obfervable that he alone gave a negative to Colonel Monk's, then a prifoner in the Tower, having a commiffion in the parliament army given to him. Mr. Ludlow calls him " an able " and ancient member of parliament." He had a family; William, his eldeft fon, was of the committee for the county of Suffex.

The Life of THOMAS CHALLONER, *Esq.*

THOMAS CHALLONER, Esq. was a younger son
of Sir Thomas Challoner, Knt. tutor to Henry
Prince of Wales, by Elizabeth daughter of Sir
William Fleetwood, Knt. and was born near
Staple-Claydon in Buckinghamshire. At the age
of sixteen he was sent to Exeter College, in Oxford, which was in the early part of the year 1611;
before he took any degree he left college, and tra-
velled into France, Italy, and Germany; upon
his return to England he went and resided at
Gisborough in the county of York, where the family estate lay. About 1643 he procured a seat
in the long parliament for a borough in Yorkshire, and being a person of great acquirements,
and of an active disposition, the parliament gave
him a commission in 1647, with Colonel John
Temple, to govern the province of Munster in
Ireland. It was very unfortunate for him that he
was not detained longer there; for coming over
to England, he was named a commissioner of the
high court of justice, and having a decided preference for a republican government, and great
prejudices against his majesty, he sat in the court,
and was peculiarly busy in carrying on the sad
catastrophe, being one of the committee appointed
to manage the business; his name is also to the
public meetings upon the 8th, 10th, 12th, 13th,
15th, 19th 20th, 22d, and 25th days of January
in the Painted Chamber; and in Westminster

Hall the 20th, 22d, and 23d; but he did not attend the laſt day when ſentence was given, though he ſigned the death warrant.

Upon the eſtabliſhment of the commonwealth he obtained very conſiderable conſequence, being appointed of the council of ſtate in 1649-50, and in the following year, and was one of the maſters of the mint. He neither approved of, nor I believe, was truſted, by the elder protector; but in 1659 he was again of the council of ſtate. He ſurrendered himſelf in obedience to the parliament's proclamation, yet like the others he was excepted both as to life and eſtate, though the great and good Earl of Southampton objected to it, as a forfeiture of the public faith; but he was over-ruled by Sir Heneage Finch, his majeſty's ſolicitor-general; however Mr. Challoner ſoon after found means to eſcape out of the kingdom, and retired to Middleburg in Zealand where he died in 1661.

Few of the regicides were more culpable than this gentleman, whoſe family had been foſtered in the royal boſom; they had been beloved, truſted, honoured. King James I. had confided the heir apparent of the crown to the care of his father, and had created another of his relatives a baronet, and his great mental accompliſhments ought to have ſhewn him the danger of deſtroying, what it was impoſſible to build up again: ſuch a wild fanatic as Carew was, might have been ſuppoſed to have ſwept away all that oppoſed his viſionary ſyſtem, but Challoner had no ſuch chimæras to combat with.

The Life of JAMES CHALLONER, *Esq.*

JAMES CHALLONER, Esq. was a brother of Mr. Thomas Challoner, whom I have juſt mentioned. He unfortunately embarked in the ſame ungrateful, as well as traitorous buſineſs; he ſat in the Painted Chamber, as one of the king's judges, on January the 8th, 10th, and 20th, and in Weſtminſter Hall the 20th, and 21ſt days of the ſame month.

He was a moſt determined republican, but, like General Fairfax, he had a great love for the fine arts, and the works of antiquity; ſentiments very oppoſite to moſt of thoſe of levelling principles, none of whom were agreed indeed how far they ought to go. Some were for lopping off a few of the exuberant branches, as they ſuppoſed they were; others were for deſtroying the venerable trunk; whilſt the moſt violent were for taking away both root and branches, that there never might be a poſſibility of its putting out again.

After the decapitation of the great and wife Earl of Derby, who fell a victim to duty, the Iſle of Man was taken from the Stanley family, and given by the parliament to General Fairfax, who ſent Mr. Challoner over as his agent or governor, where he employed his leiſure in procuring materials for a hiſtory of that little kingdom, as it was then, and until lately ſo remained.

He was recalled from Man, and again mixed in all the buſy ſcene which was acted preceding the reſtoration ; and, having declared for the intereſt of the parliament in oppoſition to that of the army, he was ſent to priſon by General Fleet-wood.

He had but juſt eſcaped from this misfortune, before another of even a worſe nature overtook him ; for though his life was ſpared, the parlia-ment confiſcated his eſtate, leaving him a prey to poverty and wretchedneſs. He ſunk under ſo great a calamity. We muſt lament the fate of a man of ſcience, who was equally an object of compaſſion and abhorrence. His ingratitude muſt ſtamp his character with peculiar baſeneſs, and he lived to feel the ſtigma.

(R.)

The Life of GREGORY CLEMENT, Esq.

GREGORY CLEMENT, Esq. was a citizen and merchant of London, who, by trading to Spain, had raised a very considerable estate, though the royalists say he had failed; but I suppose Mr. Ludlow is right in the first statement. He came into the long parliament about 1646, says Mr. Ludlow, and discharged that trust with great diligence, always joining with those who were most affectionate to the commonwealth, though he was never possessed of any place of profit under them *.

The army and parliament juntos put him upon the commission to try the king; and he, who was entirely a republican, said, upon that occasion, " he durst not refuse his assistance." He attended the high court of justice all the days in Westminster Hall; and in the Painted Chamber January the 8th, 22d, 23d, and 29th; and set his hand and seal to the warrant to put the king to death.

He had, by purchasing the estates of the bishops, acquired a very considerable fortune in land. It

---

* The Mystery of the Good Old Cause says, he had scarce been two months in the house of commons, before he protested he had not more than cleared the purchase-money, which was but fixty pounds; but said, as a comfort for himself, that he hoped times would mend. This tale is deserving of little credit; we cannot suppose, that a seat in parliament, at a time when it was most valuable, would be so easily procured; nor he so weak to mention what would have been so little to his credit to have been known.

is very evident he was more avaricious than ambitious; he forgot, however, that the strictest hypocrify was proper, whilst a multitude of self-
elected faints on all fides furrounded him; for
not managing his intrigues with fecrecy, he was
proved to have been frail with his female fervant
at Greenwich, which was fuch a falling from
grace, that he was deprived of his feat in parliament, and not reftored until after Oliver's death,
when the fin was no more remembered. Should
fuch an inquifition now take place, how greatly
would it thin both houfes!

The method of taking Mr. Clement was very
remarkable, as mentioned by Mr. Ludlow, in
whofe words I fhall give it: " Mr. Gregory Cle-
" ment, one of the king's judges, had concealed
" himfelf at a mean houfe near Gray's Inn; but
" fome perfons having obferved that better pro-
" vifions were carried to that place than had been
" ufual, procured an officer to fearch the houfe,
" where he found Mr. Clement, and prefuming
" him to be one of the king's judges, though
" they knew him not perfonally, carried him be-
" fore the commiffioners of the militia of that
" precinct. One of thefe commiffioners, to whom
" he was not unknown, after a flight examina-
" tion, had prevailed with the reft to difmifs
" him; but as he was about to withdraw, it hap-
" pened that a blind man, who had crowded into
" the room, and was acquainted with the voice of
" Mr. Clement, which was very remarkable, de-
" fired he might be called in again, and demand-

" ed, if he was not Mr. Gregory Clement? The
" commiſſioners not knowing how to refuſe his
" requeſt, permitted the queſtion to be aſked;
" and he not denying himſelf to be the man, was
" by that means diſcovered."

He was ſeized upon May 26, 1660, and ſent to
the Tower, at which time an order came to ſecure
the property of all thoſe who had ſat in judgment
upon the late king. At the return of Charles II.
he was abſolutely excepted from pardon, both as
to life and eſtate; and he was brought to his trial
October the 12th, ſucceding his commitment, with
Colonel Jones, another of the regicides; at which
time, though he had pleaded not guilty, yet ſoon
after he preſented a petition in court, upon his ar-
raignment; the Lord Chief Baron addreſſing him,
ſaid, " If you do confeſs your offence, your peti-
" tion will be read;" to whom he replied, " I
" do, my lord." His lordſhip then told him,
" Mr. Clement, if you do confeſs (that you may
" underſtand it), you muſt, when you are called,
" and when the jury are to be charged; you muſt
" ſay (if you will have it go by way of confeſſion)
" that you wave your former plea, and confeſs the
" fact." The clerk of the crown then ſaid, " Gre-
" gory Clement, you have been indicted of high
" treaſon, for compaſſing and imagining the death
" of his late majeſty, and you have pleaded not
" guilty; are you content to wave that plea, and
" confeſs it? He ſaid, " I do confeſs myſelf
" guilty, my lord." And, when aſked what he
had to ſay, why ſentence ſhould not be pro-

nounced? he only replied, " I pray mercy from
" the king."

Such a conduct would extremely intereſt one in
behalf of a criminal; and we ſhould wiſh to have
ſuch a perſon ſaved, had he been real in his ſorrow
for the crime; but his ſubſequent conduct ſhews
he was undeſerving of it: for, when he found he
muſt die, he ſaid, that nothing troubled him ſo
much as his pleading guilty at the time of his
trial, to ſatisfy the importunity of his relations,
by which he had rendered himſelf unworthy to
die in ſo glorious a cauſe. He was put to death
at Charing Croſs, October the 16th, going in the
ſame ſledge as Mr. Scot; and Colonels Scroop and
Jones in a ſecond. He ſaid nothing at the place
of execution; " for though," remarks Mr. Ludlow, " his apprehenſion and judgment were not
" to be deſpiſed, yet he had no good elocu-
" tion."

Mr. Clement was certainly a perſon of no abilities; his ſituation in the Houſe of Commons
ſerved him to lay out his money to greater advantage, which ſeems all his aim; and he was probably led by ſome ſuch conſiderations to act in
that cauſe which led to his ignominious end,
though it is evident he hated the kingly office.
It is probable he was a cadet of a knightly family, in Kent. I ſuppoſe Major William Clement, in the London Militia, was his ſon.

The Life of Sir WILLIAM CONSTABLE, Bart.

SIR WILLIAM CONSTABLE, Bart. was defcended of as ancient, knightly, rich, and loyal a family as moft in Yorkfhire, though that county boafts fo many. He was eldeft fon and heir of Sir Robert Conftable of Flamborough, by Dorothy, daughter of Sir John Widdrington, Knt. relict of Sir Roger Fenwick, Knt.

Sir William fucceeded his father in his eftate of Flamborough ; and when a young man, he ferved under the Earl of Effex, in Ireland, going thither in 1599; and, diftinguifhing himfelf againft the Irifh rebels, that nobleman conferred the honour of knighthood upon him.

When the Earl of Effex returned into England, and was led away by his furious ungovernable paffions to confpire the dethronement of his royal miftrefs, he joined in his treafon, and was arraigned for the crime, in 1601, which muft have occafioned him an ignominious death, if it had not been for the mercy her majefty fhewed him, by fending a fpecial letter, commanding him and others to be remitted the difgrace of trial, gracioufly urging, that he was drawn in by Effex ; and, March 20, following, the queen's warrant was fent to Sir John Popham, Knt. lord chief juftice, to admit him to bail.

As King James looked upon Effex as his martyr, as he was pleafed to call him, he regarded

with great affection all who had fuffered for him ;
this occafioned his majefty to look upon Sir William with efpecial favour, and, June 9, 1611, he
raifed him to the rank of a baronet. In the parliament called in the twenty-firft of this reign, he
was returned one of the reprefentatives for the
borough of Knarefborough.

In the reign of King Charles I. he had very
confiderable intereft in Yorkfhire, owing at firft
to his profufe extravagance and high living, and
afterwards for his fetting up as the leader of thofe
who oppofed the blameable conduct of the court ;
he was therefore returned to ferve for the county
of York, in the firft year of this reign, and for
Knarefborough in all the fucceeding parliaments,
except the long parliament, when he fat for Kel-
lington in Cornwall. As he fet himfelf in oppofition to the government, it drew him into many
inconveniencies ; he was imprifoned about fhip-
money, which he judged illegal ; and the expences
he had put himfelf to, obliged him to difpofe of
his eftates for twenty-five thoufand pounds, to Sir
Marmaduke, afterwards Lord Langdale.

The opening of the long parliament difplayed
him a difappointed, enraged, ruined patriot, ready
to execute whatever could gratify his anger, pride,
or avarice. When the Earl of Effex (the fon of
that nobleman for whom he had fo nearly loft his
life) drew his fword againft the king, he accepted
a commiffion from the parliament, to fight under
his banners, and foon rofe to the rank of colonel;

K 2

in which situation he performed essential service to his employers.

He was sent with Colonel Brown in 1642, with his regiment, to oppose the king's marching to London, the parliament being conscious that whoever got that city, would become in the end triumphant. In the following year, he routed three regiments of the Marquis of Newcastle's horse, took three hundred of them, with many officers, obtained Stamford Bridge in Lincolnshire, and seized there three pieces of ordnance, with powder, shot, and arms, sufficient to furnish several troops of horse, besides provisions; and in 1644, he went and laid siege to Scarborough Castle, in his own county, being sent thither by General Fairfax.

In the year 1646, he was appointed one of the commissioners to preserve the peace between the kingdoms of England and Scotland, and obtained an order from parliament to pay him the sum of one thousand nine hundred pounds, in full of the arrears due to him as one of the officers in their army. In the beginning of 1647-8, he was sent, with Lieutenant-colonels Goffe and Salmon, to guard the Isle of Wight; and as the captive king was imprisoned there, a commission was sent to him and Colonel Hammond to place and displace such attendants about his majesty as they judged most proper for the security of his person. Soon after his regiment marched into Gloucester, but part of which, in June, commanded by Lieutenant-colonel Read, assisted in storming the suburbs of Tenby in Pembrokeſhire, in which they were ſuccefsful; and about a week afterwards, the town and caſtle alſo ſurrendered to the mercy of the parliament.

He was nominated one of the high court of juſtice for trying the king, and it ſeemed a moſt grateful employment to him; he was one to whom the care of making all neceſſary preparations was given.   He ſat as a commiſſioner or judge in the Painted-Chamber, on the 13th, 15th, 17th, 18th, 20th, 22d, 23d, 24th, 26th, 27th, and 29th, and every day that the court ſat in Weſtminſter Hall, and he ſigned the warrant for execution.

The ſervices he had rendered both the parliament and army demanded a grateful return; he was put in the council of ſtate in 1649 and 1650, was gratified with a conſiderable command in the north, and appointed governor of Glouceſter, in which city he died full of years, and loaded with infamy.

His wickednefs in procuring the ſequeſtration of the eſtates he had ſold for ſo large a ſum, from the loyal Sir Marmaduke Langdale, that it might be given back again to himſelf, ſhews as unprincipled a mind in private life, as his ingratitude to the crown, which, when young, had with peculiar delicacy given him his life, and ſince then granted him hereditary honours; but this, and his ill-gained poſſeſſions, were alike forfeited at the reſtoration, when he was excepted out of the general pardon as if living.

Sir Philip Conftable, defcended from a junior branch of this family, feated at Everingham, was created a baronet by King Charles I., to whom he proved as loyal as Sir William was traitorous; but this title is become extinct from want of male heirs.

The Life of MILES CORBET*, Efq.

MILES CORBET, Efq. was a gentleman of an ancient family in Norfolk, who had applied him-felf with great feduloufnefs to the ftudy of the law in Lincoln's Inn, and what was a rare circum-ftance, had been chofen in all the parliaments for thirty-feven years; he was burgefs of, and re-corder for, Great Yarmouth in the long par-liament; and having great prejudices both againft the court and the hierarchy, he took the moft de-cided part againft his majefty.

He early became a committee-man for the county of Norfolk; at the commencement of the civil war, he had but a fmall fortune, but he foon improved it, not as many gentlemen of the law did by drawing the fword, but by obtaining lu-crative places in his original profeffion. The parliament in 1644 made him clerk of the court of wards.

---

* The Corbets are originally of the county of Salop, and were ancient barons; there have been fome of them ennobled and the title of baronet has been conferred upon feveral of the branches; there is no family of higher antiquity, nor greater gentility than this. There was one of them feated in the county of Norfolk; of this line was Sir Miles Corbet, Knt. in the beginning of the feventeenth century, who had a brother, John Corbet, Efq. he married Mary daughter of Sir Roger Wodehoufe, Knt. who fur-viving him, re-married to George Kemp of Tottenham in Mid-dlefex, Efq. he was feated at Shrowfton in Norfolk, as was Sir Thomas Corbet, knighted by King Charles I. at Royfton, Oc-tober 11, 1634.

In March 1647-8, he, with Mr. Robert Goodwin were made regiftrars of the court of Chancery, in the room of Colonel Long, one of the eleven impeached members; this place was worth feven hundred pounds a year to him.

He was put in the commiffion to fit at King Charles I.'s trial. Mr. Ludlow fays that though one of the high court of juftice, yet " he ap-" peared not amongft the judges by reafon of " fome fcruples he had entertained, till the day " that fentence was pronounced; but upon more " mature deliberation, finding them of no weight, " he durft no longer abfent himfelf; coming early " on that day into the court, that he might give " a public teftimony of his fatisfaction and con-" currence with their proceedings;" this gentleman's memory here betrays him, for Mr. Corbet feems to have had no fuch fcruples; and inftead of only appearing the laft, he was in the Painted Chamber the firft day, January the 8th; and alfo the 15th, 23d, and 26th; and fat as a judge both upon the 23d and the 27th in Weftminfter Hall when fentence was given, and he figned the warrant to put his majefty to death.

He had the principal management of the office of fequeftration to pillage the loyalifts, to enable the parliamentarians to carry on the war againft the king; fpeaking of which, Lord Hollis fays, " the committee of examinations where " Mr. Miles Corbet kept his juftice feat, which " was worth fomething to his clerk, if not to " him. What a continual horfe fair it was I ever

" like dooms-day itfelf, to judge perfons of all
" forts and fexes." This made him fo very odious in this kingdom that he was glad to change
the fcene.

The parliament therefore in Auguft 1652 put
him in the commiffion for managing the affairs
of Ireland with the Lord-general Cromwell, Lieu-
tenant-generals Fleetwood and Ludlow, Colonel
Jones, and Mr. Weaver. In this fituation he remained during all the changes of government
until January 1659-60 when he was fufpended
by Sir Charles Coote, and then impeached of
high treafon, after having received no lefs than
ten feveral commiffions for this office. He foon
after returned into England, but was fo alarmed
by the proceedings againft Sir Henry Vane and
Major Salway, and from having fo great a charge
preferred againft him, that he would not appear
publicly, much lefs go to the houfe, until, in-
fpired with fome confidence by Ludlow, he went
thither to give an account of his conduct; in
which it is moft probable he acted with great
merit; for Ludlow who was part of the time upon
the fpot, and fome while employed with him,
avers that " he manifefted fuch integrity, that
" though he was continued for many years in that
" ftation, yet he impaired his own eftate for the
" public fervice, whilft he was the greateft huf-
" band of the treafure of the commonwealth."
Perhaps this injury done to his private fortune
did not include what he received in debenture
lands, or fome other of the many ways the long

parliament, as well as Cromwell, contrived to reward such who served them ; for his original fortune was but small, and he it is known had acquired very considerable property.

At the restoration he made his escape to the continent, and after travelling through many parts of Germany, settled with Berkstead and Okey, two other of the regicides, in Hanau in the circle of the Lower Rhine, and where they were admitted burgesses of the city ; a sufficient proof that they had taken much property with them.

Not content to remain in a place of perfect safety, he most imprudently left it with his companions to come to Delft in Holland, where he was secured by Sir George Downing the English resident, their former friend ; and who had remained in that situation under Cromwell and the commonwealth ; but had made his peace with the king, for having, it is supposed, in as secret as wonderful manner, preserved his majesty's person whilst in exile ; be this as it might, he now, to shew he acted with a steady fidelity to his sovereign, procured leave to secure them ; and sent them over in the Black-a-more frigate, and as they had all been excepted both as to life and estate in the act of indemnity ; they were brought up to the King's Bench bar April 16, 1662, and sentenced to die as traitors, for they could not plead having submitted to the proclamation, as they, instead of surrendering themselves, had fled.

The day previous to his death he assured his friends " that he was so thoroughly convinced of

" the juftice, and neceffity of that action for
" which he was to die, that if the things had
" been yet intire, and to do, he could not refufe to
" act as he had done, without affronting his rea-
" fon, and oppofing himfelf to the dictates of
" his confcience;" adding, " that the immo-
" ralities, lewdnefs, and corruptions of all forts
" which had been introduced and encouraged
" fince the late revolution, were no inconfiderable
" juftification of thofe proceedings." The li-
centious court of Charles II. was a great contraft to the folemn hypocrify of the republicans;
it feemed general throughout England, from the
excefs of joy that pervaded all orders of men, to
have the re-eftablifhment of the religion and government of their anceftors, with the exception of
a very inconfiderable part of the nation. The
conduct of King Charles II. had certainly nothing to do with that of his father, whofe moral
behaviour was as irreproachable as any of his moft
virtuous enemies, and that without either fpiritual
pride or bafe hypocrify; perhaps Charles II. as
he determined to indulge in licencioufnefs, did it
openly from the difguft he entertained for that
fanctified wickednefs which fo fhockingly difgraced the republicans.

Mr. Corbet was executed at Tyburn, being
drawn thither upon a fledge from the Tower; his
quarters were placed over the city gates and his
head upon London Bridge. It is a melancholy
idea to fee a character that might have been a great
ornament to fociety thus flying in the face of the

laws of God and man, and having fuch an infatuation, as to juftify his conduct when going to be
launched into eternity.

I fuppofe Major Miles Corbet, a member of the
long parliament, who in 1648 was affaulted and
wounded by fome cavaliers in a boat upon the
Thames, for which there was an order iffued to apprehend the offenders, was a fon of his. The
heir-general of the regicide married the late Reverend Thomas Whifton of Ramfey in Hunting-
donfhire, nephew of the well-known clergyman
Wifton, who, made fo much noife at the beginning of this century.

The Life of JOHN CORBET, Esq.

JOHN CORBET, Esq. was, I presume, a relation, probably a near one, to the last person whose life I have given.

Very little is known of him. He was named one of the king's judges; but he only sat on the first day in the Painted Chamber; not from any tenderness of conscience, for he sent a message to the commissioners, at their sitting in that place, on January the 22d, by colonel Harvey, one of them, who delivered it in these words : " that he " was desired to signify unto the court in the be- " half of Mr. John Corbet, member of this " court, that his absence is not from any disaf- " fection to the proceedings of this court, but in " regard of other special employment that he " hath in the service of the state."

Mr. secretary Thurloe, in a letter addressed to Henry Cromwell, then major-general of the army in Ireland, dated February 19, 1655-6, says, " There is some discourse here of sendinge over " to you Mr. John Corbet, the lawyer, for a " judge, and it is alsoe thought he would doe well " in the councell. It is certayne, he is an ho- " nest man, and *mediocritor doctus*; but weither " this will be resolved on, or weither he will ac- " cept it, I am not able to say."

I have not discovered whether he did go into

Ireland in that, or any other capacity. But if he furvived the reftoration, the bufinefs which fo occupied his time as to prevent his going to the high court of juftice, faved him at leaft from ruin, if not from death.

The Life of OLIVER CROMWELL, Esq.

OLIVER CROMWELL, Esq. was descended from a younger branch of a very ancient, rich, and powerful family, originally Welch. At the commencement of the long parliament, of which he was a member, he was greatly dissatisfied with the court and church, and entered into the army to effect what he thought a proper reform in each; but he soon saw the real views of each party, that they both aimed only at aggrandizement; and from seeing things generally, he dived with wonderful celerity into the minds of the individuals who were at the head of all the opposing interests, and, dropping his prejudices, he resolved to bend every transaction to his own peculiar advantage; he once bounded his ambition: the order of the garter, title of earl of Essex, and vicar-general, possessed by his maternal relation, was his aim; had the king offered him these, and acted with sincerity, he would have been restored to his crown, which indeed would have lost some of its finest jewels; but had Charles afterwards still farther gratified his more than wishes with a dukedom, he might have regained even these; and it had been the part of wisdom to have complied; it was little more than what his son gave for the whole.

Cromwell saw the danger of putting the king to death; saw that he lost by it all the fond hopes of gratifying his ambition with rank, and a permanent fortune; but when he could not fway the heads of the army, and knowing the king's infincerity towards him, he complied, and then left nothing undone to effect what otherwife he would never have confented to.

Soon after this, he obtained the command of the army, being faluted general, and openly directed, what he before had covertly done, all the movements in the war; and having conquered by his prowefs every oppofition in the three kingdoms, he refolved to make himfelf the fovereign of them, and which his own fecurity imperioufly demanded. To lay down his authority, and become a private citizen, was not to be expected; and the parliament was become fo jealous of him, that they only waited for an opportunity of ruining him, and to call in the fon of that monarch whom he had fo largely contributed to ruin, was fraught with many hazards; he therefore, with a refolution that no danger could vanquifh, fpurned from the government that very parliament which had ufurped the fovereignty, and had employed him in effecting it, and feated himfelf in their room, and evinced to an admiring world that he was born for empire, governing thefe nations with a fuccefs that has never been exceeded, and which wanted only legality to have made it defervedly praifed. At home, he was hated, courted, feared by every party; abroad, revered by the Proteftants, and dreaded by the Roman Catholics; the fcourge of all his foes.

Though a military character, yet humane; wherever he could be fo with fafety to himfelf; though an ufurper, tender of liberty. A perfe-cutor by his fituation of epifcopalians, yet often honouring, and not feldom, perhaps, fecretly re-lieving the neceffities produced by their conftancy and firmnefs. Always obliged to court thofe moft whom moft he defpifed, the wild fanatics; thefe he knew were averfe to every form of go-vernment but the republican, and even fome to all but the fpiritual one of Chrift, whom they ex-pected foon to come down, and perfonally reign over them.

In fine, blot out the deep-engraven words Re-gicide and Ufurper, Oliver was a character that never more than once has been exceeded by the ancients, nor equalled by the moderns. With thefe great blemifhes he muft be always recorded as a wicked man; but not like Roberfpiere; he can never be called a monfter, which that moft infamous of wretches ever muft; like the tyger, he feemed pleafed with flaughter; was unfatisfied if he could not roll and wallow in blood: car-nage to him was paftime; oceans of human gore would not have fatisfied the thirft of this exe-crable tyrant. He had no other pleafure than feafting his eyes upon the dying agonies of youth, beauty, manhood, and venerable age. Of the many who confpired againft Cromwell, very few were put to death, and they by the cleareft evi-dence, and with all the decorum of the moft re-gular government. There is no analogy between

the Englifh and the French ufurpers; one had
not a fingle requifite for a great prince, the other
was deficient in fcarce any one to make him a
moft exalted monarch.　The one having cut the
arteries of France was, by univerfal confent, maf-
facred to fave expiring nature, in a few months
after the commencement of his fanguinary triumph; the other died, after governing with reputation feveral years, September 3, 1660, admired by all.

As few of king Charles the I.'s enemies had
Cromwell's excufe for their conduct towards him,
there was no one perfon who more fincerely defpifed them than himfelf; indeed none in general
are fo defpicable as tools, and they muft appear
more particularly fo in the eyes of thofe whofe
dupes they have been.

The Life of Sir JOHN D'ANVERS, *Knt.*

SIR JOHN D'ANVERS, Knt. was the third and younger son of Sir John D'Anvers, of Dantsey, in the county of Wilts, knt., by Elizabeth, fourth and youngest daughter and co-heir of John Lord Latimer, and grand-daughter of Queen Catherine Parr by her first husband. Lady D'Anvers' mother was Lucy, daughter of Henry, Marquis of Worcester*.

The eldest brother of Sir John was Sir Charles D'Anvers, who being deeply implicated in the Earl of Essex's treason, in the latter end of the reign of Queen Elizabeth, was put to death for it.

The second brother was Sir Henry D'Anvers, seated at Stowe, in Northamptonshire, and who was restored in blood by a special act of parliament, in the third year of the reign of king James I. on account of his brother Sir Charles' attainder. He first distinguished himself by his gallant conduct in the low country wars, whilst serving under prince Maurice of Nassau. Going from that service, he was in the army of Henry the Great of France, who knighted him for the

---

* Lady D'Anvers, re-married to Sir Edmund Carey, third son of Henry Lord Hunsdon, and died aged 84. 1630; upon the monument she erected for herself in Stowe church, is added this sentence: *Sic familia præclara, præclarior prole, virtute præclarissima.*

good fervices he had rendered his majefty. He was employed in the Irifh wars, ferving under the Earl of Effex and Charles Lord Montjoy, where he rofe to be lieutenant-general of horfe, and ferjeant-major of the whole army. King James I. in the firft year of his reign, created him a peer of the realm, by the title of Baron Dauntefey, and afterwards appointed him lord prefident of Munfter, and governor of the ifland of Guernfey: King Charles I. alfo, at the commencement of his reign, raifed him to a higher title, by creating him Earl of Danby; and his lordfhip was alfo called to the privy council, and elected knight of the garter. He died unmarried at his feat of Cornbury, in Oxfordfhire, January 20, 1643-4. The phyfic garden in Oxford is a monument of his munificence, his repairing and beautifying the church of Stowe of his piety.

The fifters were Ann, married to Sir Arthur Porter; Lucy, to Sir Henry Baynton; Eleanor, to Thomas Walmefley, of Dunkenhalgh, in Lancafhire, efq.; Elizabeth, to Sir Thomas Hobby; Catherine, the favourite of her brother the Earl of Danby, to Sir Richard Gargrave, of Noftel Abbey, in Yorkfhire, knt.; Dorothy, to Sir Peter Ofborne, knt., anceftor of the baronets of that name; and Mary, who died very young.

Sir John was feated at Chelfea, where the family had a freehold eftate valued at fixty pounds a year, fo early as the reign of queen Elizabeth; the manfion was called D'Anver's Houfe, and was taken down about the year 1696, when D'Anver's ſtreet was built upon its ſcite*.

Never were two brothers more oppoſite in character and ſentiments than Sir John and Lord Danby; though honoured by his majeſty king Charles I. with a place near his royal perſon, as a gentleman of the privy chamber, yet he was ever averſe to his intereſt, which he took every method in his power to injure. When the Scots had broke into the kingdom in 1639, he refuſed the application of the crown to contribute any ſum towards raiſing an army to drive them home again.

He was returned one of the repreſentatives for the univerſity of Oxford in the two laſt parliaments of king Charles I.; and being thus ſeated in the latter, he commenced the open and decided enemy of his majeſty; and when the war was agreed to be carried on by them, he immediately accepted a commiſſion; but, though he became a colonel, he never diſtinguiſhed himſelf in the field.

Such a conduct as this muſt have been extremely diſtaſteful to the king, and no leſs mortifying to the loyal Earl of Danby, whoſe family were under ſuch great obligations to King Charles and the late monarch; this occaſioned him, though he was his heir at law, to leave his property to Lady Gargrave, his ſiſter, in preference to him; this exaſperated him ſtill more, as by his vain ex-

---

* Sir Henry D'Anvers' name is in the catalogue of adventurers to eſtabliſh a colony at Virginia, printed in 1620.

travagance he had contracted a vaft debt, which
he then could never pay, unlefs by fome ill
fcheme, the reward of his profligate defection; he
therefore continued with the party, though it
feemed only to lend them a name; for when he
was appointed a commiffioner to treat of peace
between the king and the parliament, in 1646,
he requefted the parliament to excufe him, and
Mr. Robert Goodwin was put in his place.

When the army determined to deftroy the fallen monarch, he was felected to be one of their
chief inftruments. They appointed him one of
the truftees relative to the "agreement of the
" people," fettled at a general council of officers,
preparatory to the trial of the king, and they put
his name as one of the judges; and, to fhew his
pleafure in the horrid office, he fat every day the
high court of juftice lafted, except in the Painted
Chamber on the 22d and 29th, and he figned the
warrant to behead the king.

Lord Clarendon makes this obfervation upon
his nefarious conduct: " Between being feduced,
" and a feducer, he became fo far involved in
" their councils, that he fuffered himfelf to be
" applied to their worft offices, taking it to be a
" high honour to fit upon the fame bench with
" Cromwell, who employed and contemned him
" at once. Nor did that party of mifcreants
" look upon any two men in the kingdom with
" that fcorn and deteftation as they did upon
" D'Anvers and Mildmay."

Superadded to all this, we muft confider that

his whole aim now centered in obtaining the eftate of his late brother, Lord Danby, which he
knew could never be done but by the parliament,
who were become the fovereign power, and who
had fo early as April 1646, appointed a committee to confider of the differences between Lady
Gargrave and him, refpecting the eftate in queftion.

As he had given all the little confequence he
poffeffed to deftroy the king, and alter the conftitution, the parliament named him one of the
council of ftate, which they fet up as a kind of
privy council, and which they invefted with the
executive power. This was the more acceptable
to him, becaufe it enabled him the better to purfue his fcheme of obtaining by fraud the eftate of
his late brother, which he had loft by his wilful
and ungrateful conduct ; and May 17, in this
year, he procured the parliament to take up the
matter. The debate lafted the whole day, when
the property, valued at thirty thoufand pounds,
was to be decided ; and he had fo many friends in
the houfe, and Lady Gargrave fo few, on account
of the political fentiments of each, that the houfe
declared the will to be void, and referred the matter to a committee. On the 14th of the following
month, much time was fpent upon the bufinefs in
the houfe, when it was refolved, upon the queftion, that " Sir John D'Anvers was deprived of
" that eftate by the will of the earl his brother,
" for his affection and adhering to the parlia-

" ment." We find him this year, with the Earl of Salifbury and Sir Henry Mildmay, deputed to receive the Dutch ambaffadors.

When Cromwell affumed the fovereign power, they took mutual leave of each other, the one hating, the other defpifing his former companion. D'Anvers fhewed the firft paffion of malice, by his holding cabals in the army, in March 1655-6, inciting them to revolt from the protector, who, by his fpies, difcovered and defeated it; but, I apprehend, took no other notice of it, than to fet a watch upon his conduct; and he died neglected, and in contempt with all parties. At the reftoration, his name was inferted in the act, excepting him from pardon as if living, by which means all that wealth he had purchafed by fo many crimes was loft to his heir. Had he furvived the return of King Charles II. he would undoubtedly have forfeited not only property but life, for no man could have fewer friends; he had neither relation nor connection that would have ftept forth to foften juftice. Lord Clarendon juftly calls him " a proud, formal, weak man."

He married Magdalen, daughter of Sir Richard Newport, afterwards Earl of Bradford, and widow of Sir Richard Herbert, and mother by him of the famous Lord Herbert of Cherbury. Lady D'Anvers was buried at Chelfea, June 8, 1627; Dr. Donne preached her funeral fermon. He afterwards married Elizabeth, grand-child and heir of Sir John Dauntefy, of Lavington, in Wilts, knt,

By the former lady he had no iffue ; by the latter
he had thefe, baptifed at Chelfea : Elizabeth, May
1, 1629, who became the wife of Robert Vifcount
Purbeck, eldeft fon and heir to * John Lord Vif-

* John Villers Vifcount Purbeck was eldeft brother of the
whole blood to the great Duke of Buckingham, the favourite of
kings ; he was created Baron of Stoke, in the county of Buckingham, and Vifcount Purbeck, in Dorfetfhire, in 1619, by King
James I. He died February 18, 1657, and was buried at Charton,
near Windfor, having married twice, Frances, daughter of Sir
Edward Coke, lord chief juftice of the King's Bench ; and Elizabeth, daughter of Sir William Slingfby, of Kippax, in Yorkfhire, bart. His fucceffor was Robert Lord Vifcount Purbeck,
his only furviving fon, mentioned above ; who, from having married a daughter of that infamous chara&er, Sir Henry Mildmay,
going from one extravagance to another, changed his name to
D'Anvers, his own being, he pretended, obnoxious to liberty ;
and in 1660, he paffed a fine to the king to enable him to furrender his peerage, as equally unworthy to be retained by a patriot.
The Villers were as much beloved by the Stuarts, as the Dudleys
had been by the Tudors. His mean and bafe ingratitude was every
way unpardonable. He left a fon, who, June 5, 1678, claimed
his title of Vifcount Purbeck ; the caufe was folemnly argued in
the Houfe of Peers, and as, no attainder had paffed, but only his
father's furrendering his title by levying a fine, it was fettled on
the 18th of that month, that " Forafmuch as upon the debate
" of the petitioner's cafe, who claims the title of Vifcount Pur-
" beck, a queftion in law did arife, whether a fine levied to the
" king by a peer of the realm, of his title and honour, can bar and
" extinguifh that title ? The lords fpiritual and temporal in par-
" liament affembled, upon very long debate, and having heard
" his majefty's attorney-general, are unanimoufly of opinion, and
" do refolve and adjudge, that no fine now levied, nor at any
" time hereafter to be levied to the king, can bar fuch title of ho-
" nour, or the right of any perfon claiming fuch title under him
" that levied or fhall levy fuch fine." The court, however,

count Purbeck; Mary, September 29, 1631, who died an infant; Charles, February 14, 1632-3, who alfo died in his infancy; Henry, December 5, 1633; and John, fo late as Auguft 10, 1650.

treated this branch with deferved neglect. There was one of the defcendants of Lord Vifcount Purbeck living at the former part of the prefent century, I think, in the army; and on that account our fovereigns did not give the title of *Buckingham*, as it was fuppofed that they were entitled to the limitation of the earldom of that name; there being a remainder granted to the Duke of Buckingham to the heirs of his brother, John Vifcount Purbeck, of the earldom, though not of the dukedom.

The Life of RICHARD DARLEY, *Efq.*

RICHARD DARLEY, Efq. was a member of the long parliament, an officer in their army, and much in their confidence. He, or his brother Henry, was appointed in 1643 one of the commiffioners to go into Scotland, to bring in an army to affift them againft the king; but, for fome reafon I have not feen explained, Henry was in the following year imprifoned in Scarborough Caftle, and, though alfo a member of the houfe, he was fecluded until 1649, when in the month of May, in that year, he was re-admitted to fit again in the houfe, having firft fatisfied the committee touching his abfence. Both the brothers were returned, but not fuffered to fit in Oliver's parliament, called in 1656; they were extremely averfe to his government, being entirely republicans. The Myftery of the Good Old Caufe fays, they had five thoufand pounds granted to their ufe, but given in the name of their father. Richard only is named as one of the king's judges; but he had no manner of concern in that wickednefs.

The Life of RICHARD DEANE, *Efq.*

RICHARD DEANE, Efq. is faid to have been a fervant to one Button, a toyman, in Ipfwich, and to have himfelf been the fon of a perfon in the fame employment. When the civil war broke out he entered the parliament army as a matrofs in the train of artillery; and rendering them fo much fervice, particularly at Exeter, he gradually rofe to be a captain in the train, and afterwards progreffively, though rapidly, to be a colonel.

He was one of thofe who December 18, 1648, met Sir Thomas Widdringten and Mr. Whitlock at the Rolls, with Lieutenant-general Cromwell, and Lenthal the fpeaker of the houfe of commons, under pretence of getting fome fettlement for the nation, and, as it were, combine both parliament, the army, and the law, in one common intereft; but this was only a plaufible matter to give time to the army to effect the dreadful purpofe they meditated againft the facred perfon of the king, and it was therefore fpun out for fome days; though it does not appear that he was called upon again in the matter, which was chiefly left to Cromwell.

That a man who had rifen fo greatly in the army fhould be devoted to their intereft is not furprizing, for in it his own was concerned; and the heads of the army perceived, that if the king and parliament made up the quarrel between themfelves, they would be difbanded; and hav-

ing left their own profeffions, or like him acquired confequence and new habits in life, they
fhould be left deftitute; to ward off, therefore,
what of all things they dreaded, they determined
to cut off the king, after modifying the parliament to their own mind, and lay the ground work
for making them their tools in future. Cromwell
confided in Deane to take a very material part in
this, which he did, and none was more active in carrying things to the laft extremity; he
therefore was named one of the judges in the high
court of juftice, and he was moft attentive to go
through with the odious office; he attended every
fitting, except in the Painted Chamber on the 12th
and 13th of January, and in Weftminfter Hall
the 20th. He alfo fet his hand to the warrant
for the king's execution.

As a reward for this dreadful villany he was, in
the month fucceeding that in which it was acted,
appointeft one of the commiffioners of the navy,
with Popham and Blake; and in April he became an admiral and general at fea, and went
with Admiral Blake in a fquadron in the Downs,
whilft his regiment of horfe was appointed by lot
to go to Ireland, to fubdue the rebels there; and
he and Blake foon after fet fail for Ireland, and
put into Kinfale, to take the fhips which were
there, commanded by Prince Rupert and Prince
Maurice: leaving Blake in that port he with a
fquadron lay upon the weftern road. In February
1649-50 he returned to Portfmouth in the Phœnix,
and gave information to the parliament that fe-

veral veſſels with recruits were caſt away upon the coaſts of Ireland in their paſſage thither.

He was placed in a new ſituation in October 1651, being appointed one of the commiſſioners for Scotland, at which time he had the rank of major-general; and in December following he was ordered to go with the other commiſſioners into that kingdom; his province chiefly was to negotiate with the Marquis of Argyle, whom the parliament were very fearful intended to join with the exiled king in his intended attempt to recover his crown. In March he held a conference with his lordſhip, at which none were admitted but ſome of the marquis's relations and Major Salway, another commiſſioner, when the Scotch peer, who then had vaſt influence, profeſſed nothing but " love and kindneſs;" but in the following month he particularly inſiſted upon the intereſt of the kirk; but all his conduct was duplicity, for he privately urged the Highlanders to take up arms againſt the Engliſh, yet they, as well as himſelf, continued their hypocriſy.

The Dutch war breaking out he was again ſent to ſea in his naval capacity, and joined with Blake and Monk in commanding the navy; meeting with Van Tromp, the Dutch admiral, near the North-Foreland, they reſolved to give him battle. Blake was to the northward when he firſt ſaw the Dutch navy off the coaſt of Flanders; the ſtrength of both republics was called out to diſpute, which of the rivals was to command, and govern at fea. Tromp had to affift him Admiral Evertfen, De Wit, and De Ruyter.

Vice-admiral Lawfon, at the head of the blue fquadron, made the attack, by charging through the Dutch fleet with forty fhips; the fquadron of De Ruyter were principally fufferers in this furious onfet; Van Tromp therefore hafted to his affiftance. Blake and Deane, who were both in the fame fhip, perceiving the admiral's movement, attacked him with the main body; the fleet continuing engaged until three in the afternoon, when the Dutch fled, and were purfued by the lighteft of the Englifh frigates; but, unfortunately, Deane fell at the firft fire of the enemy, a cannon ball dividing his body at the onfet. The fecond day the battle was renewed, and a moft complete victory gained; but as Deane had no fhare in it, the particulars do not belong to this work. The battle was fought September 28, 1652.

A public thankfgiving was given for this victory, in gratitude to Providence for the firft fruits of thofe naval conquefts that afterwards were to be fo greatly illuftrious. To evince the great efteem that the protector had for private merit, a public funeral was decreed by him for the remains of the deceafed admiral and general at fea. The corpfe was carried in a barge from Greenwich to Weftminfter, attended with many other barges and boats in mourning equipages; as they flowly paffed along, the proceffion was faluted by the guns from the fhipping, at the Tower, and ordnance planted for that purpofe in the way to

2

Weftminfter Abbey, where the body was buried, attended with many perfons of the greateft confequence in the government, invited by cards fent from the council; befides large bodies of the military; and to do his memory ftill more honour the protector in perfon affifted. At the reftoration his body, with many others, was taken up and buried in a part of the cemetery of St. Margaret's church, adjoining the Abbey precincts.

When we contemplate the life of this man, we cannot but wonder at his fingular fuccefs, and the wifdom and prudence with which he conducted himfelf in fo many, and fuch oppofite offices, and all fo widely different to what was his original and mean deftination; it is one of the many inftances of great abilities being called forth from obfcurity, that often happens in the time of civil commotions. Happy had it been for him, if he had not blackened his character by that vile act of deftroying his prince, to whom he owed allegiance. He was a devoted creature firft to the army, and afterwards to Cromwell, who knew his great capacity, and ever promoted his intereft, and had he lived would have multiplied upon him ftill farther honours and promotions.

The wealth that he gained was as great as his fucceffes had been extraordinary; amongft the eftates he poffeffed was the manor of Havering at Bower, in the county of Effex, the park of which he demolifhed, after it had for fo long a fpace been appropriated for the chace, by our fovereigns, and where King Henry VIII. often came; it was in an eminent degree, likewife, the retiring place of our monarchs.

At the reftoration all his eftates were feized by government, his name being inferted, though he was dead, in that part of the bill which excepted from pardon thofe more immediately concerned in the murder of King Charles.

He left a widow and children, who, from the time of the general's death to his funeral, had 100l. per day; and 600l. per annum in land was fettled upon Mrs. Deane in reward for his public fervices. In 1654 an act of parliament paffed relative to an ordinance for allowing debts and incumbrances upon the eftate, which was fettled by order of the council of ftate upon " Mrs. " Mary Deane, relict of General Deane, and her " children." Colonel Salmon was upon the point of marriage with this lady in 1654, and probably fhe was foon after united to him.

M

The Life of JOHN DISBOROUGH, *Efq.*

JOHN DISBOROUGH, Efq. was originally a very private gentleman, but obtaining a commiffion in the parliament army, under the patronage of his brother-in-law Cromwell, whofe fifter he had married, he rofe to be a colonel, and went conftantly in the army intereft ; but it is extraordinary that he wholly declined fitting as one of King Charles I.'s judges.

The protector Oliver heaped upon him every truft and every honour, but nothing could make him decline his predilection for the commonwealth; yet he wifhed that to be directed by an army, in which he fhould have a principal command: he was one of Oliver's major-generals, an office that made all who were entrufted with it extremely odious.

He greatly contributed to ruin the Cromwell intereft, in the perfon of Richard the protector; yet after he was dethroned he avowed that one of the caufes of his difguft to the long parliament was, becaufe they had not made a more ample provifion for him. His conduct was as impolitic, as his behaviour was rude and uncourtly.

Having fpoken fo amply of him and his family in my Cromwell memoirs, I fhall only add, that fince their publication I perceive that he married a fecond time; for Mr. Swyft, the fecretary to Lockhart, the ambaffador to France, writes to his excellency in a letter dated London; April 11,

1658, " I have delivered all the letters which I
" received in one packet, two days fince, accord-
" ing to their feveral directions; except that to
" General Difbrowe, to whofe prefent lodging
" his fervants in the Spring Gardens would not
" direct me. His lordfhip was married on Mon-
" day laft, and hath ever fince continued at his
" lady's houfe."

Notwithftanding he was not mentioned in the
claufe of pains and penalties extending either to
life or property, yet he was fo dangerous a
character that it was with difficulty he could be
preferved; and during the remainder of a long
life he was always watched with peculiar jealoufy.

M 2

The Life of JOHN DIXWELL, *Efq.*

JOHN DIXWELL, Efq. is generally, by the royalifts, faid to have been of a mean family, but they do not fay where fituated ; on the contrary, he appears to have been a cadet of the Dixwells, which, dividing into two branches, became feated in Kent and Warwickfhire, and each raifed to the baronetage. This gentleman was, there is little doubt, of the former; for Sir Bafil Dixwell, of Barham, in that county, though created a baronet by King Charles II., was a great parliamentarian, and a committee-man in Kent ; and Mr. Dixwell, the regicide, was a member for the port of Dover, in the long parliament, and alfo one of the committee for Kent.

He went into the army, and rofe to be a colonel of foot ; and, fiding with that intereft in preference to any other, was put in the commiffion of the high court of juftice, and attended there on January the 10th, 13th, 19th, 22d, and all the fubfequent days, in the Painted Chamber, and all the days that they fat in Weftminfter Hall, and figned the fatal warrant of execution.

We may fuppofe his confequence by the truft repofed in him, for he had the cuftody of Dover Caftle ; but adhering to the republicans, and ftill more to the army, he was little in the confidence of Cromwell when at the helm ; but upon the deftruction of the protectorial intereft, he again became confiderable, and in 1659 was appointed one of the council of ftate.

Seeing that every thing tended to the return of the exiled monarch, he prudently withdrew from the kingdom, and, with his fellow-regicides, Barkftead, Okey, and Wauton, refided fome time at Hanau, in Germany, and became a burgefs there; but the two former falling into the hands of the fon of that fovereign whom they had impioufly doomed to die, and had been offered up as an expiation to his manes, he and Wauton privately embarked to America; here he lived in conftant fears of being betrayed to government; but amongft his friends, exulting in the crime that had banifhed him from his country and family. He finally fettled at New-Haven, in Connecticut, near Maffachufet's Bay, where he died, March 18, 1688, at the advanced age of eighty-two. At the head of his grave is an unhewn ftone of a coarfe kind, called barr, with I. D., the initials of his names, which is all that reminds pofterity that fuch a one ever was in the land of the living, and from which he would have been cut off by an act of the greateft public juftice, had he been feized in his own country, having been excepted both as to life and property in the act of indemnity paffed at the reftoration.

M 3

The Life of JOHN DOVE, *Esq.*

JOHN DOVE, Esq. was of the county of Wilts, where he was early a committee-man; he served in the parliament army, and rose to be a colonel. He was named one of the king's judges, and sat in the Painted Chamber on the 12th, 13th, 19th, and 26th of January, but never in Westminster Hall, nor did he sign the warrant for execution.

In 1655, he was nominated sheriff of the county of Wilts. He wrote a letter, dated from Sarum, March 29, in that year, addressed to Secretary Thurloe, whom he tells, that he hears there is a commission of oyer and terminer issued out for trial of the *rebels* in the west, and that there was a mistrust of his under-sheriff, but promises that there shall not be one of either jury but what he can depend upon as well affected to his highness and the present government; and recommends Mr. Secretary to proceed capitally against the " chief actors that were commissionated, as they " said, by *Charles Stuart.*" The letter is written in a peculiar stile; it begins with " Deere " Sir;" and each break-off also commences with the word " Sir."

He escaped at the restoration by the prudent mercy that was shewn, in proceeding only against such of the judges who sentenced his majesty, or signed the warrant, or he might have stood in need of that mercy which he wished not to be extended

to thofe who had rofe to reftore the legitimate government and laws of their country, whilft he was
implicated in having deftroyed them.

The unfortunate Doctor Bridgeman, Bifhop of
Chefter, who was deprived, with the reft of his
right reverend brethren, when the eftablifhed
church was deftroyed, was allied to the Dove family; for his fecond fon, the prebendary of the
cathedral church of Chefter, was named Dove
Bridgeman; and Richard Bridgeman, his lordfhip's fifth and youngeft fon, a merchant in Amfterdam, had a daughter, Elizabeth, married to
John Dove, Efq., furveyor of the cuftoms; but
whether the fon of the king's judge, I do not
know.

The Life of JOHN DOWNES, Esq.

JOHN DOWNES, Esq. was a Londoner, of mean family*; he was greatly attached to the parliament and army, and put in the commission to sit in judgment upon his royal master; and he attended the sittings in the Painted Chamber on January the 8th, 12th, 13th, 15th, 20th, 22d, 23d, 25th, 26th, and 27th, and upon all the days in Westminster Hall, and signed the warrant to put his majesty to death.

Having thus complied with the wishes of those who had led him forth from the humble walk of life, in which he ought, both by his family, fortune, situation, and still more, his education and abilities, to have been, he was almost totally neglected until the Cromwellian interest was ruined, when the army appointed him as one of the council of state, in 1659, and one of the city militia, as a pretended compliment to the city; but the real motive was, that they might use his name to serve their own purposes.

As he was absolutely excepted for life and estate in the act of indemnity passed previous to the restoration, and probably unable to leave the city, he surrendered himself, and was tried October 16, 1660, at the Sessions-house in the Old Bailey. The king's counsel, as an aggravation of his wick-

---

* John Downes was an adventurer to Virginia in 1620; his name is without any addition.

ednefs, alledged, that he fpit in the face of the unhappy monarch, his fovereign.

Mr. Downes, after apologizing for his having pleaded not guilty, fpoke in extenuation of his crime, faying, " My lord, though there was fuch " a thing, fuch an unparalleled thing, I was " thruft into this number, but never was in con- " fultation about the thing. God is witnefs I " was not put in till the act was ready to pafs in a " fecond commitment, by one of the fame num- " ber; I denied it, yet they faid I muft make " one, I muft take my fhare; fo I came in. Ne- " ver did I know of his majefty's being brought " to London till he came."

After faying that he thought it a happinefs to be tried before fuch wife and prudent perfons as the court confifted of, he related fome circum- ftances of what paffed upon the fatal 27th of January, when fentence was pronounced, and which is not mentioned in Nalfon's trial of his majefty. It was this: " My lord, he that was cal- " led prefident anfwered, that no notice fhould " be taken of any thing, but only whether he " would anfwer to his charge. Upon that, my " lord, his majefty, indeed, with the greateft earn- " eftnefs that ever I beheld, and yet in no un- " feemly paffion, told him, they might foon re- " pent of fuch a fentence; that he did conjure " them to withdraw once again, and confider of " it, if it were but for half an hour; or, faith he, " if that be too much for you, I will withdraw. " My lord, here I can make my appeal to him

" that muſt judge me when you have done with
" me. I had not a murderous nor a traitorous
" thought againſt him;, but, Sir, I confeſs ſuch
" deep paſſions did befal me, that truly myſelf I
" was not. I remember the perſons between
" whom I ſat, as it fell out, were one Mr. Cawley
" and Colonel Walton (Wauton); theſe two I ſat
" betwixt; theſe were the very words I ſpake to
" them: Have we hearts of ſtone? Are we men?
" They laboured to appeaſe me; they told me I
" would ruin both myſelf and them; ſaid I, if I
" die for it, I muſt do it. Cromwell ſat juſt the
" ſeat below me; the hearing of me made ſome
" ſtir. Whiſpering, he looked up to me, and
" aſked me if I were myſelf? What I meant to
" do, that I could not be quiet? Sir, ſaid I, no,
" I cannot be quiet; upon that I ſtarted up in
" the very nick. When the preſident com-
" manded the clerk to read the ſentence, I
" ſtepping up, and as loud as I could ſpeak,
" ſpoke to this effect theſe words, or to the
" like purpoſe: My lord, ſaid I, I am not
" ſatisfied to give my conſent to this ſentence;
" but have reaſon to offer to you againſt it, and I
" deſire the court may adjourn to hear me; pre-
" ſently he ſtepped up, and looked at me; nay,
" faith he, if any one of the court be unſatisfied,
" the court muſt adjourn. Sir, accordingly they
" did adjourn into the inner court of wards;
" when they came there, I was called upon by
" Cromwell to give an account why I had put
" this trouble and diſturbance upon the court? I
" did ſpeak, Sir, to this effect; it is long ago;

" the very words I think I cannot speak, but to
" this effect I did speak: My lord, I should
" have been exceeding glad if the court had
" been pleased to condescend to this gracious ex-
" pression: but it is not too late for me; I desire
" not his death, but his life, and that the nations
" may be settled in peace. The king is now
" pleased to offer to them such things as should
" be satisfactory to us all. So, said I, what
" would you have? Your pretence of bringing him
" to these proceedings was, that after such a long
" and bloody war, his majesty would not conde-
" scend to such concessions as might secure the
" parliament party; but now you hear him, that
" he will give every one of us satisfaction; I told
" them, sadly told them, I think I may truly say,
" more sadly then than at this time, that if they
" should go precipitately on and give judgment
" upon him, before they had acquainted the par-
" liament with what the king was pleased to
" offer, we should never be able to answer it;
" the rather, my lord, and that I did press with all
" the little understanding that I had, if they did
" but consider the last concluded order that the
" parliament made after the passing of the act for
" trial, that which was so called; I say there was
" this order that shut up all, that upon any emer-
" gency that could not at that time be thought
" on in the house, the court should immediately
" acquaint the house with it. My lord, I did in-
" fer as strongly as I could to them, that if this
" was not emergency, I could not tell what was.

" The king denied the jurisdiction of the court,
" and yet with all vehemency desired to speak
" with his parliament. Were not these emer-
" gencies? if not, I knew not what were emer-
" gencies. My lords, besides this, there was
" another thing I did press, that I thought was
" of greater consequence than this, as to the sa-
" tisfaction of every man's particular conscience;
" that admitting, if it might be admitted, that the
" king was liable to his subjects, that they might
" call him to an account, and might condemn him.
" I beg your pardon that I take the boldness to
" make such admissions; but if such a thing
" might be admitted, certainly it did exceedingly
" become those judges that were to give such a
" sentence, not against a common person, but
" against the greatest, to be very well satisfied in
" matter of fact, to a full evidence before them,
" that such and such things that were said were
" true. I do acknowledge this, that to the best
" of my apprehension, I wish it had been so to
" others; there was a great shortness in this, that
" not one member of the court did hear one
" witness *viva voce*. I did press, that if the court
" did give judgment against the king, without
" a fair examination, I said it was such a thing as
" no judge at any assizes would do against a com-
" mon person. What I had was from Peters,
" and from some private whispers from one of
" them that is gone, and hath received his sen-
" tence and doom. Cromwell did answer with a
" great deal of storm : he told the president, that

" now he faw what great reafon the gentleman
" had to put fuch a trouble and difturbance upon
" them ; faith he, fure he doth not know that he
" hath to do with the hardeft hearted man that
" lives upon the earth ; however, it is not fit that
" the court fhould be hindered from their duty
" by one peevifh man ; he faid the bottom was
" known, that he would fave his old mafter, and
" defired the court, without any more ado, would
" go and do their duty. Another that fpoke to
" me in anfwer was one that hath been before
" you, and hath received his fentence, but is not
" dead, and I defire I may not name his name ;
" his anfwer was to what I have faid, that fome
" men were either fcepticks or infidels. After
" this I did go into the fpeaker's chamber, and
" there I did eafe my mind and heart with tears,
" God only knows. I have an unhappy me-
" mory ; I have flipt many things."

The Lord Chief Baron humanely faid, " re-
" member yourfelf by papers, if you have any ;
" no man will hinder you." To which he replied " I have no papers ; but, my lord, for the
" truth of this I have faid, there are fome wit-
" neffes that will make the fubftance, the effect
" of this appear." When reminded that he fet
his hand to the warrant, and it was fhewn him, he
faid, " my lord, how to reconcile that which
" hath been faid before, with this that comes
" after, I leave it to you ; I am totally at a lofs.
" When thofe times were, how impetuoufly the
" foldiers, how not a man that dare either dif-

" own them, or fpeak againft them. I was
" threatened with my very life; by the threats of
" one that hath received his reward, I was in-
" duced to it. Certainly, my lord, it doth argue
" that there was not malice pre-dominant; love
" and hatred cannot be at the fame time in one
" perfon. Defign, my lord, what fhould be
" my defign? a poor, ordinary, mean man.
" Surely, my lord, I could not defign any great
" matters or places, I knew myfelf unfit; I
" humbly beg you would give me leave to tell
" you a little what I got." But here the folicitor-general ftopped him, telling him, " it would
" fave both his lordfhip's time and ours by
" making a public confeffion and evidence of
" forrow;" faying, " we cannot fpend fo long
" time to hear thefe long difcourfes; we will
" rather prove it againft every man fingly:"
which is greatly to be regretted, for much fecret
hiftory might have been got at, which could never
have otherwife been known; and which is now
by this care of time loft to pofterity. Mr.
Downes then threw himfelf upon his countrymen
the jury, and begged the king's mercy, and was
again proceeding, when he was interrupted; he
then requefted to have a witnefs or two called, but
it was denied, as he had confeffed the fact; he
therefore faid, " my lord, I do humbly beg his
" majefty's mercy; I came in upon the procla-
" mation."

I have given the whole of what relates to the
private hiftory of King Charles I.'s mock trial,

as it comes from a man of no abilities, but, from his extreme simplicity and timidity, brought to act a part in the tragedy.

He was condemned, but his majesty graciously remitted his sentence, by letting the reprieve granted him continue open; and he died in prison, but when or where is not known.

The Life of ROBERT DUCKENFIELD, *Esq.*

ROBERT DUCKENFIELD, Efq. was defcended from a long line of anceftry feated at Duckenfield, in the county of Chefter; he was the fon and heir of Robert Duckenfield, Efq., by Frances, daughter of George Prefton, of Houlker, in Lancafhire, Efq. The parliament, knowing his attachment to their caufe, appointed him in 1644 one of their committee for the county of Chefter; and he, to promote the popular party, drew his fword in their quarrel, and became a colonel in their army. In 1647 the parliament general fent letters to him and other officers, relative to difbanding fupernumeraries. In May, in the following year, he wrote to the parliament, that the gentry of Chefhire had engaged to adhere to the parliament, and to raife three regiments of foot, and one of horfe, if there fhould be occafion, for the defence of the country; this was in confequence of the royalifts thinking to renew the war; and there was at that time a univerfal wifh in the nation to have the king reftored to his juft rights, except in the army, which was manifefted by the city, the navy, and the country, in their feveral petitions; and even the Houfe of Commons voted, that after his majefty had figned the bills for fettling the militia, and for the *prefbyterian* government, and recalled his declaration againft the parliament, that then a treaty fhould be had with him upon the reft of the propofitions, at Hamp-

ten Court; but the prefbyterians, that had in fo
great a degree raifed the ftorm, were fuperceded
by men who called themfelves greater puritans than
themfelves; and the parliament, who had been
the friends and patrons of the prefbyterians, had
an imperious army who hated them, only lefs
than they did the legal epifcopal eftablifhment,
and were equally enemies to their fovereign and
the parliament; they therefore determined to deftroy the monarch, and make the parliament their
inftrument to legalize their tyranny. Colonel
Duckenfield was one of thofe deputed by the army
to be a judge in the high court of juftice, as it
was called, though a perverfion of the term; but
he was either not upon the fpot, or had prudence
fufficient to decline fo great a danger, for he had
no manner of concern whatever in that bafe wickednefs; the parliament probably faved him from
the danger by naming him fheriff of Chefhire that
year; he was certainly much in their confidence,
for they had before appointed him governor of
Chefter.

The Protector Oliver courted him to take a
part under his adminiftration, and fent him a
commiffion for a regiment of horfe to be raifed in
Chefhire; for which he wrote from Duckenfield,
March 23, 1654-5, one of the " fincereft" letters
that perhaps his highnefs ever received, in which
he declines " the proferred honour, becaufe,
" though his endeavours in that way had been
" very fuccefsful, yet they had been taken in ill.

" part, and that county efpecially was fo wonder-
" fully impoverifhed, that without deftroying it,
" not many foldiers could be raifed in the way the
" protector intended ; and becaufe the extremes
" of the levelling party running fo furioufly,
" did, as he humbly conceived, drive his highnefs
" upon direct contrary extremes; and he defired,
" he faid, to imitate Caleb and Jofhua in the wil-
" dernefs, as near as he could, and not feek a con-
" troverfey with thofe who limit God to their
" paffions, and againft whom God hath an evi-
" dent controverfy." He then tells Oliver, that
" he firmly believes that the root and tree of
" piety is alive in him, though the leaves thereof,
" through abundance of temptations and flat-
" terers, feemed to him to be withered much of
" late; yet he hoped time and experience would
" have a good influence upon his lordfhip. *Deo*
" *Juvente.*"

He then, fpeaking of his own fituation, faid,
he praifed the Lord for his extraordinary mercy
to him that way, that he was not much moved
with the actings of men, though of the better fort,
nor did he regard preferment much; yet to do
this commonwealth a pleafure, he was content to
leave his private and obfcure condition, with
which he was much delighted, for fome time, to
accept of fome *handfome* military command, if his
lordfhip thought well of it; but fo that the men
that were to ferve under him, when difbanded,
might be requited, and that they might be fe-

lected in the beft way from fuch as were the protector's fuperficial and diffembling friends, whom
he well knew, and would have little to do with
unlefs forced to it. He faid, he was not afraid of
his life or eftate; and to improve the talent he had,
he fhould be glad to ferve his lordfhip in any foreign war, within the continent of Europe rather
than within this nation.

He farther informed the protector, that thofe
remote corners of this nation were fo corrupted of
late by the fubtilties of the jefuited party, meaning the loyalifts, as few of them that will be entrufted with armies by the new committees in thofe
parts, would be found faithful to his intereft, in
cafe of neceffity or danger. He therefore recommended, as an excellent courfe, to raife about two
thoufand horfe equally out of all the counties on
the north fide of Trent; and he fhamefully propofed their maintenance to be fupported by levies
impofed upon the convicted or fufpected malig-
nants, meaning the unfortunate loyalifts; becaufe,
he argues, it would do no injury to the innocent,
nor be any inconvenience to the protector; he
urges as a reafon for this, that by doing it, the
clamours of moft men will be done away, who
fay, that his highnefs punifhed the innocent pro-
mifcuoufly with the nocent. And laftly, he tells
Oliver, that *Charles Stuart* had five hundred
friends in the adjacent counties for every one
friend to him amongft them; and he doubts not,

fays Mr. Duckenfield, to find you work enough whilft he lives.

From this very curious detail, it is moft evident, that Oliver was not fo chofen a veffel as he had been before his exaltation; and it proves how much the body of the people languifhed to have the monarchy re-eftablifhed. It is clear, that he *modeftly* wifhed to command the force he recommended to be raifed.

Major-general Worfley, in 1655, writes to Secretary Thurloe, that the report they had there, was, that Colonel Duckenfield was named high fheriff, and he thought fit to fignify, that he was the only perfon that refufed to act with the commiffioners for the county of Chefter, upon the orders and inftructions of his highnefs and council. And Major-general Bridge writes to the protector a letter, dated from Middlewyche, in Chefhire, Auguft 15, 1656; Colonel Duckenfield being one of the commiffioners for this county, although he had not acted, he judged it proper to fend him a fummons with the reft; and in return, received a letter, which he thought advifable to fend to his highnefs. What the contents were, is not mentioned; but we may reafonably prefume, that they were much fuch reafons as he had fent to the protector for declining the office; for he was, we may fuppofe, ftill more diffatisfied, as the protector had not indulged him with a command, that would have been dangerous to have put into his hands.

Upon the ruin of the protector Richard, he left the retirement he pretended so much to delight in, and became one of the most violent partizans of the army—such was his moderation and self-denial; and he procured the rank of lieutenant-colonel. The parliament, to shew their willing-ness to do him justice, presented him with two hundred pounds, as a reward for his services in quelling the rise of Sir Charles Booth in favour of the exiled king; but so far was this from obtaining his predilection for them, that he com-manded the force that stopped the Speaker Len-thall near the gate of the Palace Yard, as he was going to the house, who, having demanded whi-ther he was going, the speaker replied, to per-form his duty in the house; and turning to the soldiers, told them, he was their general, and ex-pected obedience; but disregarding this, they obliged the coachman to drive him back, and as he passed Wallingford-house, strove to compel him to drive in at the gate, saying to the speaker, " You must go to Lieutenant-general Fleet-" wood;" but Lenthall, commanding the coach-man to proceed home, and telling the officers, that if the lieutenant-general had any business with him, he might come to his house, they suf-fered him to proceed without further molestation to his residence.

The nation, at length, tired out with the con-stant opposition of interests, and eternal cabals, were alike disgusted with both this parliament

and the army, and it became the general wish to
call a new parliament; which no sooner met,
than they unanimously voted the return of King
Charles II.' to the throne of his ancestors, who,
upon his accession, determined to disband the
army, which would send the lieutenant-colonel
to the retirement he seemed so charmed with;
but he had no inclination to go thither, for he
engaged in a project, it is supposed, with several other military men, to make one attempt to
regain their lost consequence; the pretence was,
the return of the queen-mother, a very de-
servedly unpopular character; and it was meant
to seize the king, and the Tower; to kill the
queen, and all the French nation they could find,
and to restore the parliament, no doubt, again to
sanction these enormities. But before things were
ripe for acting, they were secured and sent to
prison. This plot perhaps hastened the breaking up of the army, which was effected upon
Tower-hill, February 14, 1660-1.

Thus ended the career of this gentleman, who,
if he had possessed prudence enough to have been
quiet after his majesty's return, he might have
gone to his paternal domains, and remained in
perfect security.

He married Martha, daughter of Sir Miles
Fleetwood, Knt. receiver of the court of wards,
by whom he had seven children, four sons, and
three daughters. One of the sons, I suppose,
was Captain Duckenfield, who so gallantly dif-

tinguished himself under the command of Sir Charles Coote, in Ireland, in 1650; probably it was John, the eldest, who died without issue. The other children were, Robert, William, Charles Ann, Elizabeth, and Mary.

Robert, the second, who succeeded to the family estate, was raised by King Charles II., June 16, 1665, to the rank of a baronet.

The Life of HUMPHRY EDWARDS, *Esq.*

HUMPHRY EDWARDS, Esq., was a younger son of Thomas Edwards, of Shrewsbury, who died March 19, 1634, aged 79; and was buried in St. Chad's church, in that town, by Ann, daughter of Humphry Baskerville, Esq., alderman of London, and relict of Stephen Ducket, Esq.

He had a seat in the long parliament; and having been refused a place by his majesty, who thought him improper for it, he, in resentment, went all the lengths that the junto in the parliament, who were the tools of the army, desired; and having been named one of the commissioners of the high court of justice, he sat in all their meetings, except in the Painted Chamber on the tenth, twelfth, twenty-second, and twenty-fourth of January, and signed the warrant to murder the king.

He is one of the several instances here given, that revenge was the passion that actuated some of King Charles' judges, to pursue, with unrelenting cruelty, his destruction.

We have no farther relation of this gentleman, who does not appear to have had any one striking feature in his character. He, fortunately for himself, died before the restoration, leaving no issue; but his name is inserted in the exceptive clause of the bill of indemnity, so that his property would be confiscated. I apprehend, the names occurring in that manner was partly for fear that some of the regicides might have impofed upon the world by fecreting themfelves; that their friends might pretend that they were dead, for the.double reafon of faving the fhame of their families, and fecuring the wealth they had obtained as the reward of their infamy; but if any did thus impofe upon parliament, it only faved life; for, by the opperation of the act, all their wealth was forfeited to the crown.

Henry Edwards, Efq., the eldeft brother, alfo died without iffue; as did Jonathan, the youngeft. Thomas, the fecond brother, was a committee-man to the protector, for the county of Salop; though he had received a patent for a baronetage in 1644 from King Charles I., but which was not allowed during the ufurpation, nor claimed until 1678, when it was exemplified to Sir Francis, his oldeft fon.

The Life of ISAAC EWER, Esq.

Isaac Ewer, Esq., was of the ennobled family of the Barons Ewer, in Yorkshire; he went into the parliament army, to the interest of which he was devoted to the greatest degree; and he then betrayed that ferocity of character which afterwards, upon all occasions, shewed itself. By a conference he had with Colonel Grosvenor, when they were together at an inn in Windsor, one Everard heard them, with others, declare that " they doubted not but the Scots would come in, " and that the city of London would join with " them; for the preventing of which they found " no way but to disarm the city friend and foe: " that such as were friends to the army should be " armed, and keep the rest in awe; and that they " would make the city advance a million of " money, or else would plunder them; and that " they had been acquainted therewith." Everard told this to the magistracy of London, in consequence of which a common council was held April 24, 1648; but it did not sufficiently alarm them, by convincing the city it was intended to make them " the beast of burden," as they were emphatically called.

In May following he took Chepstow Castle, in Monmouthshire, where was killed Sir Nicholas Kemish, and one hundred and twenty taken prisoners: for which the parliament sent him a letter of thanks, and gave the meffenger who brought the news, one of their officers, fifty pounds.

When the army was refolved to feize and facrifice the king, to promote their having the abfolute government of the three kingdoms, Cromwell, and the other cabal of officers, fixed upon him to effect the firft part of their object: the general, therefore, fent a letter to Colonel Hammond, who had the care of the royal captive, to give up his charge and repair to the army at Windfor. Hammond fent off an exprefs to the parliament; who, alarmed at the king's, and ftill more at their own, danger, voted that Colonel Hammond fhould return to the Ifle of Wight and refume his former fituation; and that letters fhould be fent to the admiral to fend fome fhips for the fecurity of the Ifle of Wight, and that they fhould obey Colonel Hammond.

But the army, who knew that whomfoever could feize their unhappy fovereign would command the kingdom, took too effectual care to fecure the rich prey; for before all things could be re-eftablifhed, Ewers, who was a colonel, had punctually obeyed what he went rejoicingly to perform. The cabal at Windfor paid very little attention to a fubfequent order directed to the general; for Ewer kept poffeffion of his majefty, who removed him to Hurft Caftle, of which they had made him governor. Both parties now came to iffue; the parliament voted, that the feizing upon the perfon of the king, and carrying him prifoner to Hurft Caftle, was without the advice and confent of the houfe; and that his majefty's conceffions to the propofitions of the parliament upon the treaty were fufficient grounds for fettling the peace of the kingdoms : the officers alfo fent forth their declarations; and backing them by the army, with the general at their head, who marching into London, and having garbled the houfe of commons, eafily procured the act to try their fovereign; and with the fame eafe might have obtained one to condemn him, without the folemn mockery of law and juftice. The army was fo grateful to their bafe agent, that they foon after voted him two hundred pounds as governor of Hurft Caftle, from whence the king was foon taken away to be facrificed.

Colonel Ewers was appointed one of the judges, and was conftant in his attendance, omitting being there only on the tenth, twelfth, and eighteeenth, in the Painted Chamber; and he figned the death warrant.

As the lot fell upon the regiment he commanded to go to Ireland, he failed in April 1649; where he greatly diftinguifhed himfelf at the taking of Drogheda and Fredah, both of which were won by ftorm; but in the latter he loft almoft all his officers. In this kingdom he died poffeffed of a large eftate, procured him there through the patronage of Cromwell, whofe devoted creature he always had been, and whom he had ferved in his vileft offices.

His nephew, Captain Ewer, was, I believe, heir to his property, and whom he had taken with him to Ireland. Secretary Thurloe gives him an excellent character, both for fobriety and valour, and recommended him to Henry Cromwell, Major-general of the army in that kingdom, in a letter to him, dated from Whitehall, May 21, 1656: the fecretary fays, he takes upon him this boldnefs, the rather becaufe he is *the only perfon of my kindred that I have ever moved for in any cafe.*

The Life of JOHN FAGG, Esq.

JOHN FAGG, Esq., was son of John Fagg, of Rye, in Suffex, by Elizabeth, daughter of —— Hudson, of that county. He joined the parliament army, and became a colonel in it. His name is amongst the commissioners of the high court of justice; he appeared in the Painted Chamber on the tenth, twelfth, and thirteenth of January, but at no other time; so that he appears rather as one who assisted in preparing for the trial, than acting as a judge; neither did he sign the warrant for execution.

Cromwell made him one of the committee for Suffex, and courted him to support his government, which he appears not to be desirous of doing. Major-general Goffe writes to secretary Thurloe from Lewes, November 7, 1655, that he had not put in Mr. Fagg's name, because he was observed to be gracious with disaffected men; besides he would not stir an hair's breadth without Colonel Morley: and in 1656 he was one of the members in Oliver's parliament, who were precluded from sitting in the house, because not approved by the protector's council.

The commonwealth being restored in 1659, the council of state, July 31, put him in power to command the militia in the county of Suffex, and sent him particular instructions how to act; by which it appears that an implicit reliance was placed in him. He was directed to take every care to fecure Chichefter and Arundel; and he was empowered to pay thofe who voluntarily joined him in the militia, as if in actual fervice; and they directed him to hold correfpondence with the forces of the army and militia that were in Kent, Surrey, Hants, and Wilts, as there might be occafion; and to give frequent intelligence to the council of his proceedings.

At the reftoration he not only made his peace, but was created by King Charles II. a baronet, December 11, 1660. There was a great conteft between him and Dr. Thomas Shirley, whofe anceftors had poffeffed Wifton, the eftate which he then held: it was, at length, taken up by the houfe of commons, who committed Dr. Shirley for breach of privilege.

Sir John Fagg married Mary, daughter of Robert Morley, of Glynd, in Suffex, by whom he had fixteen children. The prefent Reverend Sir John Fagg, of Miftole, in Kent, Bart., is his defcendant.

The Life of THOMAS *Lord* FAIRFAX.

LORD FAIRFAX was the third nobleman of that title. His grandfather was Sir Thomas Fairfax, knighted for his bravery by the Earl of Effex, in France, whilft fighting under the banners of Henry the Great, when oppofing the holy league, as it was impioufly called; and who was created many years after, May 4, 1627, Baron Fairfax, of Cameron, in the kingdom of Scotland, by his majefty King Charles I. being one of the very few Englifh families who received Scotch honours; his lordfhip died at the advanced age of eighty years. By Helen, daughter of Robert Afk, Efq. he had Ferdinando, the fecond Lord Fairfax, who being in the parliament intereft, was at the commencement of the civil war appointed their general for the affociated county of York, where his feat and eftates lay. Whilft intrenched at Tadcafter, in Yorkfhire, he was attacked, in December 1642, by the Earl of Newcaftle, whom he obliged to retreat with the lofs of part of his forces. His lordfhip routed Lord Byron in January following, who was at the head of a body of Irifh that had lately landed. The engagement was at Namptwitch, in Chefhire, and was memorable, not only for the great numbers deftroyed, but for taking prifoner Colonel Monk, who by a fucceffion of extraordinary events, was enabled by this difafter to gain the confidence of the enemies

of royalty, and yet, to be the inftrument to reftore the crown to its legal owner, after every
hope had been loft of fuch an event taking place.
He was, however, in June 1643, totally routed
by the Earl of Newcaftle at Adderton Moor. In
April 1644 he defeated Lord Bellafyfe, at Selby,
in Yorkfhire, whom he took prifoner; with fix
hundred of his forces; but in September in that
year, a corps of fifteen hundred horfe of Chefhire,
making an incurfion into the Weft Riding of
Yorkfhire, beating up the quarters of his Lordfhip, defeated two regiments of his horfe at Fer-
rybridge, and remained there fome time, expect-
ing the affiftance of the garrifon of Newark; he
therefore folicited fome of the Scotch forces to be
fent to him, who were lying before Newark to
ftop their farther progrefs; but he foon relieved
himfelf from all inconveniencies on their account,
breaking through the king's forces with his horfe
and his foot marched quietly to Southampton,
where he was joined by the Earl of Manchefter
and Wallis' troops. He commanded in the main
battle with the Earl of Leven, at Marfton Moor,
fought July 3, 1644, where Prince Rupert was
defeated with fuch great lofs; and after this victory his lordfhip was appointed governor of the
city of York, which capitulated in confequence
of it. He was alfo in the commiffion for pre-
ferving the peace of the Britifh kingdoms. This
nobleman married Mary, daughter of Edmund
Earl of Mulgrave, anceftor of the Sheffields, Dukes
of Buckingham.

Sir Thomas, the third Lord Fairfax, the fubject of this article, was the eldeſt ſurviving ſon
of the preceding peer, who inheriting the war-
like difpofition, and violent prejudice againſt
King Charles I. became a moſt ſtrenuous enemy
to his majeſty, and whoſe deſtruction was greatly
attributed to his implacable diſlike to that monarch, owing, it has been ſaid, from an offence
to his pride, which was never forgiven. It is
certain Charles I. wanted that eaſy condefcenſion
which was ſo diſtinguiſhing a feature in the character of his ſon and ſucceſſor. It is evident
that the Fairfaxes and their alliances roſe a dreadful phalanx againſt the king, from the moment
the ſword had left the ſcabbard ; and their military ſkill, their valour, and prudence, made all
the Fairfaxes conſpicuous characters, but far the
moſt ſo was this nobleman.

His ſucceſſes were brilliant to the greateſt degree. I ſhall follow him, to ſhew with what
ſeeming eaſe and rapidity he ſubjected all oppoſition to his arms. In January 1642, he obtained
the town of Leeds, in Yorkſhire, then under the
government of Sir William Savile, and took 500
of the royaliſts priſoners. April the 3d following, he ſuffered a check at Bramham Moor, in the
ſame county. June the 29th, he was worſted in
an engagement fought at Adderton Moor, where
the Earl of Newcaſtle obtained the advantage.

He and his father made an attack upon Colonel Belafyſe, governor of York, at a place called
Selby, and took him priſoner, with many of his

officers, befides one thoufand fix hundred of the
common men, and gained four pieces of cannon,
two thoufand arms, and more than five hundred
horfes. For this great and important fuccefs the
parliament in London proclaimed a folemn
thankfgiving.

Purfuing his victory, he hafted, with Lord Fairfax, his father, to join the Scotch army, and laid
fiege, April 20th, to the city of York, whither the
Marquis of Newcaftle was retreated; but Prince
Rupert raifed the fiege July 2. His highnefs, who
was always too precipitate, not fatisfied with having done well, muft follow up his advantage by
attacking the parliament army where the Earl of
Manchefter was the head of the Englifh, and the
Earl of Lefley commanded the Scotch; and on
the 3d he was defeated at Marfton-moor near
Wetherby and York, with the vaft loft of ten
thoufand of the king's forces flain, or made prifoners, with all the artillery, arms, and ammunition; in gaining this fplendid victory Sir Thomas was greatly inftrumental; one of its many
and great confequences was York falling into the
hands of the parliament upon the 16th of the
fame month.

He had rendered himfelf fo confpicuous for his
great and tried fervices to the parliament, that
April 3, 1645, when he was only in the 34th year
of his age, he was advanced to the rank of general, immediately upon the parliament's having
paffed the felf-denying ordinance; but it was remarked that in his commiffion of generaliffimo of

all their forces, the prefervation of the king's perfon and name was omitted, he being conftituted general to the parliament only; and not to the king and parliament, as the preceding commiffions had run; and a very different method of carrying on the war now commenced, the army by him and Cromwell was new modelled, and the deftruction of the perfon, as well as the authority of the king, feemed aimed at.

The greatnefs and rapidity of his victories cannot be exceeded. The general marched from Windfor April 30, 1645, fought the famous battle of Nafeby in Northamptonfhire, where he defeated his majefty in perfon, who loft eight hundred men, four thoufand five hundred prifoners, twelve pieces of cannon and two mortars, eight thoufand ftand of arms, and one hundred and twelve colours, and all this in the fpace of two hours; and he obtained his majefty's cabinet of letters and other things of great value, which the parliament very meanly refufed to return; and even after reading the letters in the houfe of commons, publifhed the private correfpondence between their majefties. He invefted Oxford on the 22d of May, and Leicefter June the 18th, which had been taken by ftorm by the king juft preceding the battle of Nafeby, and was then left to the care of Lord Haftings; the lofs was very trifling to the royalifts, who knew it impoffible to make any refiftance; the general here took fourteen cannon, two thoufand fix hundred ftand of arms, and eight colours; on the 27th, in three hours, he took Highworth garrison in Wiltshire, commanded by Major Ken, killed four, took feventy prisoners, one hundred and eighty arms, and two colours; July the 3d, he a second time relieved Taunton in Somersetshire; after spending five weeks in performing this service, with the lofs of one thousand of the royal forces, and four hundred prisoners, Lord Goring opposing him; on the 8th he took the garrison of Ilchester, commanded by Colonel Philips; on the 10th, he defeated Lord Goring at Langport, in a moft decisive manner, with the lofs to his lordship of sixty killed, one thousand six hundred taken prisoners, two pieces of ordnance, two thousand five hundred arms, and thirty-two colours. On the 23d he stormed Bridgewater, defended by Colonel Windham, which he won in eleven hours, and killed thirty, took one thousand six hundred prisoners, forty-four pieces of ordnance, three thousand arms and nine colours.

Leaving Somersetshire, he marched to Sherborne in the county of Dorset, which he stormed on the 15th of August, and though it made a good defence, Sir Lewis Dives killing him two hundred men, yet it was obliged to submit, with the lofs of three hundred and forty prisoners, nineteen pieces of ordnance, six hundred arms and two colours.

He invefted Briftol the 21ft of that month, which was well provided for a gallant defence, and the greateft confidence was placed in Prince Rupert, the governor; but the fteady valor of

O 3

Fairfax prevailed, and with the inconfiderable lofs of about one hundred and fixty of his men, he took it by ftorm in eighteen hours; two hundred of the royal troops were taken prifoners, one hundred and fifty-one pieces of ordnance, fix thoufand arms and eight colours; nothing more raifed the reputation of the one, or funk that of the other, than the conqueft of this fecond city in the kingdom; King Charles I. never more would give his royal confidence to his nephew, who could thus eafily give up a place of fuch great ftrength and importance : it has ever been a furprize to all Prince Rupert's friends, and he felt fo much concern for it, and its confequences, that he foon after left the kingdom, but returned again.

The general in perfon affaulted the Caftle of Devizes in the county of Wilts, which was furrendered September the 23d, by Sir Charles Lloyd, with only feven killed, and five prifoners; but he took in it two pieces of ordnance, and four hundred arms; on October the 20th he took the Caftle of Tiverton in Devonfhire by ftorm, defended by Sir Gilbert Talbot, obtaining there two hundred prifoners, four pieces of ordnance, four hundred arms and two colours, with only two of the loyalifts killed, it is faid.

His next advance was to Plymouth, whither he came January 16, 1645-6, and raifed the fiege of that very important place, where he was oppofed by Major-general Sir John Digby; here he took twenty-two prifoners, found five pieces of ordnance, which Sir John had left in his hasty retreat, and eighty arms.

January the 19th he stormed Dartmouth, and in seven hours took it; killed twenty, took eight hundred prisoners, one hundred and six cannon, one thousand six hundred arms and fourteen colours; Sir Hugh Pollard being obliged to yield to the constant career of success that attended the arms of this great man. February 16, he acted the same part against Torrington, and with the same good fortune, though he was opposed by Lord Hopton, Lord Wentworth, and Lord Capel, who lost sixty men, four hundred prisoners, sixteen hundred arms, and nine colours; in this tremendous attack and defence, eighty barrels of gunpowder were consumed.

His attention was next directed against the garrisoned places in Cornwall: February the 25th, Launceston fell, after an hours dispute, and the loss of three men killed, one hundred and sixty prisoners, and two hundred arms. He then marched to Saltash on the 28th, where he found three pieces of ordnance left in the works; the next day he obtained the town of Lisard, both of which had been quitted upon his approaching them. Mount-Edgcomb yielded to him on March the 3d, Colonel Edgecomb surrendering the place to him, where he obtained five pieces of ordnance; and the same day the town of Fowey was yielded to him without any opposition, where he made sixty prisoners, gained ten pieces of cannon, and one hundred and forty arms. St.

Mawe's Caftle, which commanded Falmonth Haven, yielded upon the 13th, where he found twelve cannon, one hundred and fixty arms and two colours; on the following day he obliged the loyal and gallant Lord Hopton to difband his army, according to the treaty at Truro, which he had that day fettled with him, permitting his lordfhip, however, to pafs into France; and all the arms, amounting to two thoufand, and the feventy colours belonging to the cavalry, were the general's; this was a moft fevere ftroke upon his majefty's intereft in this part of the kingdom, for by it was loft to him a body of four thoufand five hundred horfe.

Dennis Fort yielded to his excellency on the 16th, where he got twenty-two pieces of ordnance, two hundred arms and two colours; on the 13th the very large and opulent city of Exeter was furrendered to him by its governor Sir John Berkley, with the lofs of one hundred royalifts killed, forty taken prifoners, and feventy cannon, and one thoufand five hundred arms, fell into his hands. On the 20th the town, caftle, and fort of Barnftaple yielded, with the flaughter of twenty; and here he gained thirty-five pieces of ordnance, and four hundred arms; the governor was Sir Allen Apfley. Sir Thomas having now entirely defeated all in the weft, and fubjected the whole country to the jurifdiction of the parliament, he left that part of the kingdom, and marched to Rorfhall-Houfe in Buckinghamfhire, which had a garrifon under Sir William Compton;

but it yielded to him June 10, after it had fuſtained a fiege of eighteen hours; in it he took five pieces of cannon and three hundred arms.

The important work of getting Oxford only remained to make the parliament triumphant, thither therefore he went, and began the fiege May the 2d, his majefty having previoufly left it, and took fhelter and afylum in the Scotch army, where he was promifed every protection; and as his whole reliance was in their punctual obfervance of their promife, and not farther to widen the breach between him and the parliament, by unneceffarily carrying on a war which he faw was in vain much longer to continue, he permitted all the garrifons to make the beft terms they could, and fubmit to the orders of the parliament; in compliance with thefe commands, the lords of the privy council, and Sir Thomas Glemham, the governor of that city, furrendered it, June the 24th, after lofing fixty men; in it were three hundred pieces of ordnance, and two thoufand arms; but it was ftipulated by the treaty, that neither the colleges fhould be demolifhed, nor their revenues fequeftered; but great was the triumph of the parliament to receive all the public feals ufed by his majefty, which had been entrufted to the care of the privy council when he withdrew from the city; thefe were all broken in the prefence of the two houfes, who might well look upon themfelves as having, in like manner, deftroyed the whole power of the crown.

Fairfax now fet forwards to London; but in his

way thither he took in Wallingford Caftle, in Berkfhire, which had a garrifon under the command of Colonel Thomas Blagge, who yielded July the 27th, having loft five men; and left in it feven pieces of cannon, eight hundred arms, and feven colours; he then proceeded upon his march to London, which city he reached November the 12th, where he was received as his fervices deferved by his employers.

If we confider the conftant fucceffes of this man againft fuch a variety of brave and fkilful commanders, it is extremely wonderful; and when we add the number of prifoners, ordnance, arms, ftandards, and colours, taken by him in fifteen months, it furpaffes credibility; and the perfons who acted under his command, had alfo vanquifhed all oppofition; he had driven the fovereign into the Scotch camp, and the Prince of Wales into Jerfey, who foon after quitted it to go to France; and as the Earl of Effex, the other general of the parliament, died September the 14th preceding, the whole nation was actually proftrate at his feet; all things were at his difpofal.

The general fucceeded to the title of Lord Fairfax by the death of his father, who died in York March 13, 1647*, his own eldeft brother, Sir William Fairfax, falling in the bed of honour in September 1644, immediately after having defeated Lord Byron at Montgomery Caftle, and left no iffue. He did not however go to the North to enjoy his paternal fields, which he might with credit to himfelf have done, as the war was

* Ferdinando Lord Fairfax was buried with uncommon folemnity.

clofed, but retaining the command of the army, he might in a great meafure be faid to be the chief governor of the kingdom.

The king having been moft perfidioufly fold by the Scotch, to their brethren inarms in England, was received by the general with great attention, and it was evident that the parliament were jealous of this fuppofed friendfhip; becaufe had Charles, and the army under General Fairfax, compromifed their differences, the parliament would have been at the mercy of both; but his majefty having betrayed his diflike to Cromwell, who had a vaft fway in the council of officers, that artful man procured a plot to frighten the king away from the army, that he might lofe their confidence, and, like moft others of his deep-laid fchemes, it was fuccefsful; the king fled, and putting himfelf in the power of Hammond, a colonel in the army, and devoted to their intereft, he became what he ever after was, a prifoner, and held his life merely by the will, and at the caprice of, the grandees of the army.

Compaffion for the royal captive, difcontent at there being no inclination manifefted to put an end to the unhappy divifions in the kingdom; diflike at having an army living upon the public, all contributed to make the generality wifh to have the king reftored to his authority, and as many flew to arms to obtain the objeƈt of their defires, it again kindled up the flames of civil war.

The county of Kent rofe in a large body, but were difappointed that London would not join

them; however, one party threw themſelves into
Maidſtone, and defended themſelves with an ob-
ſtinate valour that had ſcarce its parallel in the
whole war; thither the general had haſtened though
he was ill, and he commanded at the attack of the
place, notwithſtanding he was ſuffering greatly
from the gout; the action was fought May 31,
1648, in which many were killed, and the purſuit
was very hot in the neighbouring pariſhes; the
bodies of theſe unhappy fugitives are conſtantly
being diſcovered in the places where they fell,
chiefly in the fields adjoining the ſides of the
roads.

Succeſs followed his ſtandard; having finiſhed
this duty, he went to Colcheſter, where the royaliſts of Eſſex had put themſelves under the government of Lord Goring; this was a much longer buſineſs than the other, for his excellency
ſat down before the town June the 13th, and
he did not obtain it until Auguſt the 28th; ſo
that the place ſuſtained a ten-weeks ſiege; here
he ſtained his laurels by ſhooting Sir Charles Lucas and Sir George Liſle, two young gentlemen
greatly beloved, and their deaths were neither according to the rights of war, nor the ſemblance
of juſtice; and ſo little was decency obſerved towards them, that they were not permitted time
ſo much as to write to their friends, or make any
preparation whatever for the change that was
doomed them. Their deaths created an univer-
ſal pity; even his majeſty forgot his own ſufferings to drop the tear of compaſſion for their un-

merited fate; when a gentleman came into the royal presence, who wore mourning for one of them, the king wept.

The general took up his quarters at Windfor, where he prefided at the confultation of the chief officers of his army, in what manner they fhould fatisfy themfelves for their fervices in the war. It was evident to them that the parliament was defirous to clofe with the king, and that his majefty wifhed to fettle their quarrel without applying to the army, not perceiving that the parliament could be annihilated by the nod of a general at the head of a victorious army.

Preferring the interefl of the army to every other, he turned from the parliament; and it was by his orders that his fovereign was feized when the treaty with his parliament was drawing to a conclufion; it was by him that the king was brought up to London; it was by his command that the parliament was garbled, that an act paffed to try him as a malefactor; by his permiffion he was led ignominioufly to a mock trial, infulted, derided, fpit upon, in going and returning to an infamous tribunal, of which he was a judge, and had fat in the Painted Chamber, January the 8th, to fanction it; and it was he who fent forces to guard him from efcape, to fee this moft unjuft and infamous murder openly committed in the face of day, in the midft of the capital, and before one of his own palaces, without expreffing one fingle fentiment of compaffion for fallen majefty, of that fovereign to whom he had taken the oaths of allegiance, and had fworn to protect at the expence of every thing dear to him, and whofe virtues, for he had many, he was well acquainted with.

How extremely different was the conduct of the general to that of his lady; who, when Lord Fairfax's name, as a commiffioner, was called over, who ftood firft in the lift of judges, and no anfwer was made; and it was repeated a fecond time, a fhrill voice from one of the boxes where the ladies were, was heard, faying, " He has more " wit than to be here." And afterwards, when the charge was read, " In the name of all the " good people of England," the fame voice cried out, " No, nor half of them; it is falfe; where " are they, or their confents? Oliver Cromwell " is a traitor ;" in which fhe was joined by Mrs. Nelfon, fifter to Sir Purbeck Temple. Surprize feized the court; and that vile wretch, Captain Daniel Axtell, who then commanded the foldiers that guarded his majefty, ftanding up, faid, " What drab is that, that difturbs the court? " Come down, or I will fetch you down ;" and turning to the foldiers, faid, " Fire at the " w——s ;" and the foldiers directing the muzzles of their pieces, her ladyfhip was perfuaded to retire to Mr. Bodurdo's chamber, from which the gallery led. Thefe particulars were fworn to at the trial of Axtell, who met his moft deferved fate at the reftoration.

After this dreadful cataftrophe, he continued at the head of the army, but he gradually loft his

confequence in it.   Cromwell artfully drew him
on to adopt thofe projects which he wifhed to
have carried : Fairfax was as far from being able
to cope with him in the cabinet as the king had
been to contend with the general in the field.
Under pretence, therefore, of not being fatisfied
in his confcience to go againft the Scots, who had
broke into the kingdom in 1650, June the 12th,
he refigned the command of the army; and the
following day an act paffed to repeal the ordinance appointing him commander in chief of the
parliament forces, and another, conftituting Oliver Cromwell, Efq. captain-general of all the
forces raifed and to be raifed by authority of parliament within the commonwealth of England,
with a power of granting, renewing, and altering
the officers' commiffions.   One knows not which
to wonder at the moft, the pretence of confcience
in Fairfax about fighting againft the Scots, who
had taken up arms to reftore the fon of his royal
mafter, murdered by his procurement, or Cromwell attempting to diffuade him from quitting an
office that he fo much defired, and perhaps would
foon have feized, if it had not been refigned by
the general.

He now retired to his Yorkfhire eftates, greatly
enriched, and feemed to take no manner of notice
of the public concerns, or the wars that were
carried on in Scotland and Ireland.   After Cromwell had obtained the fovereignty, he remained
in the fame private retirement.   Oliver gave him
a place in fome of the trivial commiffions in the

county, but took no farther notice of him; he seemed rather to study to mortify a man whom he had once served under; and this great general, who had rose against his lawful prince, now saw the nation governed by the absolute will and command of one whom he had so little a while before thought very much his inferior.

For some time he only secretly repined at his humiliating situation; but at length, unable to bear such severe and public mortifications, he resolved, in 1654, to restore their common master, as it was more easy to bear the yoke of a lawful, than an illegitimate governor; but the protector, who was all eyes, having defeated the attempts meditated against him, his lordship was obliged, to save himself more severe usage, and the disgrace of being perhaps dragged forth to open scorn, to confess the whole design against his highness; who, probably fearful of awakening any sentiments of regard in the breasts of such of the soldiers whom he had commanded, accepted his apology, and left him a prey to still more acute feelings; a situation his behaviour to the late king justly merited.

Unable to bear a fate so conspicuous as his was in the eyes of all Europe, he could not withstand the opportunity there was of again opening a correspondence with the exiled king, dangerous as it was: it only tended to sink him still lower.

The marriage of his only child with the Duke of Buckingham, made the breach between these two famous generals still the greater; the protectorial courtiers. feemed to highly refent it, be-caufe it ought not to have proceeded until leave had been given by his highnefs, who, as chief magiftrate, was in the fame fituation, and entitled to the fame attentions as the former fovereigns; and obferved, that the duke might have been a proper match for one of Oliver's daughters. It was thought of fo much confequence by the pro-tector, that there was iffued the following order of council, dated from Whitehall, Tuefday, 17th No-vember, 1657: "His highnefs having communi-"cated to the council, that the lord Fairfax made "addrefs to him, with fome defires on behalf of "the Duke of Buckingham, ordered, that the "refolves and act of parliament in the cafe of "the faid duke be communicated to the Lord "Fairfax, as the grounds of the council's pro-"ceedings touching the faid duke, and that there "be withal fignified to the Lord Fairfax the "council's civil refpects to his lordfhip's own "perfon; that the Earl of Mulgrave, the Lord-"deputy Fleetwood, and the Lord Strickland, "be defired to deliver a meffage from the coun-"cil to the Lord Fairfax, to the effect aforefaid. "Henry Scobell, clerk of the council."—A more cool and fevere contempt could not have been paffed upon him; yet it was done in fuch a manner that he could not openly refent it.

It funk very deep in his mind. Cromwell was privately informed, that he feelingly remarked to Mr. Grimes, upon being afked, if he did not think it proper to declare himfelf openly for the royal

cause, as he was cruelly insulted by the then government, " That he felt the condition of him-
" self and family, and of the usage of the protec-
" tor ; and observed, that since the dissolving of
" the parliament, which was broke up wrong-
" fully, there was nothing but shifting, and a
" kind of confusion ; and that he knew not but
" that he might chuse, by his old commission as
" general, to appear in arms on behalf of the
" people of these nations ;" and he told Mr.
Worsnam how much he was discontented, and
said, " he had laid it up, and would remember
" it when there was occasion ;" but he felt there
was a great difference between a general at the
head of an army, and one who had quitted that
post, when all those whom he had known had received their present promotion, had looked for
more from other hands.

Lord Fairfax had still greater reason to wish
for the re-establishment of that monarchy which
he had in so great a degree contributed to destroy.
His only child was become, by marrying the
Duke of Buckingham, September 24, 1657, the
first female, the blood-royal excepted, that could
be in the kingdom ; and such a court as Oliver's
was not calculated for her to shine in, for it con-
sisted only of puritans of the strictest form, and
they chiefly military veterans ; besides, by the
duke his son-in-law's means he was certain of receiving, not only pardon, but a gracious reception
from the monarch whenever he was restored.

These sentiments were heightened when the

duke was apprehended Auguft the 24th, and committed a prifoner to the Tower, for fome attempts he had made againft the protector, but who lived only ten days afterwards : the government, however, had ftill the fame reafons for detaining his grace.

It was more mortifying for Lord Fairfax to own Richard for his fovereign, than it had been his father, becaufe Oliver was confeffedly as great a general as himfelf, but the younger protector had never even drawn his fword.

No change however procured him any refpect or confequence, for when the army had reftored the long parliament, no notice was taken of him, whilft men, every way inferior to him, were caballing for that office which he once had filled with fo much praife. His labouring under that moft dreadful of all complaints the ftone as well as gout, made him court eafe and retirement ; he therefore rather wifhed well, than was enabled to promote the reftoration of royalty.

Monk, in his way to London from Scotland, called upon his lordfhip: each of thefe taciturn generals waited for the other to fpeak, that he might know the opinion his brother in arms entertained of public affairs. Fairfax, for once, found a more filent man than himfelf, and finding that the other would not declare his thoughts firft, fpoke of the grievances of the kingdom, and betrayed his wifhes for the king's return ; but Monk remained impenetrably myfterious : however, as foon as he durft, he fhewed the confidence

he repofed in his lordfhip, by intrufting Hull
into the hands of his relation Colonel Fairfax.

As the fcheme of reftoring the king to his dominions opened, he fhewed his fentiments more;
and when the convention parliament met, and
voted the king's return, he was appointed one of
the commiffioners to attend his majefty at the
Hague, who received him with fingular kindnefs
and attention, overlooking the fhare he had in his
father's death, from the fervices he had ftrove to
render to himfelf.

He was foon after elected one of the knights
for the county of York ; but, when not in parliament, he lived a private retired life upon his own
eftates in that county, far from the court, which
could very well difpenfe with his prefence. His
lordfhip died at his feat, November 12, 1671,
aged 60. He married at Hackney, June 20, 1637,
Ann, one of the coheirs of General Sir Horatio
Lord Vere, who fo greatly diftinguifhed himfelf
in the Palatinate war ; by this lady he left an
only child Mary, married to George, the witty
and profligate Duke of Buckingham, by whom
fhe had no iffue, and in whom the title of Buckingham expired. It is extraordinary that this
alliance fhould take place between fuch oppofite
families, as the fon of Charles I.'s great favourite, with the daughter of Fairfax, who, more
than any other perfon, contributed to the ruin of
that monarch.

Thofe who wifhed to reconcile Lord Fairfax's
conduct at the reftoration with it at the death of

King Charles, pretended that he was diverted from affifting the unhappy prince at his laft moments, by the length of Major-general Harrifon's long prayers, until the fatal blow was ftruck ; a more foolifh thing could not gain credit ; he not only affifted in bringing King Charles to his mock trial and judgment, but knew that the warrant was figned, knew the hour appointed to put his majefty to death, and fent the guard that was to fee the murder committed.

Lord Fairfax, if viewed as a general, demands our higheft praifes ; he had been formed as a foldier under his father-in-law, and had firft fignalized himfelf at the taking of Bois le Duc from the Spaniards ; Sir Horatio " was remarkable " for doing great things with few men, and Fair- " fax with the lofs of few." If the royalifts were to be fubdued, no one could have been better employed than this general, for he did all to foften the horrors of war ; and though fhockingly fevere againft his fovereign, yet mild and gentle to thofe he acted againft ; attentive and even condefcending to thofe gentlemen, who were obliged to fubmit to his arms. To him we are indebted for the prefervation of many of our works of elegance and tafte, of the venerable remains of former ages, which, unlefs he had interpofed, would have experienced the fate of the fifter kingdom.

None made a greater figure in the field, none a more contemptible one in the cabinet ; there was a weaknefs in his perception that is fcarce credi-

P 3

ble, in a perfon of his rank and education, much
lefs in a foldier.

The elegance of his tafte made retirement
pleafant to him ; he was formed for the fociety of
the learned, whom he loved and patronized ; Mr.
Roger Dodfworth, who was chief compiler of
the Monafticon, received a penfion from him.

The general's collections were valuable; amongft
them we are told was a fet of engraved portraits
of warriors ; and his coins and medals formed
afterwards a part of the fplendid cabinet of Mr.
Thorefby.

He alfo employed his pen fometimes ; he wrote
memorials of his own life ; he even courted the
mufes, by attempting a new verfion of the Pfalms
of David, but as thefe have never been printed
we may fuppofe he far better deferved the laurel
than the bays. What a contraft muft this
prefbyterian puritan general be, to his fon-in-law
Buckingham !

As patron of the fine arts, and as one who alfo
underftood them, he defervedly has very many
and beautiful portraits taken of him in the precious metals, upon canvas, and by the graving
tool. As a regicide, for fuch undoubtedly in
every fenfe, he muft be pronounced, though he
did not give fentence, nor fign the warrant for
execution; that print engraved, probably in Holland, is the moft appropriate, which exhibits him
holding the head of Charles I. by the hair, in his
right hand, and an axe in his left ; infcribed,
Carnifex Regis Angliæ. I fufpect that Lord Fair-

fax never forgave the Earl of Newcaftle's proclaiming him and his father traytors in the
year 1642.

The title of Baron Fairfax of Cameron defcended to his nephew, Henry Fairfax, Efq. fon
of Henry, the fecond fon of Thomas, who was
the firft nobleman of this title; which Henry
Lord Fairfax was fucceeded by Thomas his eldeft
fon, the fifth of the title, who left three fons
Thomas, Henry, and Robert, who all became
poffeffed of the barony, which expired in the laft.

The vaft poffeffions that they had acquired in
America, the largeft perhaps of any fubject in the
world, were loft by that revolution which cut off
the United Provinces from the mother country.
Henry, the feventh Lord Fairfax, left the Britifh
court to exift in a wigwam, repofing in the arms
of a fquaw; the laft nobleman, his brother, who
after living in the moft extravagant profufion, I
faw buried in a manner more humble than the
corpfe of one of the meaneft cultivators of his
eftates would have been.

There is a diftant branch of this family now in
America, who is permitted, I believe, to retain
fome inconfiderable portion of the wide-extended
domains of the Fairfaxes in that quarter of the
globe.

The Life of GEORGE FENWICK, Esq.

GEORGE FENWICK, Esq. was of the Baronet family of Fenwick, in the county of Northumberland, so created by King Charles I. June 9, 1628, in the person of Sir John Fenwick, and which expired in another Sir John Fenwick, who was attainted and executed for a supposed design to assassinate king William III.

This gentleman early distinguished himself in the parliament cause in 1646; he, with Sir John Fenwick, who had originally been a loyalist, but made an early peace with the parliament, was appointed one of the commissioners for the performance of the treaty with Scotland, and in which it is said, any nine of them, whereof three of the house of peers, and six of the house of commons, were to be present, should be the commissioners of England for the conservation of the peace between the two kingdoms, to act according to the powers in that behalf expressed in the articles of the late treaty, and not otherwise.

He is here called only Mr. George Fenwick, though probably he was then in the parliament army, for in June, in the following year, he was ranked as a colonel, and was then in service in Ireland, where he behaved so gallantly, that the English parliament voted one thousand pounds, at the same time that they ordered a day of thanksgiving for their great successes in that kingdom.

He returned to England, and was employed in the North, in June 1648; for when Sir Marmaduke Langdale retreated to Carlisle, and had sent eight troops of horse, whereof two were composed of gentlemen, excellently mounted, towards Berwick, he and Mr. Sanderson were dispatched by Major-general Lambert to watch their motions; and though they were commanded by Sir Richard Tempest, who was regarded as a skilful and diligent officer, yet in the following month he, jointly with the major-general and Mr. Sanderson, obtained a compleat victory over him, taking many of the superior officers, who were gentlemen of the first families; and this important service was performed without the loss of one man: the names of the prisoners were sent up to the parliament, where the news was received with peculiar joy.

He went afterwards with Cromwell into Scotland, and contributed to bring that kingdom into subjection to the parliament. The general sent him at the head of his troop of horse, and some dragoons, to relieve Holy Island, near Berwick; and he afterwards stormed Fenham Castle, which was garrisoned by Scots; this was in September.

In the meeting of the officers, at the head of whom was Cromwell, with the gentlemen of the four northern counties, it was agreed that a petition should be presented to the parliament for justice against delinquents, and for a commission of oyer and terminer to be sent to try such as they should apprehend, and to pay for one thousand foot in Berwick, and a regiment of horfe under Colonel Fenwick, and for eight hundred foot in Carlifle, and a regiment of horfe. Thefe were things feemingly not much connected; but as it was only in October preceding the King's death, it is evident that the delinquents here mentioned chiefly aimed at the captive fovereign, who was very foon after called the chief delinquent, and the putting in his claim upon the parliament appears to be a fweetner of Cromwell's to win him to all the compliances he wanted of him; for he was at the beginning of the following year put down as one of the king's judges, in the act of the garbled houfe of commons, for erecting the pretended high court of juftice, but he declined taking any fteps in that moft infamous tranfaction; for I fuppofe him to have been upon the fpot; as it is not reafonable to believe any were named who were not in London, or the environs.

He feems from this time to have feparated himfelf from Cromwell, and to have never more been in his confidence; he was one whom the protector's council would not permit to take his feat in the parliament called in 1656. The time of his death I have not feen: his two daughters and co-heirs were, Elizabeth, married to Sir Thomas Heflerigge, of Nofeley, in Leicefterfhire, Bart.; and Dorothy, to Sir William Williamfon, of Eaft Markham, in the county of Nottingham, Bart. " who to the great grief of not only her faid huf- " band, but likewife to all relations, friends, and " neighbours, departed this life on the 4th of

" November 1699, which was the day of her
" birth, and the 54th year of her age."

The family of Fenwick were peculiarly favoured
by the Protector Oliver, who in an eminent man‑
ner courted their fervices. Major Fenwick, in
1655, was one of the commiffioners of Suffex,
for the execution of the orders of his highnefs,
and the council for the prefervation of the peace
of the commonwealth. Captain Fenwick, whom
Mr. Edward Rolt left at Farnborough, with Mr.
Swift, to convey the letters fent by Secretary
Thurloe to him, as he was to follow the Swedifh
camp; and Lieutenant-colonel Fenwick, who
was fhot through the body at Mardike, in June
1658: General Lockhart, when he left that place,
waited on him and Colonel Drummond, alfo mor‑
tally wounded, to know if he could any way ferve
them; to whom he and his dying friend only
afked his promife that they fhould be buried in
Dunkirk. Probably this gentleman was the fame
perfon as was left at Farnborough, and in 1657
the protector had thefe committee-men of this
family in the county of Northumberland: Sir
John Fenwick, Knight and Baronet; William
Fenwick, of Wallington, Efq., who fucceeded
his father as baronet; Edward Fenwick, Efq.,
Martin Fenwick, Efq., and Cuthbert Fenwick,
Efq. They muft have been very numerous, as
they were a moft ancient family; for Blome, in
1673, mentions, befides thefe gentlemen, Wil‑
liam Fenwick, of Bywell, Efq.; William Fen‑
wick, of Stanton, Efq; and Triftram Fenwick,

of Kenton, Gent. It was no wonder, therefore, that both the parliament and the protector were extremely attentive to them; the former, in March 1647, by an ordinance of both houses, reftored Mr. Fenwick to a fellowfhip in Cambridge; and in the preceding month had ordered Mr. Robert Fenwick, for his loffes and good affection, one thoufand pounds. In the Myftery of the good Old Caufe, are two mentioned of the name; James Fenwick, captain of a troop of horfe; and William Fenwick, whom the writer fays, " had but five hundred pound given him " by the parliament; fo fmall a fum deferves not " a Chriftian name." I fufpect he was afterwards the baronet.

The Life of JOHN FOWKE, *Alderman of the City of London.*

JOHN FOWKE was an alderman of London, who diftinguifhed himfelf againft the court; for this reafon he was invefted with fome of the moft confiderable offices in the city, and thofe the moft profitable.

Having been appointed a commiffioner of the cuftoms, and refufing to deliver up an account upon oath of what money he had received, he was committed by the other commiffioners to the Fleet prifon; but feveral of the citizens, in July 1643, joining in a petition to the parliament in his behalf, he was ordered by them to be bailed, and the bufinefs was referred to another committee; but in the next month, it was determined by the Houfe of Commons, that he fhould be accountable in the fame manner as the other commiffioners of the cuftoms.

He was of thofe who were deprived of their commiffions in the militia of the city in 1647; but when a new one was fettled, and the lift was brought into the houfe to be approved, the houfe ordered their thanks to be given to the old commiffioners.

This man was altogether treacherous and bafe, always pretending a regard for the parliament, yet ever betraying its beft interefts to the army; for when the two houfes, and the city, refolved to put

themfelves in a pofture of defence, and had for
that purpofe called a committee of lords and
commons, and another of the militia of London,
and they had determined to act both collectively
and individually to promote their common fafety
in defending themfelves againft the criminal defigns of the army, and, in conformity to which,
as Lord Hollis remarks, " the committee went,
" and did their parts, but they found Jacob's hand
" every where; the army had fo played Abfalom,
" pretending an intention to fettle peace imme-
" diately, correct the exorbitances with which
" the people had been oppreffed and abufed, re-
" ftore the king, with fuch other plaufible
" things; and their agents had fo induftrioufly
" improved their interefts, fome falfe brothers
" in the city, as Alderman Foulks and Alderman
" Gibbs, fo cunningly wrought upon men's
" minds, fometimes upon their fears, fetting out
" the ftrength and power of the army, which
" threatened nothing but ruin; fometimes upon
" their hopes and defires of peace, gilding over
" their proceedings, as all done in order to it;
" fometimes upon the diflike of the prefent con-
" dition, affuring them all taxes and payments
" would, by this means, be taken off; fome-
" times upon their credulity, making them be-
" lieve, that thofe perfons whom the army had
" in their eyes to remove, were not fo well af-
" fected to the public, but had fome particular
" ends and defigns of their own, to arm reforma-
" does, and fet up the power of another fword

I

" to rule and govern by, fo to continue the mife-
" ries and burdens of the people; by which falfe-
" hoods and jugglings, thofe two chiefly, like
" Jannes and Jambres, had generally bewitched
" the city, and lulled it into a fecurity, with-
" ftanding thofe who had no other thought than
" to deliver their brethren and themfelves from
" that fubjection and vaffalage to which they
" were then defigned; and, 'fays his lordfhip,'
" are fince brought. As the citizens refolved
" not to ftir, but looked on to fee what this
" army would do, fome few did appear, rather to
" make objection and hinder the bufinefs than
" help it; and though many good orders were
" made for putting the city into a pofture to de-
" fend itfelf, none were obeyed; fo on all hands
" the poor parliament, and kingdom, and city
" itfelf, were betrayed, and left to the mercy of
" the army, whofe aim, we foon faw, was cruelty
" itfelf, injuftice, oppreffion, violence, and rebel-
" lion in the higheft degree."

Such were the fentiments of the vile duplicity
of this man, and his brother alderman, which his
lordfhip mentions, as an excufe for the parliament and city making no barrier againft the
army; but bafely fubmitted to every indignity
and encroachment they chofe; but it is a very
difficult thing to defend a body of fenators, and
of merchants and tradefmen from a victorious
army, though that army has been raifed by the
authority of the one, and chiefly paid by the contributions of the other; for what could reftrain

them? Not duty; for both the parliament and the city had taught them that revolt and rebellion were not only neceſſary but laudable; and if they had learnt to practiſe theſe ſentiments againſt their legitimate rulers, much more would they againſt thoſe who had no juſt right to demand their obedience. Lord Hollis was a preſbyterian member of the Houſe of Commons, and could ſee the baſeneſs of the army; but could not perceive that it was only a reflected light from his own party, who had raiſed a ſtorm which they could not quell, and were obliged to ſtoop to a tenfold tyranny from the very men whom they had armed to lay their lawful ſovereign at their feet. Speaking farther of the baſeneſs of the city, he ſays, " I may ſay, they were a people prepared for ruin " and ſlavery. Gibbs and Fowke principally had " bewitched them; and agents for the army, who " were up and down, weakened men's hearts and " hands, ſo as nothing was done to any purpoſe " for putting them into a way of ſafety, or poſſi- " bility of deliverance."

It is undoubted, that none ſo greatly contri-buted to raiſe the civil war as the city of London, from ſome diſobligations ſhewn by the court; but much more from thoſe factious incendiaries that filled the pulpits in their churches, the gloomy puritans; but none lamented the death of the ſovereign more, nor had more reaſon; for the war fell, as it always muſt, moſt upon the richeſt; and war and commerce are incompatible. The city ſhould have inſiſted upon peace between the king and his parliament; and had they done it with firmnefs, both muft have decided their quarrel in the only proper mode it could have been done. The parliament demanded re-drefs of many encroachments; Charles was made fenfible that they were fuch, and had complied with their defires; but the parliament, having began to tafte the fweets of fovereignty, wifhed to render him a cypher: the city fhould have fup-ported the juft rights of the crown, and not have been cajoled by fo wicked an inftrument as Fowke, who was only the vile agent of the junto of the officers of the army.

The faction put his name in the commiffion for trying the fovereign, conftituting him one of his majefty's judges; but he was too wife to publicly act in a bufinefs that he had fo craftily promoted.

He continued his acquiefcence in all the modi-fications that the army were pleafed to adopt. Cromwell, who was at the head of that intereft, had him elected lord mayor in 1653; yet this could not prevent his fellow-citizens fhewing their juft diflike to fo hateful a character; for in October, in this very year, though invefted with the magiftracy, and patronized with the au-thority of the protector, the common-council prefented a petition againft him to the parlia-ment, which was referred to a committee.

The remains of the parliament, in derifion called the Rump, knowing how material it was to gain this man, conftituted him one of the city militia, July 7, 1659. At the reftoration, he was

VOL. I.   Q

perhaps the moft odious perfon in the city; his avarice was fo proverbial, that he was faid, from his extenfive dealings into diftant countries, to have laid Jews, Gentiles, papifts, and proteftants alike under the fevereft contributions; his arbitrary and querulous difpofition loft him even the hearts of thofe who acted with him; and his having been one of the infamous inftruments to fubject the city, and the nation itfelf, to the lawlefs controul of the army, rendered him truly and defervedly deteftable. Yet criminal as he was, the government permitted him to retain the vaft riches he had fo unworthily acquired; he funk, however, into univerfal contempt. Probably he fpent fome of his time in retirement at Iflington; for Sarah, wife of Thomas Fowke, merchant, was buried there in 1663. This infamous lord mayor bore for his arms, *Vert, a fleur de lis argent.*

The Life of GEORGE FLEETWOOD, *Efq.*

GEORGE FLEETWOOD, Efq. was the fon of Sir William Fleetwood, of Aldwincle, and Woodftock, Knt. cup-bearer and comptroller to both King James I. and Charles I., and a great fufferer for the royal caufe; and furviving the reftoration, was reftored to the places he had poffeffed under the grandfather and father of the reigning fovereign. His eldeft brother, Miles, was knighted by King Charles II.; his fecond brother, William, was a colonel in the parliament army; and Charles, his youngeft brother, became the parliament general after the death of his father-in-law, the elder protector.

Never was a family more divided than the Fleetwoods at this time; the eldeft branch, the baronets, were ftrict Roman catholics; many kept true to the church of England; whilft this gentleman, and his youngeft brother, became the wildeft enthufiafts.

Devoted to the parliament at the commencement of the civil war, he flided to the intereft of the army, and was entirely under the controul of the chief leaders in it, efpecially Cromwell. He therefore having been named in the commiffion to try his fovereign, accepted the infamous office, fitting in the Painted Chamber on the 18th, 26th, and 27th of January, and in Weftminfter Hall on the laft of them, and figned the death-warrant of that king, who had fo eminently patronized his family; an inftance of fhocking ingratitude, that muft render him peculiarly deteftable.

Though one of the long parliament, he deferted that intereft to fupport the government of his general, Cromwell, who raifed him to various diftinctions, and ultimately placed him in his upper houfe as Lord Fleetwood, where I have already fpoken of him.

I fuppofe he was the Colonel Fleetwood whom Lord Hollis fays, was, by way of fequeftration, put into the remembrancer's place of the court of wards, which his brother held, and by going to Oxford loft; and who, upon the breaking up of the royal court, had three thoufand pounds given him as a recompence.

At the reftoration, he was one of thofe excepted out of the act of indemnity, both as to life and eftate, though he had furrendered himfelf in obedience to the proclamation of the convention parliament. He was at this time a lieutenant-general in the army; but he was arraigned only as George Fleetwood, Efq.; he was fet at the bar in the Seffions-houfe, at the Old-Bailey, October 10, 1660. When he was afked, whether he was guilty or not guilty, he prudently replied, " My lord, I " came in upon his majefty's proclamation;" and when directed to anfwer in the affirmative or negative, he replied, " I muft confefs I am " guilty;" and then delivered a petition to the

court, which he faid was directed to his majefty
and the parliament, and it was received ; and
when found guily, and afked what he had to fay
why fentence fhould not pafs ? he faid, " My
" lord, I have already confeffed the fact; I wifh
" I could exprefs my forrow," and wept.

Sentence having been paffed upon him, he was
taken again to the Tower ; but through the intereft of his venerable father, and other friends, his
majefty not only refpited the fentence, but at
length permitted him to go at large ; when, feeing how odious and contemptible he was here, he
paffed over to America, and lived with thofe
whofe fentiments were congenial to his own ;
but, inftead of humble gratitude to his gracious and
merciful fovereign, inftead of humbling himfelf
before the throne of his heavenly judge, he proudly
exulted in the infamous wickednefs he had perpe-
trated. And here it may be remarked, that thefe
men, who, though they were convinced that both
their own and foreign nations looked upon them
as moft criminal, and pretended to think fo of
themfelves at the bar, yet, if they got away from
impending danger, exulted in their fhocking
breach of the rights of all civil fociety. If they
had been led, as a few were, to execution, they
would, with a very few exceptions, have triumphed in their deaths, and acted a part to
make the people believe they were martyrs for
liberty, and even the caufe of Chrift ; though it
is well known, that they were as far from know-

ing the juſt principles of the goſpel as from
practiſing them; and that their religion was
only an hypocritical form of godlineſs, uſed as
a cloak to cover the greateſt crimes and the
moſt ſelfiſh practices.

The Life of JOHN FRY, Esq.

JOHN FRY, Esq. was feated at Yarty, near Membury, in the county of Devon, and was, I think, fon and heir of William Fry, Esq. of that place, by Mary, daughter of John Younge, of Culliton, in Devonshire, Esq. anceftors of the baronets of that name ; the youngeft were as decidedly in the intereft of the parliament as they afterwards were enemies to the Cromwells.

This gentleman had great abilities, which gave him celebrity at firft ; but he had no ftability. Leaving his own church, he was conftantly fhifting his religious creed, and, like vaft numbers at this period, he could not help fhewing his weakness to the public : he was prefbyterian, independent, Arian : courted and defpifed by all parties : his works were doomed by the parliament to be burnt by the common executioner, " as " erroneous, profane, and highly fcandalous."

He was appointed one of King Charles's pretended judges ; and attended all the meetings in the Painted Chamber, from January the 8th to the 25th inclufive ; he fat in Weftminfter Hall upon the 20th, the 21ft, and 22d ; but not upon the laft, neither did he fign the warrant for execution.

He died in the year 1650, having juft been expelled parliament, and in danger of fome fignal punifhment, for his going greater lengths in religion than his mafters judged proper.

William Fry, Efq. whom I fuppofe was his brother, was a committee-man for Devonfhire; whom Major-general Defborough recommended to Secretary Thurloe for one of the commiffioners for Dorfet.

The regicide was fucceeded in the eftate and feat of Yarty, by his fon, John Fry, Efq*. His father not being mentioned in the exceptive claufe in the bill of indemnity. He married Anna, daughter of Robert Napier, of Punknoll, Efq. mafter of the hanaper to King Charles I. and King Charles II. and poffeffed many other places in the court of the laft prince, after his return to his dominions, and whofe loyalty to the former of thofe monarchs had fubjected him to plunders and fequeftrations by the ufurpers. Mrs. Fry's brother, Robert Napier, Efq. was a very confidential fervant to King Charles II. alfo clerk of the hanaper, and whom that monarch created a baronet.

* John Fry, Efq. was a member for Shaftefbury, in the long parliament; but I do not know whether the father or the fon.

The Life of AUGUSTINE GARLAND, *Efq.*

AUGUSTINE GARLAND, Efq. was fettled in the
county of Effex, and bred to the bar; but for
fome time quitted the law to join the parliament
army; he was returned a member in the long parliament in 1648; and when the idea of the army
was to deftroy the king, they put his name in the
commiffion, conftituting him one of the judges
of the pretended high court of juftice, and he
was named by the junto of the parliament, chairman of the committee which prepared the bill;
and he fat in all the public and private meetings
of the infamous court, when it met either in the
Painted Chamber or Weftminfter Hall, except
four days in the former, the 12th, the 18th, 19th,
and the 24th of January; gave fentence in this
unrighteous caufe, and figned the warrant for the
completion of the villany.

At the reftoration he was excepted out of the
bill of pardon and indemnity, and fubjected to
the lofs of life and eftate, though he had furrendered to the parliament according to their
proclamation. He was arraigned at the Seffions
Houfe in the Old Bailey October 10, 1660, and
pleaded not guilty, and tried the 16th following. When addreffing the court, he faid, " may it
" pleafe your lordfhip, I came here this day in-
" tending to have waved my plea, and referred
" myfelf to this honourable court, to be recom-
" mended to the king's mercy and the parlia-

" ment's; but hearing of fome fcandal upon me,
" more than ever I did hear till within thefe few
" days, I fhall defire your favour in my trial."
Mr. Solicitor-general, " my lord, he faith well;
" for if he had confeffed the indictment we
" fhould not have accepted it;" and then directing the witneffes to be called, Mr. Garland
faid, " I do confefs this, I fat, and at the day of
" fentence, figned the warrant for execution."
Mr. Solicitor-general then told the court, " and
" we will prove that he fpat in the king's face."
To whom Mr. Garland replied, " I pray let me
" hear that, otherwife I would not have put you
" to any trouble at all."

   Clench being fworn, and afked whether he
knew the prifoner at the bar, Auguftine Garland? faid, " I know him very well." Council.
" Tell my lords and the jury how you faw him
" behave himfelf to our fovereign lord the king
" when he was at the bar." Clench, " I was
" that day at Weftminfter Hall when the king
" had fentence; they hurried the king down; this
" Mr. Garland came down ftairs by them; to-
" wards the bottom of the ftairs he fpit in his
" face, at a little diftance." Council, " do you
" believe he did it on purpofe, upon your oath."
Clench, " I fuppofe he did it fomewhat fuf-
" picioufly in that way, I did fee the king put
" his hand in his left pocket, but I do not know
" whether the king wiped it away." Mr. Solicitor-general, " the king wiped it off, but he
" will never wipe it off fo long as he lives: he

" hath confeffed that he fat, that he fentenced,
" and that he figned ; we fay he contrived it at
" the beginning, and at laft bid defiance to the
" king ; I fhall defire he may be remembered in
" another place."

Mr. Garland, " I do not know that I was
" near him at that time ; I do not remember
" this paffage, I am afraid he is an indigent per-
" fon. If I was guilty of this inhumanity I
" defire no favour from God Almighty."

Lord Chief Juftice, " I will tell you this doth
" not concern the jury ; but this circumftance
" poffibly may be confidered in another place."

Mr. Garland then took leave of the court, by
faying, " I refer myfelf whether you be fatisfied
" that I did fuch an inhuman act, I fubmit that
" to you : I dare appeal to all thefe gentlemen
" here, looking upon the prifoners, or any other,
" whether they ever heard of it, nor was I ever
" accufed for fuch a thing till a few days fince ;
" but I wave my plea, and refer myfelf to the
" court. Now, my lord, this is the truth of the
" cafe, there is that honourable gentleman the
" fpeaker of the houfe of commons, knows I
" lived in Effex in the beginning of thefe trou-
" bles, and I was inforced to forfake my habita-
" tion ; I came from thence to London, where I
" have behaved myfelf fairly in my way. After-
" wards in 1648 I was chofen a member into the
" parliament ; in June 1648 I came in a member
" of the parliament. My lord, after the divi-
" fions of the houfe by the infolency of the

" foldiery, fome came to me and defired me that
" I would go to the houfe; I was then in my
" chamber at Lincoln's Inn; I forebore a week
" and more; faid I, I do not expect to be ad-
" mitted, for they look upon me as another per-
" fon; faid they, if you will go you fhall have
" no contradiction; I went, I went in; when I
" was in, the firft bufinefs that came was the
" bufinefs of trial of the king, and it was put
" on me to be chairman for bringing in this act
" for trial; I did not know how to contradict that
" power or authority, be it what it will, but I
" muft obey; I fear my ruin will follow it; in
" that refpect, my lord, when I came there, I was
" forced to run throughout what they had im-
" pofed upon me. Having feen me, I could not
" fhrink from them for fear of my own deftruc-
" tion, and thereupon I did go in, and did that
" which I have confeffed to your lordfhips, not
" out of any malignity to his majefty; I never
" had any difrefpect to him in my life; my lord,
" I did not know which way to be fafe in any
" thing; without doors was mifery, within doors
" was mifchief. I do appeal to all that had any
" thing to do with me, that I never did any
" wrong to any that was of the king's party, but
" helped them as I was able. My lord, when
" the government was thus toffed, and turned,
" and tumbled, and I knew not what, and the
" fecluded members came into the houfe, I knew
" not what to do in that cafe neither. As foon
" as this parliament had declared the treaty,

" which was the 8th of May, the 9th of May I
" appeared before the Right Honourable the Lord
" Mayor of London, and did claim the benefit
" of his majefty's gracious declaration, and to
" became a loyal fubject, as in my heart I always
" was; and my Lord Mayor being there, I hope
" he will teftify that as foon as I heard of the
" proclamation, I rendered myfelf according to
" the proclamation. My lord, this hath been
" the carriage of me, being always under fear and
" force: I refer myfelf to your lordfhips."

Sentence was paffed upon him, but he was
faved by the fon of that monarch to whom he
had fhewed none, as appears by the king's trial,
in which he feemed over fedulous; where or
when his death happened, is not I believe known.

This man has all the appearance of being extremely weak, the tool of the party throughout,
and as timid as weak. The inhumanity alledged
againft him, was not well fubftantiated. Such indignities, with quaffing tobacco fumes in the face
of the fallen degraded king undoubtedly did
happen in his way to and from his trial, and
whilft in confinement, a little time previous to
his death; but thefe brutal acts were committed
by the foldiers, at the inftigation of their vile officers. The royal fufferer bore thefe indignities
with a manly and meek carriage, as one who then
looked only for reft and peace in thofe realms
which lie beyond the grave.

Mr. Garland's excufe, that he was obliged to go
through this perverfion of juftice was highly im-

proper; others were named, yet did not act, and were not injured for declining what their confciences dictated was the higheft crime the law knows; and as he was bred to that profeffion, he of all others ought to have withftood every attempt to forfeit that allegiance he owed his fovereign. The very men who afked him to go into the fnare would have fecretly honoured him for refufing to obey their commands.

He fhould not have advanced what no one could believe, that he was " always a loyal fubject in " his heart;" no faith could be fo ftrong to credit what fo contradicted his actions; for it was not a fingle day's erration, but a deliberate treafon of the moft flagicious nature, and fuch as none could be ignorant of, nor of the punifhment annexed.

So little did the parliament, the army, the protectors, even the rump, value this man, that he was fuffered to remain in obfcurity; and his infignificance happily protected him after his life became forfeited.

The Life of WILLIAM GOFFE, *Esq.*

WILLIAM GOFFE, Esq. was the son of the puritanical rector of Stanmer, in Suffex, the Reverend Stephen Goffe. He was bred to the trade of a dry-salter in London; but leaving that for the profession of the army, he rose to the rank of a colonel in the parliament service; was named one of the commissioners of the high court of justice, erected to destroy his sovereign under a legal form, and assisted every day in promoting so vile an act, but on the 10th, 12th, 18th, 20th, and 23d days of January, in the Painted Chamber; and not only gave sentence against, but signed the warrant to murder the king.

He rose to great honour under the Cromwells, and was one of the few who remained true to their interest throughout. Of his farther history I forbear to speak, having already given it amongst the Protector Oliver's Lords, in my Cromwell memoirs. I shall therefore only observe, that being excepted out of the act of indemnity at the restoration, both as to life and estate, he thought it better to fly than surrender himself to justice, as the proclamation ordered; he effected his escape to North America, where, cut off from all human society but his father-in-law Whalley, equally implicated in this blackest crime, he spent forty years of as great misery and wretchedness as can be paralleled. Dreadful as their sin

2

had been, none can read their fufferings without commiferation, and the endearing foftnefs, the firm yet gentle conftancy of his amiable wife to her parent and her hufband, in their years of captivity, muft melt any heart that is not impenetrable to pity, and ought to be a leffon written in brafs, to deter men from enormous vices, that leave only the wretched alternative of a painful and ignominious death, or a life of infamy, dread, and mifery, feparated from all thofe connections that render exiftence defirable; that here have no hope; that hereafter can have no profpect, but of ftill greater inflictions, unlefs their crimes are redeemed with the fevereft and fincereft repentance.

The Life of JOHN GOURDON, *Efq.*

JOHN GOURDON, Efq. was feated at Affington, in the county of Suffolk, was returned one of the reprefentatives for the borough of Ipfwich, in that county, and became one of the parliament committee-men there.

Lord Hollis fpeaks of him with much contempt, as a favourer of the army, and one who made a party in the houfe of commons to perform what-ever their mafters of the fword dictated. For when the parliament required, " that the houfes be " purged, thofe who have appeared againft them " not to be theirs, and the kingdom's judges, " whofe names they *faid* they would fpeedily " give in ; they told the parliament what fort of " men they will have preferred to power and truft " in the commonwealth ; then (which was a " crime fome fix weeks before), to move in par-" liament, and in a parliamentary way, fo as that " fagacious gentleman, Mr. Gurden, flood up in " a rage, and faid it fmelt of Oxford, and it was " much decried by all the crew, but is now of " public merit, and very pious, coming from " their mafters, the army, they would have a de-" terminate period of time fet to the parliament, " and fome provifion made for the continuance " of future parliaments."

It is certain that the army cajoled the parlia-ment into what terms they pleafed, even before they put that violence upon them, previous to his Majefty's death, which this gentleman, as much a friend as he was to their meafures, would never promote by accepting the infamous office they had allotted him, of fitting upon his fovereign as a judge.

We know fo very little of this perfon, that we muft fuppofe him extremely infignificant in every other refpect, than as a member of this extraordinary parliament. He appears as one of Oliver's committee alfo for his own county, and was continued in that unpopular office, probably until the reftoration, which he furvived. In May 1649, Dr. Gourdon, the phyfician, was made mafter of the Mint, in the room of Sir Robert Harley, who refufed to ufe the republican type for the coin.

The Life of ROGER GRATWICK, Esq.

ROGER GRATWICK, Esq. was, I apprehend, son of William Gratwick, Esq. by Amphilis, the youngest daughter of Sir Benjamin Tichborne, Knight and Baronet, a gentleman of the privy chamber to King James I. several of whose sons were greatly distinguished in the civil war as the partizans of the parliament, which might induce this gentleman to unite in the same cause; but his name is so little known at this time, that was it not from his being mentioned as one of the commissioners of the high court of justice, history would be silent respecting his ever having exifted. He had, however, resolution to withstand the plot laid to make him infamous to posterity; for he never in the least assisted in any part of the odious and impious act.

The Life of THOMAS *Lord* GREY.

THOMAS LORD GREY was of a very illuftrious family, being defcended from a younger branch of the Greys, who had enjoyed the title firft of Marquis Dorfet, and afterwards Duke of Suffolk; but they loft this pre-eminent rank by the attempt to place Lady Jane Grey upon the throne, after the death of King Edward VI.

King James I. compaffionating a family who had been by this fatal ambition levelled to the ftation of gentry only, raifed Sir Henry Grey, of Pergo, in Effex, fon and heir of John Grey, of the fame place, Efq. a younger brother of the Duke of Suffolk, to the peerage, by creating him Lord Grey, of Groby, a barony that had defcended to the Greys by marrying an heirefs of the De Ferrer's family; this nobleman died in 1614, and was fucceeded by

Henry, the fecond Lord Grey, of Groby, and created by his majefty King Charles I. March 26, 1628, Earl of Stamford; who, by Ann, youngeft daughter and coheir of William Earl of Exeter, had Thomas Lord Grey, the fubject of this memoir, Anchitel, John, and Leonard; Elizabeth, married to Sir George Booth, created by King Charles II. for his diftinguifhed loyalty, juft preceding the revolution, Lord de la Mere; Diana, to Robert Earl of Aylesfbury; Joan, Ann, and Mary: neither of the two latter ever married.

His Lordſhip, from his birth, his expectations, the gratitude his family owed to the royal
houſe of Stuart, and particularly to his majeſty,
might have been ſuppoſed the laſt to have
riſen up againſt his ſovereign ; and that if he had
been led away by the heat of paſſion from his
duty, would, when he ſaw the adverſe party take
decided means to deſtroy the monarch, and abo-
liſh the kingly office, have retraced, with the
ſwiftneſs of an eagle, and the fury of a lion, his
devious ſteps ; but, like a rebel againſt his royal
maſter, and an enemy to that order which he was
born to inherit, or bequeath to his poſterity at
leaſt, he was foremoſt in throwing down every
thing ſacred, every thing that he, in a peculiar
manner, was bound to have upheld and ſup-
ported ; and painful as it is, I am obliged to deliver him down to poſterity with an ignominy that
has ſcarce ever been paralleled in the Chriſtian
world.

This nobleman having been returned a member
in the ever-memorable long parliament, immediately diſtinguiſhed himſelf by going into the moſt
violent courſes that the worſt enemies of the court
adopted ; he ſigned the Proteſtation, and ſought
every mean to make the wound between the ſovereign and his people ſo deep, that nothing ſhort
of ruin could enſue.

The moment, to him wiſhed-for moment, came,
that the war was decreed : he ſignalized himſelf
by collecting his men, and joining the ſtandard of
revolt. The parliament, proud of a young noble-

man to affift in their caufe, gave him every confidence they could, little fufpecting that in the end
he would prove as faithlefs to themfelves as he
had done to the king; round whom was collected
the fons of moft of the ennobled families in the
kingdom. The few on the parliament fide, efpecially
in the commencement of the war, made him more
confpicuous, and gave him a confequence that was
extremely flattering to his pride : he loft fight of
all decency and moderation. However, fituated
as he was, he might have been excufed entering
in the war on the parliament fide, when fo large
a proportion of the nation at firft were fo inflamed
againft the court, and the Earl of Stamford took
that fide of the caufe, and even became a general
of their army in the Weft, though he never made
any diftinguifhed figure in the field, that was referved to this, his fon. The earl was contami-
nated by every crime; his fon feemed ambitious
to excel him as much in profligacy as in arms.

The parliament gave Lord Grey the command
of Leicefterfhire, and of the affociated midland
counties, and appointed him governor of the
town of Leicefter, where a ftrong garrifon was
placed.

His Lordfhip was under many obligations to
the Earl of Effex, the parliament generaliffimo,
who was appointed to go and relieve Gloucefter,
then befieged by his majefty in perfon, as having a great defire to obtain a place which commanded the Severn ; anxious therefore to prevent
what would give fuch a vaft fuperiority to the

middle of the kingdom, Effex was ordered to go
down and fecure it for his employers. Lord
Grey, to fhew his refpects to his fuperior commander, and one to whom he had a peculiar de-
voir, with Colonel Harvey, marched to that nobleman's rendezvous at Aylesfbury, Auguft 29, 1643,
at the head of a large body of forces belonging to
the affociated counties, and a number of volun-
teers; and the parliament, who before had much
neglected their general, ftrove by every mean to
gratify him to the full; and to recruit his army,
completed the regiments by frefh levies of foldiers raifed in London; the trained bands alfo
were in part fent, and the fhops fhut up, until
the whole complement wanted were raifed; and
the army fet out on their way to Gloucefter, which
was immediately relieved, juft in time to prevent
its furrender, and having ftaid there three days,
the whole army returned to London, having in
their march obtained a victory at Newbury over
the royal army.

The parliament and the city were extravagant
in their joy upon this occafion; the Scotch covenant was embraced with a kind of holy furor by
all ranks of men; from the church they removed
to the camp, offering the moft fulfome addreffes
to Effex, the vaineft of the vain; the mayor and
his brethren, with the train bands, faluted him,
as the protector and defender of their lives and
fortunes, and of their wives and children.

Thofe who had contributed to this fuccefs were
alfo publicly thanked by the houfe of commons;

amongst them the Lord Grey stood the foremost, for his good service done in the late relief of Gloucester, and victory of Newbury; and they ordered that this should be entered in the parliament journals for an honour to them and their posterity.

That standard which the army had taken at Newbury was certainly very significant of him, in both senses; for it displayed the house of parliament, with two traitors' heads fixed upon the top of it, with this motto, *ut extra, sic infra*; because he was alike disloyal to his sovereign, both in and out of the house.

In the middle of the ensuing year his lordship and Sir John Gell united their forces to reduce his majesty's garrison at Wilney-Ferry in Derbyshire, which had been very successful in their sallies; to effect this, they used a stratagem; they took sixty cart loads of hay, and other things that would easily take fire, and conveyed them with their troops to the fort they meant to gain; the forces protecting the men who drove the carts, to enable them to overturn, and set their contents in a flame; and the wind sitting that way the garrison were so annoyed, that the Governor, Captain Robinson, offered to quit the place with his baggage; but this was denied him, and a resolute defence was preparing, until the men, overcome with the smoke, threw down their arms and surrendered. His lordship and his friend then obtained Wingfield and Shelford manors, in the same county, whose mansions were garrisoned for the king. For thefe fucceffes his lordfhip, and Sir John received the thanks of parliament.

In the year 1644 there arofe fome mifunder-ftanding between his lordfhip and the affociation in the county of Leicefter; and foon after, he being abfent, probably in London, they prefented a petition to the parliament, requefting he might be fent down into the country as commander in chief, which was occafioned by the fear of his majefty, who aimed at gaining Leicefter; and their common danger made them quit all alterca-tion to withftand the royal arms.

Thefe fears were not groundlefs, for the place was taken by ftorm by the king, who entered the town June the 1ft, in the year 1645; and there were taken in it, Colonel Grey, the governor, proba-bly one of his lordfhip's brothers, and Captain Hackar, who afterwards became fo infamous for the part he took in the king's death, both of whom were wounded; but the place foon after-wards fell into the hands of General Fairfax, who reinftated the Greys in the government of it.

We hear little of his lordfhip for a confiderable time after this; probably he remained chiefly in the government of Leicefter; but in the middle of the year 1648, fearing another difgrace, he, without the authority of parliament, with Captain Temple, raifed a confiderable body of troops in the county of Leicefter; which afterwards was approved of by a vote of the houfe of commons.

The Duke of Hamilton having been defeated at Uttoxeter, and having furrendered himfelf

upon articles, Lord Grey came up, and fhamefully took him out of the hands of Lambert, to
whom his grace had figned the treaty, and then
pretended that he was a prifoner without any fti-
pulation for life, or liberty; and the parliament,
to fhew their fanguinary difpofitions, in exact oppofition to juftice, adjudged the duke a prifoner
to Lord Grey, that they might have a pretence to
deftroy him; and to affect this the better, they of
the houfe of commons paffed a vote of thanks to
his lordfhip, for taking his grace a prifoner, and
difperfing a brigade of his horfe; and though the
unfortunate duke applied to the honour of Grey
to fave him at his trial, it was to no purpofe; his
death had been decreed, as his royal mafter's, before he came to his trial, and he fell a facrifice to the fhamelefs policy of the times. He
mocked God by a day of thankfgiving for this
victory over the Scots, and feafted one hundred
and fifty of his officers for it at Leicefter. The
Scotch had began the revolt againft King
Charles I. but in the end they paid very dear
for it.

His Lordfhip, foon after this pretended fervice,
came to town, and affifted at the call of ferjeants
at law; and with others, efpecially the Earl of
Kent, was complimented with a ring, by one of
the new ferjeants, as his peculiar friend, in compliance with a very ancient cuftom. It redounds
very little honour upon thofe tools of the parliament, who continued to fit in his majefty's courts
to adminifter juftice, when their fovereign was in

the hands of men going to proftitute all laws, human and divine, by folemnly mocking juftice, with bringing him to a trial, and efpecially to take the council, and be perfuaded to fanction, as it were, the intended deed by Lord Grey, one of the moft infamous of men, becaufe they fuppofed him armed with a little paltry authority; and yet Whitlock, who well knew his character, owns, that he, and the other judges fat in the courts whilft preparations were making in Weftminfter Hall, for the trial of their unhappy king, bafely feized by the army.

Lord Grey had always been the foremoft for violent meafures, fearing, perhaps, that as he had finned paft forgivenefs. he would take every occafion to urge on the deftruction of the captive monarch, and demeaned himfelf by being, not only fecretly in the council of officers, but openly the particular inftrument to accomplifh it: for when it was refolved that they would oblige the houfe of commons to fanction their unheard-of impious deed, he, with a pride that diftinguifhed itfelf in wickednefs, undertook to perform the dirty office by garbling the houfe of commons.

This has been called Colonel Pride's purge, but he was only the inferior inftrument, for when that officer's foot were drawn up in the court of requefts, upon the ftairs, and in the lobby before the houfe, juft preceding the time the houfe was to meet, his lordfhip ftood near to direct him in what he was to do, and though Pride had a paper in his hand of the names of fuch members as were too honeft to give any fanction to the murder of their fovereign; yet, as he did not perfonally know them, this office was performed jointly by his lordfhip and the door-keeper; and as each obnoxious member came, he was pointed out, fecured, and fent away by fome of the foldiers to the queen's court, court of wards, and other places, according to the imperious commands of the general and council of the army. Thefe were men who dared to fay that they drew their fwords for the protection of the king, the freedom of the parliament, and the liberty of the fubject, and could mock the Almighty by pretending that it had his fanction.

He fat in the Painted Chamber January the 8th, 15th, 17th, 18th, 20th, 22d, 23d, 24th, 26th, 27th, and 29th; and he fat every day in Weftminfter Hall, when his majefty was brought before them, and figned the warrant for execution. His prefence probably was abfolutely neceffary to give fome fanction to the infamous proceedings, and to overawe fuch as might be refractory.

After this ever-to-be-lamented cataftrophe, and they had changed the monarchy into a republic, he was named one of the council of ftate for 1649, and continued in the fame place of truft and power in the years 1650 and 1651.

As he had advanced confiderable fums probably, and much was owing him in his military capacity, his difburfements and arrears that he had prefented to the houfe, were taken into confideration June 25, 1649, and they were referred to a committee to confider how they might be fatisfied; and on the 3d of the following month, they were fully paffed, and allowed to be due.

Lord Grey was now in his meridian glory; he had deftroyed the fovereign, and with him monarchy: he rofe to be one of the heads of the ftate; having gratified his ambition, and the luft of rule, he fought alfo to glut himfelf with wealth, and this he had by no means been delicate in doing before; for Denzil Lord Hollis fays, " he obtained a confiderable fum, to be " paid out of fuch difcoveries of the royalifts' " eftates, denominated then delinquents, as he " fhould make; whereupon, fays his lordfhip, " he and his terriers were long attending the " committee of examinations, in the profecution " ftill of fome game or other, till his fum was " made up." This fum he had got by the army; but now, as one of the chief governors of the nation, he gained far greater fums, and more valuable acquifitions; with part of this money he purchafed, at a very eafy rate, the largeft part of the loyal Lord Craven's eftate, particularly Comb Abbey, worth at leaft three thoufand pounds a year; and he received a grant from his brethren of the queen's manor-houfe, park, and lands at Holdenby, where he made a great devaftation in the woods.

So far he had been trufted, courted, applauded, and gratified, chiefly by Cromwell; but as that great man faw that Grey was as ambitious as himfelf, or at leaft that he could not brook a fuperior, he began to treat him with lefs confidence, and at length to watch him as a dangerous perfon; as inimical to thofe great defigns he was meditating.

They probably moft cordially hated each other; he feared Oliver, and regarded him as a revolter from the common intereft; and the other knew the wickednefs of his heart, and that a man who had been fo untrue to his lawful fovereign, could not be expected to be loyal to one whom he viewed as inferior to himfelf.

Outwardly, however, they behaved with feeming attention to each other, whilft each was watching for the favourable moment to ruin his enemy. Oliver durft not truft him in London, the feat of government; he therefore kept him in his ftation in Leicefter: but that being the central fituation of the kingdom, and, in cafe of a revolt, a very dangerous one for a perfon of Lord Grey's confequence and turn of mind, he kept conftant fpies upon him; and being fatisfied of the truth of what he had fuppofed, he fent Colonel Francis Hacker to feize his lordfhip, and convey him to Windfor.

I cannot give a better account of it, than what the colonel wrote to the protector, February 12, 1654.

"May it pleafe your highnefs,

"According to your command, I have feifed "the Lord Grey and Captain Bodell. I have "alfo according to order feifed 3 horfes, and 5 "cafe of piftols, being all the armes I could find,

" and thofe unfixed. My lord did informe mee,
" that 3 of his beft horfes was not yet come from
" Stamford, where a race was lately; but he ex-
" pected them this night, and if I would fend for
" them, they will be forth coming. The Lord
" Grey is much diftempered with the gout, and
" was defirous to knowe whither hee was to goe,
" which I concealed from him, and hee perceiv-
" ing mee not willing to declare, faid he was wil-
" ling to fubmitt to goe whether I pleafed; but
" defires to come to London. I have not ac-
" quainted him whether hee is to goe, but have
" prefumed upon the advice and confent of thofe
" with mee, in regard of his indifpofition of
" health, to let him reft at Leicefter, where will
" be three troopes for his guard, untill further
" order from his highnefs." The reft of the
letter relates to the turbulent difpofition of the
quakers, and is foreign to the prefent purpofe.
The protector, however, did not chufe to permit
a man to remain a prifoner where he had been a
governor; and therefore, notwithftanding the ill
ftate of his health, ordered him to be brought up
to Windfor Caftle, where he came the 27th of the
fame month; and we may fuppofe he entered it
with different fentiments than he left it, after he
had contrived the agreement of the people previous to the king's trial. How long he remained
in prifon, I have not feen; but he obtained his
liberty, yet funk into the moft wretched ftate of
contempt.

As a proof of this, it is fufficient to remark,

that all parties, but the moſt deſpicable, viewed him with ſcorn; and his reputation was at ſo low an ebb, that he could not get the confidence of any but thoſe wretched fanatics, the fifth monarchy-men, at the head of whom was Major-general Harriſon. So fallen was this haughty, turbulent, and traitorous man, becoming the deriſion and contempt of all ſober and rational people.

The projects of theſe deſpicable perſons were long carried on, and, as they weakly imagined, with the utmoſt ſecrecy; the ſcheme was to deſtroy the protector, ſeize Monk in Scotland, and erect the kingdom of Chriſt. Grey was to be at the head; Colonel Saxby, as leſs ſuſpected, they ſuppoſed, than Harriſon, was made the active mover of the plot.

Their chief cabal was held in a houſe near Shoreditch, where they had agreed to print vaſt numbers of declarations againſt the protector's government; five thouſand of them were to be ſent into Leiceſterſhire, where his lordſhip's chief intereſt lay; and Heſelrigge, and other diſaffected perſons of various religious principles, were invited to join them.

What raiſed their conſequence, and made them more dangerous was, that the Spaniſh court was perſuaded, that money lent to theſe fifth monarchy-men would be better employed than if advanced to the cavaliers, as more deſperate, and better calculated to the temper of thoſe who hated Oliver's perſon and government.

I

Thurloe, to whom as fecretary nothing was unknown, foon came to the information, which detected all thefe fchemes which Grey was carrying
on with his defpicable affociates ; but he did not
interrupt them until the very evening preceding
the day they meant to declare themfelves ; when,
fending a party of foldiers, they feized the chiefs,
Lord Grey, Venner, Gowler, Hopkins, Afhton,
and others, with all their apparatus ready prepared. Amongft thefe, the principal object that
arrefted their notice was a ftandard with a lion
depicted upon it, in a couchant pofture, as of
the tribe of Judah, with this motto : *Who fhall
rouze him up ?* There were numberlefs copies
of thefe printed declarations, beginning with
" The principle of the remnant," &c. fuitable
to the wild vifionary ideas of thefe expectants of
feating Chrift in the temporal as well as fpiritual
government of thefe nations. None can think that
Grey had the leaft opinion of the poffibility of
eftablifhing fuch a monarchy ; he only guided a
filly multitude to perform what he alone believed
he fhould obtain the advantage of—wealth and
power.

He was fent to his former apartments at Windfor. Ludlow affects to fuppofe, that his imprifonment was folely owing to a copy of the
" Memento" he had difperfed in Ireland ; but
Thurloe's State Papers give us better information.
By the fame mode of reafoning, the former gentleman imagines that Sexby's difgrace was from

VOL. I. S

the fame caufe; he, however, efcaped a prifon by a timely retreat; and that fo haftily, that his fervant who was conveying away his portmantua, was feized. The protector, pretending to pafs over the mifconduct of Sexby, fent him as an agent to Bourdeaux, in France; but took care to difpatch a meffenger to that government, to fay how much he wifhed him fecured. Sexby, fufpicious, obtained information of his intention, and, effecting his efcape over the city gate in the night, left the kingdom, and no more trufted to Oliver's infidious proteftations.

Lord Grey determined, if poffible, to regain his liberty: to accomplifh this moft defirable event, he fued for a hæbeas corpus, which the lord chief juftice granted; but the governor of Windfor Caftle refufed to give obedience to it; nor did he obtain his freedom until he had given fecurity, in the penalty of a large fum of money, if he ever again acted againft the government; " which he chofe," fays Mr. Ludlow, " to do, " rather than engage his parole, thereby hazard- " ing only the lofs of fo much money, and pre- " ferving his honour and integrity;" but as perhaps Oliver thought he had neither of thofe valuable properties, he took what was much bet- ter, a pecuniary fecurity; the lofs of wealth be- ing, he was convinced, the greateft evil that Grey thought he could fuffer.

The other confpirators were fent prifoners to the Gate-houfe, where they lay long in a mifetable fituation; but they were fpared to create new difturbances at the reftoration; when, fally-ing out into the ftreets of London, proclaiming *King Jefus,* they were furrounded as it were; but though they were only a few ill-armed perfons, fuppofing themfelves invulnerable, they could not be prevailed upon to fubmit, until they were fatally convinced to the contrary. The furvivors expiated their crimes at Tyburn.

Happily for Lord Grey, and for the noble family from whence he derived his defcent, he fell a victim to his own defeated wickednefs, which, with the gout, brought to a vaft height by the violence of his paffions, put a period to his exiftence in this world, juft preceding the reftoration, or he would have been held up to the infamy he feemed defirous of afpiring to, by fo many, and fuch atrocious crimes: it is not poffible to draw from hiftory a more infamous, or more deteftable character. I have confulted all our beft peerages, to find the exact time of Lord Grey's death, and the place of his inter-ment, but they are all filent refpecting thefe cir-cumftances.

There is, at Lord Denbigh's feat, of Newn-ham Paddox, in Warwickfhire, a very fine por-trait of Lord Grey, the regicide. The Earl of Denbigh of that day, was brother-in-law to this regicide, and meanly accepted of feveral places of profit under the commonwealth.

Lord Grey married Dorothy, fecond daughter

and coheir of Edward Bourchier, fourth Earl of Bath, who long survived him, and married two other husbands; Guftavus Mackfworth, Efq., who was proclaimed a traitor by King Charles I. in the year 1642; and after his death, Charles Howden.

The iffue of Lord Grey and this lady, was a fon and two daughters: Thomas, who became the fecond Earl of Stamford, fucceeding his grandfather, who died Auguft 21, 1673. King William III. appointed him chancellor of the duchy of Lancafter, lord lieutenant and cuftos rotulorum of the county of Leicefter; and Queen Ann called him to her privy council. This nobleman died January 31, 1719-20, aged fixty-feven years. He left no iffue by Mary, daughter and coheir of Jofeph Maynard, of Gunnerf-bury, in the county of Middlefex, Efq., fon and heir of Sir John Maynard, Knt., one of the commiffioners of the great feal. His eftates devolved to his two fifters, or their reprefen-tatives: Elizabeth, married to Henry Benfon, of Charlton, in Northumberland, Efq.; and Ann, to James Grove, Efq. ferjeant at law.

The earldom of Stamford came to Harry, the grandfon of John, third fon of Henry, the firft Earl of Stamford; fo that the Marquis of Stamford, the poffeffor of fo many virtues, is not, I am happy to fay, the defcendant of Thomas Lord Grey, who fo eminently difgraced his name and title.

The Life of THOMAS HAMMOND, *Esq.*
INCLUDING THAT OF HIS UNCLE,
COLONEL THOMAS HAMMOND.

THOMAS HAMMOND, Esq. was of an ancient and knightly family; a name as memorable for the distinguished merit of the excellent Dr. Hammond, as for the disgraceful part many of the family took against King Charles I. a monarch who loved, cherished, honoured, and revered the eminent divine and scholar, whose piety, virtue, and acquirements will ever render his memory respected, as an ornament to the christian world.

It is difficult to exactly distinguish the actions of the military Hammonds. I believe I am accurate in giving the following events as relative to, and belonging to the life of the regicide.

He was appointed to a regiment raised by King Charles I. to act against Scotland in 1639, but who, like many others, turned those arms against his majesty, which were put in their hands to defend him.

The parliament were pleased with his apostacy, and raised him to a far greater rank, and by a very rapid promotion; he became a lieutenant-general of the Ordnance; but I have not been able to learn any brilliant, or indeed any particular service deserving of this reward, except influencing many of his relations to take part against his royal master, as it were, to counteract the faith-

ful fervices of his brother, the good Dr. Hammond.

He was named one of the commiffioners of the
high court of juftice, and fat in Weftminfter Hall
every day of the trial, and alfo in the Painted
Chamber, with the omiffions of the 8th, 10th,
13th, 19th, 24th, 25th, and 29th of January, and
he figned the warrant for the execution.

He died before the reftoration, but his name
was inferted in the act of attainder. His hiftory
is very little, but his conduct was very confe-
quential. He was rich and powerful, and probably had no children ; this gave him it is prefumed great intereft in, and command over his
nephew, Colonel Thomas Hammnod, whofe life
is fo very remarkable, and whofe conduct was fo
momentous, that I fhall depart from my ufual
mode, in fubjoining it, and this the rather, becaufe though he was not one of the regicides, yet
he appears to have acted under the controul, direction, and, perhaps in a great meafure, command of his uncle, one of the king's judges.
If his brother, the reverend divine, had poffeffed
as great an influence over this his nephew, how
would it have turned the fate of the Britifh monarch.

Colonel Thomas Hammond, a fon of the regicide's brother, was originally an enfign in Sir Simon Harcourt's regiment, and went into the army
in 1644. He much diftinguifhed himfelf when
fent by Colonel Maffey to relieve the country
round Berkley Caftle, which fuffered greatly from

the excurfions of the garrifon, and his valour and conduct was fo confpicuoufly difplayed in this enterprize, that it laid the foundation for all his fubfequent reputation.

In the battle of Nafeby, fought in the year 1645, he performed his duty in the referve of the army, bringing it up as he was required in a moft mafterly manner; and in the fame year he was very ferviceable in the ftorming of Briftol and Dartmouth; in the latter he led the forlorn hope with great gallantry and judgment. Towards the clofe of this year he obtained Poudram Caftle, in Devonfhire, which he was preparing to ftorm when it furrendered to him.

Sir Thomas Fairfax, under whom both he and Lieutenant-general Hammond ferved, was fo well pleafed with his conduct, that upon the furrender of the city of Exeter, April 13, 1646, he made him governor of it, and wrote to the parliament for their approbation, which was given. Soon after this, Mount Edgecome furrendered to him.

It being found neceffary that fome forces fhould be fent over to Ireland, which fervice was by no means relifhed by any of the army; until at length General Fairfax declared his willingnefs to go, Colonel Hammond was the firft who fhewed a readinefs to accompany his excellency thither; and the parliament had fettled that Sir Thomas fhould go as commander in chief to that kingdom, and Hammond was greatly approved of as one of his officers; but, fays Lord Hollis, being " now a " colonel of the new model, he ftood upon his

" pantoufles, that he would not be obliged for
" longer than two or three months, have all his
" pay beforehand, victuals for fix months, though
" he would ftay but two, be abfolute commander
" of all the forces there, have a proportion of
" money over and above for contingent occafions,
" put into what hands he would appoint, a fleet
" of fhips to tranfport him, wait upon him, and
" be at his difpofing, not to ftir without leave;
" in truth he muft be admiral and general : fuch
" terms as no prince or foreign ftate that had but
" given an affiftance, could have ftood upon
" higher. This was the obedient confcientious
" army; but moft men were fatisfied if it was not
" difbanded Ireland muft be loft, and England
" undone." .

I apprehend that he made thefe conditions becaufe of the danger of going thither, as it would
preclude him from the greateft advantages, by
preventing his promotion in this kingdom; however, extravagant as his propofitions were, the
parliament, from the fears they were in, accepted
them. But the general and his officers feeing
their aim, drew up fuch a petition to the houfe of
commons that they knew was impoffible to comply with; thefe petitions were to be forwarded to
Lieutenant-general Hammond, and him; and
alfo to Colonels Ireton and Rich.

The parliament getting information of this,
and fearing the confequences, ordered that he and
others fhould refide in the army, and that fome
of their quarters fhould be removed. This was

the firſt great attempt of the army to ſet up an intereſt independent of that of their employers, the parliament. However, a compromiſe ſoon was ſet on foot, and the army ſeemed willing to do what their maſters demanded of them; and in this acclamation, " All, all, Fairfax and Cromwell, " and we all go." Both Lieutenant General and Colonel Hammond joined, and with equal ſincerity.

Inſtead of going to Ireland, he came up to London with his regiment of foot, in the train of General Fairfax when he made his magnificent entry into London, Auguſt the 6th, 1647; and in September following, he was, by an ordinance of both houſes of parliament, made governor of the Iſle of Wight, a place of great importance at the time, but ſtill of much more by the circumſtances that followed.

For his majeſty being with the army at Hampton Court, was ſo alarmed by private letters and hints given him of his danger, that he reſolved to quit the army, in whoſe hands he then was, and if poſſible get to a place of ſafety; but this was one of the moſt unfortunate ſteps he took during his misfortunes, as it was a plot laid by Cromwell and other officers to make him odious to the army, becauſe it was ſeen that the neighbouring gentry and people, as well as many of both the higher and lower parts of the military, became attached to his perſon, compaſſionated his ſufferings, and would ſoon have rendered it impoſſible to have either led the ſoldiers againſt the king, if the war was renewed, or otherwise consent to his destruction.

His majesty falling into the snare, made his escape, with Mr. John Ashburnham and Sir John Berkley. It is not known whither their royal fugitive meant to trust himself, but probably it was to get to a sea-port town, and obtain a vessel to carry himself out of the kingdom, and go to his continental friends, or transport himself over to Ireland, but the former is the more probable; but to leave conjecture, his majesty arrived at Titchfield, the seat of the loyal Earl of Southampton, November the 11th, and there reposed himself after the fatigues of his journey, having only Mr. Legge with him.

Sir John Berkley and Mr. Ashburnham were dispatched to Colonel Hammond, with a copy of the letter left upon the table by his majesty, when he left Hampton Court and two others, which he had lately received, one of them without a name, expressing great fears and apprehensions of the ill designs of the republican party against him; the other from Cromwell, of much the same import, and also to acquaint him, that to effect their purposes it was intended to have placed a new guard, consisting of men of these principles about his person the next day.

They likewise conveyed a letter, addressed from his majesty to the governor, expressing his fears of the levellers in the army; but professing the interest he took in the army in general, and of himself in particular as a gentleman who was of

good extraction, and not his perfonal enemy, and
as fuch he meant to entruft himfelf to his care;
but that he might not furprize him, he had fent
thofe two gentlemen to acquaint him with his
intentions, requefting of him to give his promife
of protection to himfelf, and them, as far as he
could, and that if he declined it, to let them all
retire in fafety.

Sir John Berkley at leaving his majefty, faid
that as he had no knowledge of the governor,
they might be detained, and therefore if they
were, and did not return the next day, he requefted
the king to think no more of them, but effect his
efcape.

Towards evening thefe gentlemen came to
Lymington, but a violent ftorm having fallen, it
rendered the paffing there impracticable that
night, but in the morning they went into the
ifland, and proceeded to Carifbrook Caftle the
governor's refidence, but unfortunately he was
gone to Newport.

Haftening to go thither they overtook him, and
delivered his majefty's meffage, at which he grew
pale, and trembled to fuch a degree that he was
near falling from his horfe. Nor did he recover
his confternation of an hour, but fometimes
breaking out into paffionate and diftracted ex-
preffions, faying, " O gentlemen, you have un-
" done me in bringing the king into the ifland,
" if at leaft you have brought him; and if you
" have not, I pray let him not come; for, what
" between my duty to the king, and gratitude to

I

" him, upon this fresh obligation of confidence,
" and the discharge of my trust to the army, I
" shall be confounded."

They assured him that his majesty meant to favour him and his posterity, by giving him this
opportunity of rendering so essential a service,
and which was no way incompatible with the
duty he owed the army, because they had so-
lemnly engaged themselves to the king; but that
if he thought otherwise, his majesty would be far
from imposing his royal person upon him.

To this he replied, " but if the king should
" come to any mischance, what would the army
" and the king say to him, who had refused to
" receive him ?" to which they said, that as the
king had not come to him, it could not be objected to him that he had refused. Collecting
himself, he desired to know where his majesty
was, wishing, he said, that he had absolutely
thrown himself upon his honour.

These raised suspicions in the king's friends,
and, fearful of consequences, they took the governor aside, and some kind of agreement was entered into by him ; Lord Clarendon tells us, that
he would give no promise of permitting the king
to retire, apologizing that he was only an inferior
officer, and must do as his superiors in the army
commanded him, but said, if his majesty would
come to him, he would treat him in the best manner he could, until he heard from the parliament.
He then asked where his majesty was, which they
did not think prudent to inform him; but said

they would go, and acquaint their master with what the colonel had mentioned, and return with his majesty's answer; he then expressed a wish to detain Mr. Ashburnham, but that gentleman declined his consent.

Mr. Ludlow makes it not so much to the governor's credit, for he says, that after some conference with Mr. Ashburnham, he got him to declare, " that he did believe the king relied on " him as a person of honour and honesty, and " therefore he did engage to perform whatsoever " could be expected from a person so qua-" lified."

Mr. Ashburnham replied " I will ask no " more;" then said Hammond, " let us all go " to the king and acquaint him with it."

When they came to Cowes Castle, where a boat lay ready to carry them over, Colonel Hammond took Captain Basket, the governor of that castle, with him, and gave order for a file of musqueteers to follow them in another boat, says Ludlow; but Lord Clarendon, that the governor took only three or four soldiers, or servants to wait upon him, and this appears most probable.

When they came to Titchfield, Mr. Ashburnham, leaving Sir John Berkley with Colonel Hammond and Captain Basket below, went to his majesty, who was in his bedchamber, and acquainted him with what had been done, and that the governor was below ready to fulfil what he had agreed to.

The astonished and alarmed monarch in an

agony of grief exclaimed, ſtriking his breaſt, " what have you brought Hammond with you? " oh, Jack, thou haſt undone me; for I am by " this means made faſt from ſtirring."

Mr. Aſhburnham, ſeeing the king's agitation, ſaid he would go and ſecure the governor if he miſtruſted him, to which his majeſty ſaid, " I " underſtand you well enough; but if I ſhould " follow that counſel, it would be ſaid, and be- " lieved, that he ventured his life for me, and that " I had unworthily taken it from him:" adding, " it is now too late to think upon any thing but " going the way you have forced me upon," wondering how he could make ſo great an over- ſight; at which Mr. Aſhburnham, burſt into a paſſion of tears.

Colonel Hammond and his companion Captain Baſket, ſurprized they heard nothing, became impatient at their long attendance in the court; Sir John Berkley therefore ſent a gentleman of the Earl of Southampton's to deſire, that the king and Mr. Aſhburnham would remember that they were below.

About half an hour after he ſent for them up, but before Colonel Hammond and Captain Baſ- ket could be admitted to kiſs his hand, taking Sir John Berkley aſide, he ſaid to him, " Sir John, I " hope you are not ſo paſſionate as Jack Aſh- " burnham, do you think you have followed my " directions?" to which he replied, " no in- " deed: but it is not my fault, as Mr. Aſhburn- " ham can tell you, if he pleaſe."

His majefty finding it was now too late to take other meafures, received Colonel Hammond chearfully, who again, fays Mr. Ludlow, having repeated to him what he had promifed before, conducted them over to Cowes. The following morning his majefty went with the governor to Carifbrook.

In their way to that place many of the gentlemen, knowing of the approach of their fovereign, ftrove with eager zeal to pay their dutiful refpects to him; and affured his majefty that the whole ifland was devoted to him except the governors of the caftles, and the officers under Colonel Hammond.

They alfo, fpeaking of him, faid, " he might " eafily be gained over to his majefty's intereft; " but if he fhould prove difloyal, nothing could " be more eafy than to bring him to fubmiffion; " for," faid they " the caftle being full day and " night of thofe who were attached to the royal " intereft, and that the king might ufe his own " time of quitting the Ifle of Wight, having " had liberty granted him of riding in the coun- " try every day."

A ray of hope therefore beamed forth upon the king and his confidential friends, and alfo upon fuch who were in his intereft; and his majefty and Mr. Afhburnham applied themfelves to the governor, with fuch good fuccefs, that he and thofe with him were defirous only of having a meffage fent by the king to both houfes of parliament, acquainting them how defirous he was

of peace ; and with which requeſt the unfortunate
ſovereign complied.

There has ever been a myſtery in this unaccountable buſineſs, that has never been un-
ravelled ; and yet no treachery has been fixed
upon theſe two confidential ſervants : it may not
be impoſſible, but that Cromwell, who planned
the eſcape might have alſo in an artful manner
hinted the ſecret wiſhes of both himſelf and his
relation, the governor, to ſerve his majeſty, if he
was once out of the immediate care and controul
of the army, and the parliament ; this is but conjecture : their conduct muſt have been owing to
ſome peculiar perſuaſion of Hammond's devotion to his majeſty, more than what they could
preſume upon from his being the nephew of the
pious Dr. Hammond ; eſpecially as the Colonel
was more under the command of his other uncle,
and himſelf bore arms on the parliament ſide.

It is impoſſible to expreſs the conſternation of
the parliament and army at the news of loſing
the rich pledge, through whom each hoped to
ultimately be the predominent power in the ſtate,
by obtaining from him a ratification of their demands ; unſpeakable therefore was their joy when
Hammond wrote a dutiful letter to the parliament, acquainting them what had happened, and
of his having removed the king, by his own deſire into the Iſle of Wight.

As to Cromwell he expreſſed more pleaſure than
ſurprize, exulting no doubt in the ſucceſs of his
deep-laid ſcheme.   He wrote to the houſe of com-

mons, that he had received letters from Colonel Hammond relative " to the manner of the " king's coming into the Ifle of Wight and the " company that came with him, that he re- " mained there in the Caftle of Carifbrook, till " the pleafure of the parliament fhould be " known;" and then affured them, that " Co- " lonel Hammond was fo honeft a man, and fo " devoted to their fervice, that they need have no " jealoufy, that he might be corrupted by any " body :" " and all this relation he made," fays Lord Clarendon, " with fo unufual a gaiety, that " all men concluded that the king was where he " wifhed he fhould be."

The king certainly was greatly injured by this flight ; he was ftill a prifoner to the army, and in a detached fituation where he was intirely at the difpofal of any fecret wickednefs ; befides he irritated his beft friends in the army, and reaped no other advantage, than making the parliament more ready to liften to reafonable terms, now they faw him wholly in the power of the army ; for whenever their dangers were great, then they were for a treaty, when there was little caufe of fear they were extremely unwilling to have any terms offered that could be accepted ; and they would have been well contented to have let the king have remained a prifoner during his life ; amufing him, as Elizabeth did Mary Queen of Scots, with hopes of reftoring him to his throne.

Colonel Hammond, who now had this richeft jewel in his hands, if he had poffeffed a loyal heart, or, what was more to have been expected, had that ambition that a soldier generally cherishes, who goes into such a war, he might have been the instrument, under Providence, of replacing his sovereign in the legal authority he had been deprived of; his own name would have been handed down with honour, and his descendants, with distinguished rank, might have shone for many centuries the objects of respect and favor of grateful princes; but, as he managed his delicate situation, it became a misery to himself, and disgraceful to his memory.

The parliament rewarded the colonel's messenger, and dispatched a letter of thanks for his care, and instructions to him to govern himself by.

Colonel Hammond was courted, caressed, feared, and hated, by the king, parliament, and army, and their several partizans. It was impossible to satisfy any two of them, but he did not please any one of them. It is probable that he had wisdom enough to see that the army was all-powerful, and had the absolute command, not only of the king and parliament, but of the whole kingdom: however, it was in his power to have made a prodigious difference in this respect; but fear of displeasing his relations and friends at the head of the army, and perhaps determining to stand or fall with the military, might induce him to sacrifice all to that interest.

The army, who sent a letter full of respectful attention to his majesty, professing their duty to his person and family, and regard for regal government, had their cabals to treat with the parliament about the fettlement of the nation; in which the colonel's name was inferted amongft the heads of the army: and, in fine, they took every method to win and cajole the king. Hammond fent a letter to the parliament, through the hands of the general, that he had given orders already not to permit any to come near the king who had been in arms for him; and that he would comply with the other commands that had been given him; but that he had not ferved their warrant for apprehending Mr. Afhburnham, Mr. Legge, and Sir John Berkeley; defiring the ferjeant's deputy to defift until he had their farther orders: becaufe, if he did, it would be with difficulty he could fecure the king's perfon, for his majefty had faid, " if thefe gentlemen fhould " be taken from him, and punifhed as evil doers " for councelling him not to go out of the king- " dom, but rather to come to this place for the " more conveniency as to settlement of peace; " and for endeavouring it accordingly, in attend- " ing him hither, he cannot but expect to be dealt " with accordingly, his cafe being the fame. " That thefe gentlemen have engaged their ho- " nours not to depart from him; and having caft " themfelves upon him, in cafe they fhould be " removed from thence, it would much reflect " upon him." There is fomething peculiarly pleafing in Charles's conduct to his friends; for, after facrificing Lord Strafford, which to the laft defervedly lay heavy upon his confcience, he never could be prevailed upon to defert them.

The governor now paid the utmoft attention to his charge, omitting nothing that could prevent an efcape, and this the rather as his majefty had withdrawn himfelf from reftraint before. He had, previous to the meffage he had laft fent to the parliament, called the gentry of the Ifle of Wight, who had expreffed their readinefs to preferve the king's perfon, and to obey the authority of parliament: at the fame time he gave peremptory orders to reftrain any from leaving or entering the Ifle without paffes, or being examined by himfelf.

When the treaty was broken off with the king, he was ordered by parliament to be particularly careful of the fecurity of the monarch; the general alfo fent him the fame meffage. This made him redouble his vigilance, and treat the royal prifoner with greater ftrictnefs and feverity, becaufe he feemed abandoned by both the two houfes and the army, no more addreffes being allowed to be fent to him.

It became very neceffary for him to act with great caution, if he determined to detain the king; for the people of the Ifle, notwithftanding what they had profeffed to him, fhewed fo marked a deteftation of the parliament's conduct in breaking off the treaty, that for two days there was an open infurrection throughout it; but, like all injudicious matters of this nature, it only injured thofe whom it was meant to ferve.

His Majesty's guard was doubled, his friends denied all access, the whole Isle put in the best state of defence, all the supernumeraries removed from the castle of Carisbrook, and ships were stationed to prevent any others coming into the harbours. Sir William Constable, Lieutenant-colonels Goffe and Salmon, were sent to guard the Isle, and, perhaps, to be a check upon the governor himself, if he should waver in his duty to the army. An order was also dispatched to try the revolters in the military by a court martial, the others by a commission of oyer and terminer.

A ship had been prepared by Mr. William L'Isle to transport the king out of the Isle of Wight; happily that gentleman effected his escape. This attempt to quit the situation in which his servants had thrown him, is a convincing proof that his majesty looked upon himself as lost, if he could not get out of the governor's hands.

Hammond now acted the part of a jailer: every day some privilege was abridged, and the king feared he should lose Dr. Sheldon and Dr. Hammond, who were great comforts to him in his afflictions; and though the latter was uncle to the governor, yet he paid no manner of attention to his sentiments; and the parliament having voted that he and Sir William Constable should have power to place or displace such attendants as they thought proper, it was extraordinary they were not sent away with the foremost.

The royal sufferer at length, irritated beyond his

patience, addreffing him, afked, " why he had
" given order for difmiffing his fervants; and
" whether it ftood with the engagement to them,
" who had fo freely caft themfelves upon him,
" and with his honour and honefty?"

To whom the governor replied, " that his ho-
" nour and honefty were, in the firft place, to
" them that employed him; and, next, that he
" thought the king could not but confefs that he
" had done more, as things ftood, for him than
" he himfelf could have expected."

To this his majefty afked, " Do the commif-
" fioners know of this order?" He replied,
" No." " Then," faid the king, " by what
" authority do you do it?" " By the authority of
" both houfes of parliament; and which, I fup-
" pofe your majefty is not ignorant of the caufe of
" its being done." The fovereign profeffing the
contrary, he concluded the altercation by faying,
" that I plainly fee your majefty is actuated by other
" councels than ftand with the good of this king-
" dom." Meaning, I prefume, that if he could
efcape from the power of both the parliament and
the army, he certainly would. The one wifhing
to ufurp his authority, and keep his perfon as a
pledge for it; the other, equally defirous of rule,
would deftroy him, the better to eftablifh their
power.

The parliament, who had been lavifh to profufion in their own expences, and in their grants
to each other, now meanly ordered a retrench-
ment ftill farther, in the already-fmall eftablifh-

I

ment of the king, appointing only eight perfons, until the general fhould fix upon others to his fatisfaction ;. but thefe were not to exceed thirty; and all the old faithful fervants of his were difmiffed in February, 1647. But the parliament allowed one thoufand pounds for the repairs of Carifbrook Caftle, where he remained in confinement, more to make it a place of greater ftrength than to accommodate the unhappy fovereign, who often wanted fuitable linen for his perfon.

Every month brought fome frefh mortification to the dethroned monarch; yet, profcribed as loyalty was, it would ftill manifeft itfelf; for little papers were conftantly thrown over the wall where his majefty ufed to walk, in which fuch information was conveyed that would either ferve or pleafe; and fometimes letters were conveyed to him, notwithftanding the utmoft vigilance of this Argus of a governor; but every inftance of fuch kinds of attentive duty fhewn the illuftrious captive, if difcovered, brought down ftill greater feverities.

The temper of the governor was feen by this circumftance, and ftill more, that of the parliament and the army. Sufpecting Major Rolfe of a defign againft his life, he complained, and the major was fent to prifon; but the grand jury were fo felected by the governor, at the defire of thofe in power of the civil and military departments, that the bill was thrown out as malicious. At the same time, one was found against Captain Burleigh for beating a drum as a signal to attempt rescuing the king, and he was found guilty, and executed as a traitor; whilst Rolfe was publicly honoured, and pecuniarily rewarded: this needs no farther comment.

Whitlock writes, that the king " declared to " his friends, that the governor was a man of " honour and trust, and had carried himself ci- " villy and respectfully to him; that Osborne had " unjustly and ungratefully asperfed the gover- " nor; and, as touching the preservation of his " person from poison, or any such horrid design, " he was so confident of his honesty and faith- " fulness, that he thought himself as safe in his " hands as if he were in the custody of his own " son." This ill accords with what the king told Sir Philip Warwick, a writer of great veracity, and much in his majesty's confidence, that " the governor was grown such a rogue, that " he could not be in worse hands;" and in June, 1648, Charles attempted to escape from Carisbrook; but, after several ineffectual efforts to get through the iron bars of the window of his bed-chamber, he was obliged to desist. Had the bars been some little farther apart, he would have got through, and then he might soon have reached a place of safety, because every thing had been prepared for his advantage with the greatest care.

His majesty was still farther flattered with being fet at liberty from Hammond's care, as it was the intention of the parliament to permit him to go to Windfor to attend another treaty; but changing their defign, they ordered that it fhould be held again at Newport, in the Ifle of Wight.

The governor received particular inftructions for his conduct during this treaty, allowing him to give his majefty many of thofe privileges he had long been deprived of; but they were conditionally, that he would " give his royal word not " to go out of the ifland during the treaty, nor " twenty days after, without the advice of both " houfes of parliament ;" and as the king was permitted to go at large in the ifland, fearing an efcape, the governor afked, and obtained an addition of horfe and foot to be ftationed there; and the parliament granted him an additional falary, as his expences would neceffarily be increafed. He received the parliament commiffioners at Cowes, with efpectful attention, and complimented their arrival with the difcharge of the ordnance.

The parliament, who had long out-fhot their policy in not coming to terms with their fovereign before the army had acquired that fuperiority and contempt for their authority, as to obey their commands only when it was their intereft, were prevented obtaining the fruits of all their defigns by the determination of their real mafters to fnatch from their hands the royal prey, juft at a time when, from their own danger, they began to fhew a real wifh to reftore the monarch to his crown.

It is a very old and a very true obfervation, that there is no friendfhip among the wicked; it is equally fo, that there is no reliance upon them. This is exemplified in the cafe of this governor, who, contrary to his allegiance, contrary to the regulations the parliament had been pleafed to prefcribe themfelves, had ever been altogether the moft devotedly obfervant to the army; yet now was neither confided in, nor trufted by them; for, determined to facrifice the king, they feared he would oppofe the removal of his majefty from Carifbrook.. The general, therefore, fent him a letter, dated November the 27th, requiring him to repair to his excellency, at the head-quarters at Windfor, acquainting him at the fame time, that Colonel Ewers was appointed to take charge of his majefty's perfon in his abfence.

The houfe of commons, hearing this, voted that he fhould remain in his truft, and that the general fhould be acquainted with their determination; and they fent letters to the admiral of the fleet, to difpatch fome fhips for the fecurity of the Ifle of Wight, with an exprefs order to pay obedience to the commands of the governor.

Thefe were only weak efforts to prevent confequences which all men had long feen muft happen. The army publicly fpent their time in prayers, and in privately laughing at the pointlefs weapons of the parliament.

Hammond went to Windfor, and Ewers gained the perfon of the devoted victim. The fuperceded governor fent all the correfpondence which had paffed between him and the general, to the parliament; who, on the 29th, fent a letter to Fairfax, faying, that the inftructions which Colonel Ewer had received from his excellency, were contrary to their refolutions, and the orders they had tranfmitted to Colonel Hammond; and that it was their pleafure that General Fairfax fhould recal his orders, and permit him to attend his charge in the Ifle of Wight.

This had no other effect, than their fending, on the following day, Major Cromwell to the parliament, to declare, in the governor's name, that he was ftill detained at Windfor, and that Colonel Ewer remained at Carifbrook Caftle. The houfe of peers feemed particularly ftruck with this pofture of affairs, which muft, they were convinced, ruin the conftitution; but it. was now out of their power to alter it; for what had they to oppofe to a victorious fanguinary army?

The king was foon after removed to Hurft Caftle, and his fad cataftrophe foon followed. None more contributed to this than Lieutenantgeneral Hammond, by the conftant influence he kept over this his nephew, to keep him fteady to the intereft of the army; and, as a prelude to

the king's mock trial, prefenting the " Agree-
" ment of the People." As to the governor,
he was only the inftrument in his uncle's hands,
who thought he was promoting the caufe of the
military, to which he was devoted; but Cromwell, who guided him, had only his own aggran-
difement in view, and in the end reaped all the
advantage of every party, over all of whom he
eftablifhed a defpotic tyranny.

It muft here be obferved, that no fooner was
the king immolated, than Hammond, who had
forfeited the firft of civil duties to ferve his
employers, was regarded by them with fcorn
and contempt: however dear the treafon is, the
traitor is always detefted.

There could not be any thing bafer than the
conduct of Hammond towards the king, who
threw himfelf, by Afhburnham's means, entirely into his hands. If he would not have
given him an afylum, he fhould at leaft have
declined taking him under his protection: his
duty to the army was not legitimate; that to
his fovereign was undoubtedly fo. Had he
acted wifely, he fhould have quietly fortified
the Ifle in the beft poffible manner, and procured veffels to lie in the harbours, if neceffary;
he might then have defied every attempt againft
him, efpecially as the people in the Ifle were
confeffedly loyally devoted to Charles's perfon
and juft rights. The army and parliament then
would have ftrove which fhould have offered the

beft terms to his majefty; the kingdoms would
have hailed him the inftrument, under Providence, of giving domeftic peace to nations, fo
long imbrued in the blood of their own fons.
He died before the reftoration : his widow was
married to the anceftor of the Earl of Buckinghamfhire.

The Life of Sir JAMES HARRINGTON, Knt.

Sir James Harrington, of Merton, in Oxfordshire, was knighted by King Charles I. at Whitehall, December 23, 1628. He was of great descent, and of still greater abilities, but they always bordered upon the romantic.

He acquired a seat in the long parliament, and became one of the committee for Middlesex; his sentiments of goverment always leaned to a republican system, but he did not avow them in King Charles the Ist's life-time. In the year 1647 he was appointed one of the commissioners to receive his majesty at Holdenby, in the room of Sir William Airmine, Bart. who had declined that office.

Sir James was named one of the judges of his ill-fated sovereign; compassion, or some other motive, prevented his attending more than one day, the 23d of January, but then he went both to the Painted Chamber and to Westminster Hall; the same motive that kept him from going again, instgated him to refuse signing the fatal warrant.

The parliament, in April 1659, gave Sir Edward Harrington, of Rutlandshire, a relation I presume of his, the important trust of having the charge of such of the children of the late king as were in England, with an allowance of three thousand pounds a year for their maintenance; this gentleman was elected to the appointment becaufe he was not a member of parliament, none who were fo being eligible by a vote of the houfe; but he declined it, and in the following month the care of them was transferred to the Countefs of Carlifle. From this circumftance it may be prefumed, that the Harringtons were generally in the parliament intereft.

An extraordinary occurrence happened to Sir James in July 1649: a woman, for fome reafon not affigned, gave him moft grofs abufe; and he having become a member of parliament, and complaining of the infult, that immaculate body, who had deftroyed their fovereign, difgraced themfelves by wreaking their vengeance upon this inconfiderable idle perfon, by firft fending her to the Marfhalfea, and afterwards to the houfe of correction.

The republicans had a very high opinion of his merit, electing him of the council of ftate in 1649-50, and in 1653, in which year he was mafter of the mint jointly with Thomas Challoner, Efq.; but when the government was feized by Cromwell, he became very difcontented; and during his protectorate he wrote his well-known Oceana, to fet forth the ideas he entertained of a commonwealth, as moft fuitable to his fentiments of perfection. I have, in the life of Mrs. Claypole, Oliver's daughter, mentioned a fingular anecdote relative to the manufcript of this work's having been feized upon, and by the interference of that lady returned to him.

He fet himfelf up in Middlefex to oppofe the protector in the election of fuch as he wifhed to

have returned for that county; but his fuccefs was
fuch as might have been fuppofed by any lefs vifionary than himfelf.

At the deftruction of the protectorial power he
fhone out again in great fplendour; he was named
of the council of ftate in the year 1659, and alfo
of that of the officers, which took the executive
government into their hands; and he was appointed one of the nineteen commiffioners to treat
with General Monk on the part of Scotland.

The reftoration immediately fucceeding, he fell
into great difgrace, the government was fearful
of his enthufiaftical projects; to difgrace him, he
was degraded from his knighthood, and was not
permitted to receive any benefit from his eftates,
and made liable to any punifhment that the legifla-
ture fhould think proper to inflict upon him.

To foften the rigour of his fate, he ftrove to
find amufement in travel, fpending much of his
time upon the continent.

He married Catherine, daughter of Sir Marmaduke Darrel, of Buckinghamfhire; this lady
was greatly admired for her perfonal and mental
charms: fhe was both beautiful and witty. It is
remarkable that fhe rejected his addreffes when
in the bloom of youth, but from prudential mo-
tives, gave him her hand when more advanced in
life. Such a union was not likely to prove happy; his conftitution by application to his ftudies,
by a tedious imprifonment, harfh treatment, and,
as it was apprehended, the effects of poifon, was
greatly emaciated, nor were his intellects lefs in-

jured; a feparation enfued, but it was followed
by a reconciliation, and he behaved afterwards
with great civilty, if not tendernefs.

There are three portraits of him, one by Mar-
chi, half-fheet, metzotinto, from an original pic-
ture in the poffeffion of John Hudfon, of Beffing-
by, in Yorkfhire, Efq. A fecond, infcribed æt.
45, 1654, by Faithorne, 4to. The third by Hol-
lar, from a painting by Sir Peter Lely, 1658, 4to,
which has been copied by Vandergucht. He is
called efquire in the firft and laft, and it has been
fuppofed, though erroneoufly, that he was not
really a knight.

There is alfo an engraving of " Katherine, wife
of Sir James Harrington, by Faithorne, æt. 36,
1654. She was not married to him until after
the reftoration, and therefore Mr. Granger is
wrong in giving it to her; it belongs to Catherine,
daughter and coheir of Sir Edmund Wright, Lord
Mayor of London, who was married to Sir James
Harrington, Knight and Baronet.

The Life of THOMAS HARRISON, *Esq.*

THOMAS HARRISON, Esq. was a butcher or grazier's son : Lord Clarendon says he was born near Namptwich in Chefhire ; but in the preface to the trials of the regicides, it is said he owed his birth to Newcaftle-under-Line in the county of Stafford, and I am inclined to think that was his native place.

After he had received some grammar learning, he was sent to a gentleman of the name of Hofelker, an attorney in good eftimation in Clifford's Inn, who had an employment under the king, and, Lord Clarendon says, difcharged his duty faithfully.

Politics engaged every mind at this momentous period, and young Harrifon much diftinguifhed himfelf by his energy ; as foon as he had ferved his clerkfhip, he joined the company of the ftudents of the law, who under the command of Sir Philip Stapylton, became a guard to the Earl of Effex, the parliament general..

He foon after ferved as a regular foldier in the army raifed to oppofe the king, as a cornet, and by his fobriety and ftrict attention to his new fituation, he rofe to have a commiffion ; but he attracted no particular notice until the army was new modelled.

At the furrender of the old palace of Woodftock in the year 1646, he was appointed one of the commiffioners to receive it : at that time he

I

was a major. He got fo far into the good opinion of Colonel Sydney, Lord Lifle's fon, that he patronized him, as a good foldier; and at his requeft in January 1646-7 the commons voted that he fhould accompany that gentleman thither, and his conduct was fo meritorious, that when Lord Lifle and Sir John Temple reported the ftate of that kingdom, the houfe included him and Colonel Sydney in their thanks, when they gave it that nobleman and his colleague.

He was raifed to the rank of Colonel foon after his return, and became fo confpicuous a character, that he was named one of the commiffioners of the army appointed to treat with thofe deputed by the parliament, relative to a good underftanding between them.

His regiment was one of thofe which in November following fhewed an inclination to mutiny, on account of that fanatic fpirit which their commander was afterwards fo diftinguifhed for, but which at this time he did not dare to openly avow; he had fo great an intereft in the army, that he procured the pardon of his troop which they fubmiffively afked; and in the following year they fhewed their gratitude by performing gallant fervice, at the battle of Prefton, in Lancafhire, where the Duke of Hamilton was defeated.

When the junto in the army determined to publicly deftroy the king, he was fixed upon by them to bring the victim up to Windfor, their head quarters. He went to Hurft Caftle with a ftrong party of horfe, and fhewing his commif-

fion to Colonel Ewer, the governor, that gentleman delivered up the miferable fovereign into his
hands; he received his majefty with outward refpect, and uncovered, fays Lord Clarendon; but
others fay he kept his hat on; but it is of little
confequence, be that circumftance how it may;
it was indeed very immaterial when he was going
to conduct his deftined prey to a fcaffold*.

He was extremely ftrict in his attention to
every thing that paffed, and was " not to be ap-
" proached by any addrefs, anfwering queftions
" in fhort and few words; and, when importuned,
" with rudenefs."

The king ftrove to make an effort to efcape
from the deftruction he faw, by requefting permiffion to dine at Bagfhot, the little park of
which had been the fpot where his majefty had
ufed to fpend fome of his pleafanteft hours. To

* Sir Richard Worfley in his hiftory of the Ifle of Wight has
from an authentic MS. given all the tranfactions which happened at Hurft Caftle, when Harrifon came to feize King Charles;
it is too long for this work, or I fhould have given it. It would
melt any heart but that of a ftern republican to read. Charles
could not be prevailed upon by the Duke of Lenox his relation,
and other devoted fervants, to attempt efcaping, " No" faid he, " I
" have given my word to the parliament, and I will not break
" it;" but when he was taken from under their protection he
thought himfelf at liberty to fave his life if poffible. The night
Harrifon came there was extremely dark and tempeftuous, the
garrifon in the greateft diforder, and a veffel was ftationed for the
king's ufe, fo that it is far from improbable that had he put himfelf under the care of his grace he might have efcaped; but
Charles never knew the precife moment to act in, without which
no man can be a politician.

get Harrifon to confent to his requeft, he told him that Lord Newburgh, the ranger, knew he defigned to take his dinner at a lodge there, and that he would fend a meffenger to let his lady know, that he certainly would come, as fhe would be, the better pleafed, as giving her an opportunity of providing a fuitable table for him, to which the colonel gave his affent the preceding night.

This nobleman had always been extremely loyal, and his lady, the widow of Lord Aubignè, flain at Edge Hill in Charles's caufe, was eminently fo; fhe had been very near falling a victim to her fentiments: this dutiful pair had married with his majefty's approbation; and ever fince the king had been a prifoner at Hampton Court had contrived means to convey letters to and from Charles and his Queen; and, to crown their fidelity, had fent by the fame means they had other letters, one to Hurft Caftle to requeft his majefty if poffible to contrive and dine at the lodge at Bagfhot, in his way to Windfor, and to take occafion if he could, to lame the horfe he rode upon, or to find fuch fault with the creature's going, that it might afford a plea to take one out of his lordfhip's ftables to continue his journey upon.

Lord Newburgh was a great admirer of horfes, and had one of the fleeteft in his ftud, of any in the kingdom, and it was defigned that this fhould be given to his majefty, that he might, if poffible, get an opportunity to fet fpurs to the animal's fides, and efcape by its fwiftnefs, from the com-

pany that furrounded him; and it was rendered
the more feafible, becaufe his majefty fo well
knew all the intricacies of the moft obfcure parts
of the foreft, and therefore might convey himfelf
to places in view of fome of his lordfhip's attendants who were to wait with three or four
horfes, all famous for their fpeed.

The Colonel who knew the importance of his
commiffion to the army, and fearing fome fcheme
was intended to take the king out of his hands,
fent fome horfe and an officer to fearch the houfe,
and every part of the park, that he might be certain he had nothing to apprehend from a fur-
prizal.

His majefty in his way to Lord Newburgh's
conftantly difcovered a pretended uneafinefs at the
movements of his horfe, and faid " he would
" change it and get a better." All things proved
unfortunate relative to the attempt meditated,
for upon his majefty's arrival, dinner was prepared, and he was given to underftand that this
fine animal, by a kick of another horfe the preceding day, was rendered lame; and though
other horfes were procured, yet from the conftant
vigilance of Harrifon and thofe with him, all attempts muft be impoffible, for he was furrounded
by one hundred horfemen, all excellently mounted,
and every one of his guard armed with a piftol,
which they held with their finger upon the trigger
ready at an inftant's notice to fire; fo determined
was this body of infamous mifcreants not to let
their prifoner efcape the ruin they fought.

The king after paffing three or four hours at Bagfhot with every caution that could be devifed, was obliged to purfue his journey: Harrifon never fuffering any one to be in the room where he was, unlefs in company with fix or feven foldiers, nor would he permit any thing to be fpoken, unlefs fo loud that all might hear it.

At quitting the lodge he permitted Lord Newburgh to ride with his majefty for fome miles in the foreft, and had given the king another horfe, as the other had been fo much complained of; but after his lordfhip had rode fometime he was required by this ferocious colonel to retire. The king was conveyed by him that night to Windfor, and the next morning to St. James's; though he had been told what public difgrace was defigned, and that he was to be led to a mock trial, yet he could not diveft his mind of fome fecret and premature tragedy, and, wholly occupied with fuch melancholy ideas, he faid to the colonel, how odious and wicked fuch an affaffination and murder would render a man, and that the perfon who undertook it, would never afterwards be fafe, to which he indignantly replied, " you need " not entertain fuch imaginations or appre- " henfion, for the parliament had too much " honour and juftice to cherifh fo foul an inten- " tion; for whatever the parliament refolved to " do, will be very public, and in a way of juftice, " to which the world will be witnefs; for they " will never endure a thought of fecret vio- " lence." Yet this declaration, fignificant as it

was, the king could not be prevailed upon to believe true, he ftill fuppofed his enemies would not
dare to perform fo monftrous a deed in the open
face of day.

. Such a fcene as this, as a prelude to a worfe, is
painful to relate, and the mind contemplating it
is furprized that men could act fo deliberate a
wickednefs, to promote their own ambition,
when its gratification would be fo extremely dangerous; it is wonderful that compaffion fhould be
fo entirely buried in the human breaft, as not to
revive at beholding fo great a character fallen,
and efpecially when that perfonage was their fovereign, againft whofe life a few years before they
would not have fuffered even their thoughts to
have ftrayed; and as whole nations would exe-
crate the abominable deed, it is extraordinary
that fear of fhame, if not the fear of punifhment,
did not deter them from fo monftrous a crime.

. To quit fo melancholy a fubject, I fhall only
remark, that Harrifon, as one of the king's judges,
fat every day upon the trial except the 13th, 15th,
17th, and 24th of January, in the Painted Chamber, and his hand and feal is to the infamous deed
to put his majefty to death.

This man, whofe origin was fo mean, and his
profpects fo low at the commencement of his going to the war, now by a ftrange turn of affairs,
was only lefs in confequence than Fairfax, Cromwell, and Ireton; he was a good officer, very refolute, always collected, and of a mind that
fcorned compaffion, as unfit for fuch times.

Bifhop Burnet juftly ftiles him, "a fierce and bloody enthufiaft;" but one of the greateft re-quifites that he had for pre-eminence was his fup-pofed gift of expounding the fcriptures, and wrefting all the prophetic writing from their meaning to fuit the times; this won greatly in an army of fanatics; even fenfible well-informed men at that period received pleafure from fuch extravagances. Whitlock, who was remarked for underftanding, fays that when Cromwell was go-ing as lord lieutenant to Ireland, " three mi-" nifters prayed, and the lieutenant himfelf, and " Goffe, and Harrifon, expounded fome places of " fcripture excellently well, and pertinent to the " occafion:" we muft fuppofe Mr. Whitlock was prefent.

In the year 1650 he was become a major-gene-ral, and was fent to Ireland, and again diftinguifhed himfelf; but he came over with Cromwell, and affifted at the famous confultation with Fairfax, about his tender fcruples in commanding the army againft the Scots, who were attempting to re-inftate King Charles II. upon their throne, and intended to conduct him into England; the parties who held this council were Fairfax, Crom-well, Lambert, and himfelf, in the army, and Sr. John and Whitlock as lawyers. He had told the lord-general that he was fatisfied of his faith to the parliament caufe, and that he was certain the Scotch nation meant to attack them; and con-cluded the whole by faying, " it is indeed, my " lord, the moft righteous and the moft glorious

" caufe that ever any of this nation appeared in ;
" and now when we hope that the Lord will give
" a glorious iffue and conclufion to it ; for your
" excellency then to give it over will fadden the
" hearts of many of God's people." But this
did not fatisfy the " tender confcience " of the
general, who refigned the command, which fell
into the hands of Cromwell.

He was making a brilliant figure, October 22d,
in drawing out the trained bands, and other bodies
of men, to the number of eight thoufand, in Hyde
Park, where the fpeaker and the members of parliament met, and were faluted in a military manner by them, preparatory to his going into the north
with Cromwell to attack the Scots, with a body
of horfe and foot which the parliament foon after
voted to be put under his care. In June he was
advanced as far as the extremity of Cumberland,
and thence proceeded to Berwick. He fent the
parliament advice that the Scots were advancing
into England, and that he had acquainted the
commiffioners of the militia in Lancafhire, Cumberland, and other counties, to raife what forces
they could to join him ; and that he had obtained
three thoufand horfe, and hoped to prevent the
enemy's march into England : concluding his
letter with defiring " fome provifion of four or
" five hundred godly men for two or three months,
" if he can get them mounted." This curious
letter is dated in the fame manner as the modern
quakers write, " 7th of the 6 moneth, 1651, at 11
" o'clock, forenoon."

As the Scotch army obtained an entrance into the kingdom, he followed them, and with Lambert sent a body of troops to Worcester, fearing the king should make it " a quarter or garrison." And in the battle fought near that city, in which his majesty was entirely defeated, he behaved in a manner that gave the greatest satisfaction to the general and the whole army.

This was " a crowning victory " to Cromwell, as he himself termed it: and now the army having conquered all opposition in the three kingdoms, chose to reap the entire benefit of it, without even the mask that they had continued to wear after the death of the king.

A consultation was held, December 10, 1651, between the heads of the army, the parliament, and the law, what settlement was to be had; Cromwell opening the conference with asking, " That now the old king being dead, and his son " being defeated, he held it necessary to come to a " settlement of the nation; and in order thereunto " he had called this meeting, to see what was fit " to be done, and to lay their opinion before the " parliament." The speaker complimented Cromwell, and said, " they should be grealy blamed if " they did not take advantage of his victories to " conclude a settlement." Harrison following him, said, " I think that which my lord general " hath propounded, is to advise as to a settlement " both of our civil and spiritual liberties, and so " that the mercies which the Lord hath given in " to us may not be cast away; how this may

" be done is the great queſtion." He acted here merely as the tool of Cromwell, though he was ignorant of it, who only called them together to hear their opinions, that he might the better effect the ambitious project he had long meditated.

His conſequence was augmented by being choſen one of the council of ſtate, ſo that he was every way become one of the heads of the government; and Cromwell, by humouring his diſpoſition, won him entirely to his intereſt; which he the more eaſily did, by convincing him that the aggrandizement of the general was raiſing the conſequence of the army: and inſtilling into him, that the parliament were not ſufficiently ſpiritualized for the great work; and ſhewed to him, what was extremely viſible, indeed, to all, that their firſt care was to enrich themſelves; yet with an admirable dexterity he made the projects he intended appear as if in compliment only to Lambert and him; for when he had reſolved to diſſolve the long parliament, he excuſed it to Quarter-maſter-general Vernon, and no doubt to many others, " that he was puſhed on by the two parties " to do that, the conſideration of the iſſue whereof " made his hair to ſtand an end: but," ſays he, " Lambert's merit is not rewarded as he or others " wiſhed or expected." And then directing his ſpeech towards Harriſon, he ſaid to Vernon, " of " the other, Major-general Harriſon is the chief, " who is an honeſt man, and aims at goods things; " yet from the impatience of his ſpirit will not " wait the Lord's leiſure, but hurries me on to

" that which he and all honeft men will have
" caufe to repent."

Having directed Harrifon's mind to his purpofe, he took him with him to the parliament, of
which he was a member, accompanied with a
fufficient number of foldiers, to effect what he intended ; they went, and took different fides of the
houfe ; but Harrifon being called, went to Cromwell, who told him that " he thought the parlia-
" ment ripe for diffolution ;" to which he replied,
" Sir, the work is very great and dangerous ;
" therefore I defire you ferioufly to confider of it
" before you engage in it." " You fay well,"
replied Oliver, and then fat down for a quarter of
an hour ; but the queftion for paffing the bill relative to fomething that muft neceffarily occafion
their meeting again, enraged him fo much, that
fpeaking again to Harrifon, he faid, " this is the
" time, I muft do it ;" when fuddenly ftarting
up, " he loaded them with the vileft reproaches,
" as not having a heart to do any thing for the
" public good, but had efpoufed the corrupt in-
" tereft of prefbytery and the lawyers, who were
" the fupporters of tyranny and oppreffion ;" ac-
cufing them " of an intention to perpetuate them-
" felves in power, had they not been forced to the
" paffing this act for their own diffolution ; which,
" he affirmed, they defigned never to obferve ;
" and that the Lord had done with them, and had
" chofen other inftruments for the carrying on his
" work, that were much more worthy."

The remainder of this extraordinary fcene was

confufion ; fometimes Cromwell ftamping about the room, and behaving as if infane ; treating them either collectively, or individually with contemptuous infolence : he knew their principles too well to refpect them, and now he feemed refolved that they fhould effectually be acquainted with his fentiments. " Come, come," fays he, " I will put an end to your prating ; you are no " parliament ; I will put an end to your fitting ; " call them in ; call them in." The foldiers entering, all began to be in confternation ; having reviled fome of the members for their vices, he commanded the mace to be taken away, faying, " what fhall we do with this bauble? here, take " it away."

Speaker

Harrifon, who fat quietly near Lenthal the fpeaker, now thought he ought to affift ; therefore, going up to the fpeaker, who kept the chair, he told him, that " feeing things were reduced to " this pafs, it would not be convenient for you " to remain there." The fpeaker anfwered, " I " will not come down, unlefs I am forced." " Sir," fays he, " I will lend you my hand ;" and as Ludlow fays, put his hand in Lenthal's, to conduct him down ; but Whitlock, and others, that he took him by the arm, and fo brought him down, and foon turned out all the members that were there, though they were in number from eighty to an hundred ; Cromwell having commanded the doors to be locked, they went away to Whitehall ; and he thus obtained what he had fo long aimed at, the fovereign power.

The friendſhip that had ſo long ſubſiſted between theſe two " mighty men of valour," who
had ſo often fought and prayed together, was in-
ſtantly diſſolved; Cromwell regarded him now as
his ſubject, and a very dangerous one; Harriſon
viewed him as a ſuperior hypocrite to himſelf,
who had duped him; his heart ſwelled high for
vengeance; but though Cromwell was determined
to take his commiſſion from him ſo early as two
months after this, yet he carried it fair to him,
inviting him to take his ſeat with the aſſembly of
officers, and of the council of ſtate; but this was
only a ſmothered ſtorm.

For he was reſolved to act in direct oppoſition
to Cromwell in all things; he not only ſet himſelf at the head of thoſe who were for a war with
Holland, but he even changed his religious principles. Cromwell and he had been the great
apoſtles of the independents; he now ſpurned the
ſect as not ſufficiently ſpiritualized, and went over
to the anabaptiſts, who were then a furious ungovernable ſet of men, and he ſubmitted to a ſub-
merſion from them; having thus waſhed off all
his religious, as well as political impurities, he
became quite a regenerated creature; he was
" heated one ſeven times more than he was wont
to be;" and he already had acquired no inconſi-
derable a proportion.

Such a ſect, with ſuch a leader, were extremely
dangerous in any ſtate; and Cromwell, who more
than any other had known how far ſuch principles
and practices would prevail againſt any eſtabliſh-

ment, began to moſt ſeriouſly think of providing
againſt the effects of ſuch cauſes; and Harriſon,
finding himſelf ſuſpected, determined to quit London, where he was ſo well watched, and carry on
his deſign in a leſs open, but not in a leſs decided
manner; this brought things to a criſis, for it
would have been ill policy to let ſuch a man go
at large.

He was therefore ſent for by Cromwell to the
council, in December 1655, and aſked to ſubſcribe
an engagement not to diſturb the protector's government, but he declined it; Oliver therefore
had his commiſſion taken from him, and upbraided
him with his former conduct towards him, ſaying,
he had coveted his employment when he was ſick
in Scotland; and as he was extremely reſolute in
his behaviour, he ſent him a priſoner to Cariſ-
brook Caſtle, in the Iſle of Wight, where his
murdered maſter had lately experienced ſo many
hardſhips: this was a dreadful blow to him and
his new friends; for, ſays an intercepted letter,
" as Harriſon was the head of the anabaptiſts, it
" gave him the greateſt reſpect in the world to
" gain this party, who wanted to pull down the
" miniſtry and the law; by which the proud fool
" grew ſo high, as did his party, that if the new
" parliament had been ſuffered to have ſat a week
" longer, both the one and the other had been
" voted down;" however, when Oliver had ſet-
tled his government, he ſent Major Strange for
him, and permitted him to return to his own houſe
at Highgate, but ſtill as a priſoner.

At this time he was full of his religious vagaries. Mr. Ludlow called to visit him, whom he entertained with a discourse upon many prophecies, and their fulfilment at that time; but it did not satisfy the Lieutenant-general any more, than the reasons he assigned for assisting in dissolving the long parliament; as an apology for which he said, " upon their heads be the guilt, who have " made a wrong use of it; for my own part, my own " heart was upright and sincere in the thing;" saying also, that " he had joined Cromwell, be- " cause he pretended to own and favour a sort of " men who acted upon higher principles than " those of civil liberty."

He had some confidence placed in him by the protector, in being appointed Major-general of Wales; but his conduct was such, that it greatly injured the government; for taking to his bosom Vivafor Powell, a most obnoxious anabaptist, who was so far gone in fanatical madness, that he threw all Wales in flames; and, as Harrison had taken every method of putting the gentry out of all commissions, and in their room placing the lowest of his own party, it made both him and the protector odious; but this was rectified: Powell, after various fruitless admonitions, was sent to prison, and the commissions Harrison had received were annulled.

In the year 1655 he again fell under Oliver's displeasure, and had been sent to confinement, to the great unhappiness of all his saints, who wept, prayed, and petitioned, but all in vain.

He remained in prifon from the early part of that
year at leaft, and all the entreaties of his friends
were fruitlefs with the protector to difcharge him,
until the beginning of the following one, when
he yielded to them ; but he changed his mind by
the advice of his council, and it was counter-
manded by this order :

  " At the Council at Whitehall,

   " Friday, March 7, 1655.

 " Ordered,

 " That there be a ftay of the warrants for re-
" leafing from imprifonment Colonel Thomas
" Harrifon, Mr. Carew, Mr. Courtney, and Colonel Rich, until further orders.

   " W. Jessop, Clerk of the Council."

However, in the next month, he was fent for to
London, and difcharged ; but it was only to put
himfelf, and thofe around him, to new trouble,
which ended in fending him in September, in
that year, to Pendennis Caftle, a prifoner.

Yet he again procured his releafe ; but it appeared now, that he had worked himfelf up to a
ftill greater ftate of wildnefs and infatuation ; in
fober times, it is not eafy to believe the excefs
to which the paffions led men : he, joining with
Meffrs. Pheake, Can, and Rogers, met at the
houfe of Mr. Daforme in Bartholomew-lane,
near the Royal Exchange, where they held their
confultations about an infurrection ; and thought
that then was the exact time, becaufe " the three
" years and an half were at an end in which the
" witneffes have lain dead, and that there will be

" a refurrection of them ;" and upon this delu-
fion they refolved to rebel, and deftroy all who
fhould oppofe them. To minds lefs heated, it
might, one fhould have thought, been better to
have waited until the witneffes had actually arifen
from the dead.

It muft be here remarked, that he had again
paffed through the religious furnace, and became
ftill more purified. The anabaptifts were now as
drofs and not filver in his fight; he left them to
join the fifth monarchy-men, who were become
the new, and confequently more violent fect; and
befides, it claffed better with his extravagant religious quixotifm, to fuppofe that Chrift fhould
vifibly appear amongft and own them for his
faints on earth. The particulars of this plot, in
confequence of this new change, I have already
given in the life of Lord Grey, of Groby ; and
therefore it fhall be paffed over, with obferving,
that in April 1657, he was again, for the extravagance of his conduct, fent to prifon.

Henry Cromwell, lord deputy of Ireland, writes
to Lord Fauconberg, February 10, 1657-8 : " I
" hear that Harrifon, Carey, Okey, &c. have done
" fome new feats. I hope God will infatuate thefe
" men in their further endeavours to difturb the
" peace of thefe nations, as they feem already to
" be by thofe their follies, which do fufficiently
" fhew them to have been but meer pretenders to,
" and abufers of religion ; and fuch whofe hypo-
" crify the Lord will avenge in his due time."
It is incredible to think, that a man once fo con-

fiderable in the nation, fhould fo entirely lofe himfelf by thefe unaccountable exceffes, to become the fcorn and derifion of the world. He had not been releafed more than a few weeks, if days, before he was convinced that the fifth monarchy-men had become a very defpicable party, both in numbers and confequence ; he therefore had reconciled himfelf to his former friends, the anabaptifts, and had, by a fecond baptifm by them, been wafhed from the impurity of his late apoftacy.

When the long parliament was reftored, and with it the fhadow of a commonwealth ; and even afterwards, when the army again triumphed over them, he was fo funk in contempt with all the heads of both the parliament and the army, that he was looked upon as a meer cypher.

A new fcene opened itfelf at the reftoration. Some fatisfaction was due for the blood of a monarch, inhumanly fhed by a bafe faction ; and thofe who had fpilt it were odious to an extreme that is not to be defcribed.   Of all that were living, he was the moft fo : Colonel Bowyer, therefore, at the head of a party of the Staffordfhire militia, feized him, April 27, 1660, with the horfes and arms he had provided, which he might have avoided, as he knew what was defigned againft him ; but he accounted it, he faid, an action of defertion of the caufe in which he engaged, to leave his houfe, and therefore remained quietly waiting the event.

He was conveyed to the Tower, and thence to

Newgate for his trial, having been abſolutely excepted from pardon by a clauſe in the bill of indemnity.   He was indicted as Thomas Harriſon,
late of Weſtminſter, in the county of Middleſex,
gentleman, and was brought up to the Seſſions-
houſe in the Old Bailey, October 10, 1660.

When he was called upon to hold up his hand
as a criminal, he declined it at firſt, only ſaying,
" I am here ; my lord, if you pleaſe, I will ſpeak
" a word :" but being told, he muſt firſt comply
with the practice of the court, he ſubmitted. On
the following day his trial commenced ; and, as
the other priſoners, Meſſrs. Scroop, Carew, Jones,
Clement, and Scot, could not agree about their
jury, he was ſeparately tried.   The ſame caſt of
character that had for ſo long diſgraced him, was
now moſt viſibly diſplayed ; having challenged
thirty-five, the trial commenced. Sir Heneage
Finch, the Solicitor-general, and Sir Edward
Turner, addreſſed the jury, ſhewing the enormity
of the offence of which the priſoner was accuſed ;
and it was plainly proved that he had ſitten in the
court when ſentence was given, and that he had
ſigned an inſtrument for convening and ſummon-
ing the high court of juſtice, and ſet his name to
the warrant to put his late majeſty to death.
When the warrants were ſhewn to him, he owned
that he thought the names were of his hand-
writing; but ſaid they ſhould not be produced,
as they were not records ; but when told they
were to evince that there was an overt act done,
becauſe the indictment expreſſed that he had
imagined, compaſſed, and contrived the king's

death, of which thefe were proofs; he anfwered, " I am not come to be denying any thing that in " my own judgment and confcience I have done " or committed, but rather to bring it forth to " the light."

He defended himfelf exactly as a man of his behaviour might have been expected, as one who certainly had never feared death, and now faw that it muft come upon him; he therefore regarded the opinion of the court the lefs; mercy, he knew, was fhut out from him, his crimes being too great for pardon.

He told them, that the king's death " was not " a thing done in a corner; he believed the found " of it had been in moft nations; that he had " prayed night and day for conviction; and that " he had received rather affurances of the juft- " nefs of what he had done; that *he believed ere* " *long it would be made known from heaven; there* " *was more from God than men were aware of;* that " he would not hurt the pooreft man or woman " that went upon the earth;" but he was ftopt when he began to reflect upon the activity of fome upon the bench; then he launched out of the goodnefs of the commiffions under which he had acted; for inftead of ufurping an authority, he faid " it was rather done in the fear of the " Lord."

The court again interfered; and Lord Finch told him, " he muft not be fuffered to run into " thefe damnable excurfions, to make God the " author of the damnable treafon committed."

Nothing intimidated: he argued then, that he

had not done wrong, for thefe two reafons: that it was authorized by the parliament, the houfe of commons, to which that court was inferior, and that therefore he was not to be queftioned for it; hinting at the legality of the act by the fate of King Richard II., and defired council, as " it " concerned all his countrymen."

The council telling him, " his countrymen " would cry out, and fhame him," he replied, " May be fo, my lords; fome will; but I am " fure others will not."

The folicitor-general urged, that his plea was only, as it really was, one point; that " the com- " mons had the power of bringing a king of " England to condemnation;" but, he told him, " that neither one, or both houfes together, had " any fuch right; neither was the houfe of com- " mons he pretended to have acted under, an " houfe, nor an eighth part of an houfe of com- " mons."

The lord chief baron fpoke more fully, and told him of the force that was put upon the houfe of commons, by " purging" it, as they called it, until there were not more than forty or forty-five at moft; that when the propofition was but named to the houfe of peers, another branch of the le-giflature, it was fpurned by them; that even fome in the commons' houfe gave a negative; and that all were under awe from the army; telling him, his doctrine was fubverfive of the laws; and there-fore, as he had no pretence to urge for fuch an au-thority under which he acted, his plea fhould be

over-ruled; for, fays his lordfhip, " neither both
" houfes of parliament, if they had been there;
" nor any fingle perfon, community; not the
" people, either collectively or reprefentatively,
" had any colour to have any coercive power
" over the king."

Mr. Annefley, among fome very pertinent remarks, fpoke of the violence put upon the houfe,
upon himfelf as one of the members, when the
treaty was feemingly drawing towards a happy
conclufion between his majefty and the parliament; that the houfe of commons never was a
court of judicature; it hath no power of life or
death; could not even adminifter an oath; that
no act in thefe kingdoms were valid but what had
the confent of all the three branches of the legif-
lature, king, lords, and commons.

Mr. afterwards Lord, Hollis fpoke upon the fame
grounds; concluding with telling him, " Now he
" would make God the author of his offence, fo
" likewife he would make the people guilty of
" his opinion. But," fays he, " your plea is
over-ruled;" to which the court affented.

The prifoner then allowed, that what he had
faid was only one point; and urged, that what
had been done, was done in obedience to authority; and if it were but by an order of the houfe
of commons, thus under a force, yet this court is
not a judge of that force; and faid, if it was done
by one eftate of parliament, it was not to be queftioned.

The court, Mr. Hollis, the council, lord chief

baron, the Judges Mallet, Hide, and Twifden, the Earl of Manchefter, Sir William Wild, and the court again, all attempted by the cleareft reafoning to fhew him the folly of his defence; but nothing moved, he replied, " Notwithftanding " the judgment of fo many learned ones, that the " kings of England are no ways accountable to " the parliament, the lords and commons in the " beginning of the war having declared the king's " beginning war upon them; the God of Gods," —here he was ftopped;. but continuing, he faid, " I would not willingly offend any man, but I " know God is no refpecter of perfons. His fet- " ting up his ftandard againft the people——". Here he was filenced, as not belonging to him to hold fuch words. " Under favour," fays he, " this doth belong to me; I would have abhorred " to have brought him to account, had not the " blood of Englifhmen that had been fhed——." here he was alfo interrupted; and the council faid, he ought to be fent to Bedlam until he came to the gallows to render an account of his deed; obferving too, it was in a manner a new impeachment of the king upon the throne to juftify their treafons againft his late majefty. The Solicitorgeneral requefted that the jury might go together upon the evidence.

Sir Edward Turner faid, " he had the plague " all over him, and that none fhould be near " him, but that he fhould be avoided as an houfe " infected, which had written over it, the Lord " have mercy upon him," and fo requefted the officer might take him away ; but the Lord Chief Baron, though he told him, " he had fpoken " that which is as high a degree of blafphemy, " next to that againft God, as he had heard, yet " he would hear any thing he had to offer in ex- " tenuation of his crime ; but that he muft not " purfue the language he had held."

He then faid, " I muft not fpeak, fo as to be " pleafing to men ; but if I muft not have liberty " as an Englifhman— Here the Court told him that " he had received more liberty thàn he " was intitled to, that they wifhed he had made a " better ufe of it, and defired him to keep to the " bufinefs, and he might fay what he would."

He then attempted to extenuate his conduct, and particularly what Mr. Nutley had fworn againft him ; who gave in evidence that whilft in the coach with his majefty conveying him from Hurft Caftle to Windfor, or from that place to London, the king afked him, " What do you in- " tend to do with me? whether to murder me or " no?" he told his majefty, " there was no fuch " intention as to kill him, we have no fuch " thoughts ; but the Lord hath referved you for " a public example of juftice," and the fame gentleman alfo fwore that, " when fome were " for contracting the impeachment againft his " fovereign, he faid, Gentlemen, it will be good " for us to *blacken* him, or words to that effect, " but he was fure the word *blacken* was ufed."

Harrifon, therefore, to foften this evidence, faid, " My lords, thus ; there was a difcourfe by one

" of the witneffes that I was at the committee
" preparing the charge, and that I fhould fay let
" us *blacken* him. The thing is utterly untrue;
" I abhorred the doing of any thing touching
" the blackening of the king. There was a lit-
" tle difcourfe between the king and myfelf.
" The king had told me, that he had heard that
" I fhould come privately to the Ifle of Wight
" to offer fome injury to him; but I told him I
" abhorred the thought of it. And whereas it is
" faid that my carriage was hard to him when I
" brought him to London; it was not I that
" brought him to London; I was commanded
" by the general to fetch him from Hurft Caftle.
" I do not remember any hard carriage towards
" him."

The court told him, " there were great con-
" tradictions between his affertion, and the oaths
" of the witnefs, which the jury muft confider
" of; that if he could fay nothing more that
" tended to his juftification, they muft direct the
" jury; for the end of his fpeech was nothing
" but to infect the people." To which he faid,
" You are uncharitable in that." And when reproved by Juftice Fofter for fuch language, he
broke out, " the things that has been done, have
" been done upon the ftage, in the fight of the
" fun." As if wickednefs, ceafed to be fuch, if
done openly and daringly.

The court told him that this was only a juftification of the fact; and the council faid, that
" as he had confeffed the fact, he requefted the

" jury might receive the charge ;" but the Lord Chief Baron ſtill intreated him not to perſiſt in his conduct, otherwiſe he muſt do it. To which he replied, " My lord, I ſay what I did was by " the ſupreme authority. I have ſaid it before, " and appeal to your own conſciences, that this " court cannot call me to queſtion."

Wearied out with ſuch kind of language, his lordſhip told him " Mr. Harriſon, you have ap- " pealed to our conſciences. We ſhall do that, " which, by the bleſſing of God, ſhall be juſt ; " for which we ſhall anſwer before the tribunal " of God ; pray take heed of an obdurate, hard " heart, and a feared conſcience."

He then finally replied, " my lord, I have " been kept ſix months a cloſe priſoner, and " could not prepare myſelf for this trial by coun- " cil. I have got here ſome acts of parliament " of that houſe of commons, which your lord- " ſhips will not own, and the proceedings of " that houſe whoſe authority I did own."

The Lord Chief Baron having told him, that he had ſaid that already, and that if he had never ſo many of that nature, they would not help him, and that he had heard the opinion of that court touching that authority, and therefore charged the jury; who by their foreman, Sir Thomas Allen, returned a verdict Guilty ; and being aſked whether they all agreed in, they anſwered in the affirmative ; and when he was deſired to ſay what reaſon he could give why judgment ſhould not paſs againſt him to die, according to law, he ſaid,

" I have nothing further to fay, becaufe the court
" have not feen meet to hear what was in my
" heart to fpeak; I fubmit to it."

Judgment, the tremendous judgment de-
nounced againft fuch as are guilty of high treafon,
was then pronounced againft him. The court
fhewed great patience and forbearance, and twice
reproved the audience when they openly derided
him; and expreffed the pleafure they felt at his
being brought to juftice.

The sheriff fent three clergymen to him, who
endeavoured to bring him to a fenfe of his enormities; they dwelt upon the death of the king, of
Mr. Love's execution, of diffolving the parliament, of his neglect of divine duty in his family,
and that his prefent fentence was the confequence
of them.

He defended himfelf from any malice to his
royal prifoner, by faying, " that he was very
" tender of the king," who confeffed that he
found him not fuch a " perfon as he was repre-
" fented to him, when he was brought out of the
" Ifle of Wight, and that he had fome fkill in
" faces, fo that if he had not feen his face before,
" he fhould not have harboured fuch hard
" thoughts againft him." As to the lawfulnefs
of the authority under which he had acted, he abfolutely defended it, faying, " the people in the
" three kingdoms owned it, foreign nations
" owned it." But why then did he deftroy it?
Cromwell was owned by all, yet he never acknowledged him, but as an ufurper. As to Mr.

Love, he faid, he was not in the kingdom where
he was put to death; which he juftified, by faying, " that if a godly man did fo tranfgrefs a
" righteous law, he ought to fuffer as another
" man."

Relative to his affifting in diffolving the houfe,
he faid he had not known Cromwell's intention
of doing it, until he went thither with him, that
he only handed the fpeaker out of his chair; yet
he vindicated what he had done in it; " taking
" the Lord to be his witnefs he did not do it for
" any felf-end, but in the integrity of his heart
" as to the Lord, hoping that God would have
" done his work by bringing more worthy per-
" fons upon the ftage; but when he faw Crom-
" well and his party fet themfelves up in their
" room, he abhorred them and their ways; that
" he had fuffered feverely on account of his fen-
" timents; and therefore his confcience was free
" from all guilt refpecting what happened about
" that matter."

He called upon his fervant to vindicate him,
as to his conduct relative to religion, and not
neglecting honouring the Lord's day: and the
man bore ample teftimony to his religious deport-
ment; which, indeed, was a thing of all others,
that it might have been thought he was not deficient in—fuch a religion as it was.

As to his fuffering for his fins, that feemed to
give him no trouble; for, inftead of fins, he looked
upon himfelf as not only a righteous, but a moft
chofen, fanctified veffel; and then, and at his

death, he was all raptures; that he died for Chrift:
and he more than hinted feveral times, and, no
doubt, had perfuaded himfelf, that God would
foon raife him up again, by a refurrection from the
dead, to glorify him here. In fact, he was all de-
lufion; fcorn, contempt, imprifonment, even
death itfelf, could not either intimidate or cure
him of a furious, ungovernable, fanatic frenzy,
that made him, with all his pretences that he
would not willingly injure the humbleft, the
moft dangerous perfon that arofe, in a time when
fo many abounded: and once this man, who was
little lefs than a valiant maniac, was, with three
or four exceptions, the moft powerful man in
thefe nations. It was thought, fays Bifhop Burnet, " that while the army was in doubt whether
" it was fitter to kill the king privately, or to
" bring him to an open trial, that he offered, if a
" private way was agreed on, to be the man who
" fhould do it." Which was the reafon why he
was fingled out for the firft to fuffer, and that
without the leaft mitigation of the fentence.

He was executed at Charing Crofs, October 13,
1660; and proved his words at that time, " that
" death was no more to him than a rufh." Some
feeing his hands and legs tremble very much, noticed it; when he affured them, it was an infirmity
which he had been fubject to for twelve years,
owing to the vaft quantity of blood he had loft by
wounds in the battles he had fought; and that it
had ever fince thus affected his nerves.

No man in the kingdom was regarded with fo

much deteſtation as this, by all parties, except the few remaining fanatics, who looked upon him as a faint and martyr, and firmly believed to fee him arife,—to fee, rather, his mangled fcattered remains re-unite in glory amongſt them: on this account it is that Mr. Cowley, in his Cutter of Coleman Street, makes one of the characters fay, "we ſhall fee Major-general Harriſon come in "green ſleeves," (then worn by butchers) "from "the north, upon a ſky-coloured mule;" which fignifies heavenly inſtruction. In Lord Clarendon's octavo Hiſtory of the Rebellion, is a fmall portrait of him holding a truncheon.

He had a wife and family whom he left deſtitute; to the former, he faid, he left her only a BIBLE!

The Life of EDMOND HARVEY, *Esq.*

EDMOND HARVEY, Efq. was a citizen of London; a filkman, as fome fay; but as he was a partner with Alderman Sleigh, he probably dealt in many articles of commerce. The parliament in 1645 gave him leave more than once to export great quantities of calves-fkins; which might have led one to fuppofe he had been a fkinner.

At the breaking out of the troubles, he took the parliament fide in the quarrel, and became a colonel of horfe; yet he purfued his bufinefs at the fame time, chiefly, we may fuppofe, by means of his partner. In 1643 he, with Lord Grey of Groby, joined the parliament general, the Earl of Effex, before his going down to relieve Gloucefter: foon afterwards he and Major-general Skippon had fome trivial encounters with his majefty's forces in Northamptonfhire; and at the clofe of this year, he was fent with his regiment of horfe to the affiftance of Sir William Waller.

He had taken great liberties in his conduct, we muft fuppofe; for, in January 1643-4, there were feveral petitions againft him, particularly one prefented by Mr. Squire, concerning three thoufand pounds taken from him by the colonel, or fome of his officers; which was referred to a committee to be examined.

He was ill enough advifed to purchafe the manor of Fulham, in Middlefex, in 1647, which belonged to the fee of London, and had conftantly

done from the time of the Anglo-Saxon heptar-
chy. The purchafe money, including what was
given for the leafehold lands held with it, was
7617l. 8s. 10d. which evinces that he was a perfon
of very confiderable property; fuch, indeed, that
it enabled him to make the epifcopal palace his
refidence. He likewife purchafed of the family
of Nourfe, of Woodeaton, in Oxfordfhire, the leafe
of the great tithes.

The parliament named him one of the commiffioners to try the king; he fat with the other
judges in the Painted Chamber on January the 8th,
17th, 20th, 22d, 23rd, 24th, 25th, and 27th; and
in Weftminfter Hall the 20th, 22d, 23rd, and
27th days of that month.

But on the laft day he was extremely difcontented, and publicly expreffed it to the commiffioners; and though he was prefent when judgment was given, yet he did not affent to it, as
Whitlock, who took notes, remarked; and he
could not be prevailed upon to fign the warrant
for execution: of this more will be feen at the
conclufion of his life.

After this great national calamity, he was highly
trufted by the new government, was appointed
collector of the cuftoms of London *; and in
1650 the navy committee having voted the fum
of 100l. out of the new impoft on coals in the

* As it is allowed that Mr. Edmond Harvey was collector of the
cuftoms, it is evident that the word EDWARD, page 209, Vol. I.
of Thurloe's State Papers, fhould read EDMOND.

port of London to be diftributed amongft the
poor at Fulham, he and Ifaac Knight, the Vicar,
were appointed the diftributors; and the fum of
40l. was voted in the fame manner the following
year. He, probably, was a popular character
there; for he and Maximilian Bard, Efq. gave
100l. to the poor about 1650.

When Cromwell had feated himfelf in the chair
of ftate, he joined his government; and probably
as a native, and poffeffing a landed intereft in the
county of Suffolk, he had, from the commencement of the troubles, been a committee-man;
fo now he was by the protector appointed one of
the commiffioners for fecuring the peace of the
commonwealth; and he and James Harvey, with
others, fent his highnefs a dutiful addrefs, dated
from Bury, November 20, 1655. In which it
ftates, that " the method which had been devifed,
" they thought moft likely to anfwer the end of
" fecuring the peace of the nation, and that they
" were bound to blefs God, who had moved his
" highnefs' and council's heart, to be thus careful
" of the fecurity and eafe of the good people of
" this commonwealth, and of thofe dear liberties
" purchafed with the price of fo much precious
" blood, and vaft expence of treafure; and they
" prayed, that as the Lord had been pleafed to
" make ufe of his highnefs as the inftrument of
" their deliverance from that *implacable generation*
" of men, fo he would be pleafed farther to ufe
" his highnefs as the inftrument of their prefer-
" vation and farther reformation."

Y 2

To fhew his zeal to his highnefs, he alfo gave him a moft magnificent entertainment at his *palace* of Fulham; yet he foon after was a malcontent: he thought the protector did not fet about this *farther reformation;* or, what is more probable, there might be much difpleafure in his highnefs, from having detected fome improper conduct in the performance of his place; certain it is, he was committed to the Tower in November 1655, but foon releafed; and though he was returned a member of Oliver's parliament in 1656, he was fo obnoxious to him, that he was not permitted to fit in it.

He was in a very uneafy fituation ever after. He wifhed, above all things, to have the republican government irrevocably re-eftablifhed, becaufe he was now in difgrace with the protector; and a return of monarchy, he might naturally fuppofe, would deprive him of his epifcopal eftates, and even endanger his perfonal fafety.

At the reftoration, though he furrendered himfelf, he was abfolutely excepted both as to life and property; and October 16, 1660, he was brought to the Seffions-Houfe in the Old Bailey, and tried for the part he had acted againft the late king.

When they were going to call witneffes againft him, he faid, "My lord, according to my duty, "I fhall fave this honourable court all their "trouble. I do humbly acknowledge that I was, "and did fit, in that court; but I did not fign "and feal that warrant." To which the lord chief

baron faid, " It is very true, Mr. Harvey." He
continued, " I hope your lordfhips, and this ho-
" nourable bench, will give me leave, in that time
" you fhall appoint, to fhew you my reafons that
" I did it, not in malice, and it was an error, not
" of will, but of judgment; what I have to fay
" will be, though not for the annihilating, yet
" for the extenuation of my crimes." His lordfhip then faid, " Say now what you will, only
" confider with yourfelf whether you have not al-
" ready fpoken as much as you can for the exte-
" nuation of it; fay what you can farther.—Let
" me fpeak a word—Go on, Sir."

He then made this defence : " My lords, I do
" humbly conceive, if I had conceived that I had
" then done any thing of treafon, I would not for
" all the world have been there. I was prefent
" when his majefty did not own the court, defir-
" ing that both his houfes might meet, that he
" might have a conference with them for fettling
" of the peace. My lord, heartily and unfeign-
" edly I did endeavour that that advice might be
" embraced, and that no fentence might be pro-
" nounced. I was one of thofe (with fome
" others) that did fo far promote it, that that
" which was called the high court of juftice did
" withdraw to confider of it, but the major part
" of it did diffent. But, my lord, I was fo un-
" happy as to return to the court, though with
" reluctancy; I went with a refolution not to go
" more to them, nor never did. I was fummoned
" to come to the court : I did declare I abhorred

" the thing; that my foul had reluctancy againſt
" it; and I did refuſe any more to come, or to
" conſult about any thing that followed, in order
" to his majeſty's death, and to ſign and ſeal.
" And that I may make it appear to your lord-
" ſhips, I pray I may have a witneſs or two ex-
" amined."

Lord Chief Baron. " Name them. Did he
" ſit upon the day of ſentence?" " Yes," ſaid
the counſel, " he followed it."

Mr. Corbet was then examined as a witneſs,
who ſaid, " My lord, the atteſtation which I this
" day make ſolemnly in the holy fear of Almighty
" God, and in the awful reverence of this great
" tribunal, hath only this great ſcope, that Co-
" lonel Harvey, the priſoner at the bar, upon
" that day of ſigning the warrant for that horrid
" execution of his moſt excellent majeſty, not in
" title only, but in reality; he finding me, as I
" was paſſing to the duty of my place in the aſ-
" ſembly of divines then ſitting, he ſeized on
" me, and deſired privacy of time and place, that
" he might diſburden his ſoul and ſpirit unto me;
" it was then about nine o'clock in the forenoon,
" to the beſt of my remembrance."

" What day, I beſeech you?" ſaid the lord
chief baron. Corbet replied, " To the beſt of my
" remembrance, upon the Monday. " Sir,"
ſays he, " I deſire to make known unto you the
" deep horror that ſits upon my ſpirit, the ſad-
" neſs and grief, above all expreſſions, that my
" preſent caſe has caſt me into; I have endea-

" voured Sir," fays he, " in the fight of God, all
" that I poffibly could, to divert them from the
" fentence. I could not prevail." " Sir," fays
he, " I have been this morning folicited with
" very much earneftnefs, that I would go and
" fign and feal, and order that wicked execution,
" which my foul abhors; and, Sir, that I might
" be removed and withdrawn from all tempta-
" tions and folicitations of fuch a wicked fact, I
" befeech you fpare me your time this day, which
" I did, in the prefence of another divine, till
" four o'clock that afternoon, and then I parted
" and went to Weftminfter, to fign and affift that
" which I did apprehend my bounden duty, the
" vindication of the affembly of divines, wherein
" we did teftify, that it was far from our thoughts
" to advife the parliament to any fuch unheard-
" of unnatural act."

Counfel. " We do admit, that after he fat, and
" fentence paffed, that he did not fign." Mr.
Harvey then faid, " Be pleafed to call one Mr.
" Thomas Langham; he hath heard me often de-
" clare againft the act."

The lord chief baron. " What do you fay, Mr.
" Langham, as to this bufinefs?

Who replied, " Sir, about the time that his
" majefty was executed in 1648, I was then fer-
" vant to alderman Sleigh, who was formerly
" partner with this colonel, and he frequently
" came to alderman Sleigh's every night; and the
" alderman having fome bufinefs with him, would
" afk him what news there was at the high court

" of juftice; he ufually told him the paffes upon
" any day; the alderman afked him, if fo be, he
" thought his majefty might efcape? He told
" them this, that he would do what lay in his
" power that he might, that he might not come
" to his fentence paffed; upon Saturday, being
" alfo there, he told them this, that he had done
" what lay in his power to hinder the fentence,
" but could not attain his defign; but he was re-
" folved he would never fign nor feal to his ma-
" jefty's death, for it was utterly againft his
" judgment."

Mr. Harvey then faid, " There is another, my
" lord, and but one more; that is George Lang-
" ham." To which the lord chief baron replied,
" To what purpofe? this is believed." Mr.
Harvey clofed his defence by faying, " I fhall
" only crave and fupplicate this favour of this
" honourable bench, that this honourable bench
" will be pleafed on my behalf, fince I have en-
" deavoured it two months before, to prefent my
" humble petition to his facred majefty, and in-
" tercede for mercy and favour on my behalf; and
" myfelf, my wife, and thirteen children, fhall
" humbly pray."

The court humanely received the petition, and
promifed to prefent it to his majefty; and the
" judge faid to the jury in his charge, " Mr. Har-
" vey hath pleaded feveral matters, which are not
" proper for you, expreffing his forrow and pe-
" nitence; we fhall not trouble you with that,
" becaufe they are for the confideration of ano-

" ther court; we ought all to have a tender com-
" paffion; ought to be forry with, and for them
" that are forrowful.''

After conviction, being afked what he had to
fay, why fentence fhould not pafs, he replied,
" My lord, I have no more than what I have
" faid.'' This humility faved his life, but he
was imprifoned fo long as he lived.

It was a melancholy thing to reflect that a gentleman, who if he had purfued the line of his
duty might have died in the bofom of his family,
and in the efteem of his friends; but going to
the moft criminal lengths in politics, he brought
fhame upon himfelf, ruin to his family, and grief
to his friends.

Fulham returned to its epifcopal owner; the
leafe of the great tythes became vefted in the
crown, and were granted by King Charles II. in
1664, to Anthony Eyre, Efq. in confideration of
the fervices he had rendered his royal father. The
other property of this regicide we muft fuppofe
was all diffipated and loft, and his family reduced
to the greateft diftrefs and poverty.

The Life of Sir ARTHUR HESELRIGGE, Bart.

SIR ARTHUR HESELRIGGE, of Noseley, in Lei-
cestershire, Baronet, was one of the most determined enemies of the king, and of monarchy, of
any who entered into the parliament's service, yet
he would not be concerned in the king's trial,
though named one of his judges.

He was one of the pillars of the commonwealth,
hated, despised, and plotted against the elder protector, assisted in ruining the younger one; was
the most violent man in the army, and finally was
deluded by General Monk, who after deceiving
him, as long as it was necessary, sent him to the
Tower.

He was then adjudged so dangerous a person by
government, that he was voted to be excepted out
of the act of indemnity, and would have been put
to death if General Monk had not, upon being called upon, declared that he had promised
he should not lose his life if he would remain
quiet.

King Charles II. is said by Ludlow to have rejoiced when the lords excepted him. He was undoubtedly a very obnoxious character; at that
time a very dangerous one. He died in the Tower
of a fever contracted by grief, in 1660, or 1661.
The great prelatical estates he had acquired were
forfeited to the sees from which he had obtained
them.

For more particulars of this gentleman's life, I muſt refer the reader to the Cromwell memoirs, where he will find Sir Arthur's life at length amongſt the protector Oliver's lords.

Sir Arthur is the anceſtor of the preſent baronet, Sir Robert Heſelrigge, of Noſeley.

The *Life of* WILLIAM HEVENINGHAM, *Efq.*

WILLIAM HEVENINGHAM, Efq. was a gentle-man of very great defcent, his family having re-fided at a place of that name, for many ages in the county of Suffolk; I fuppofe he was fon of Sir Arthur Heveningham, Knt. Seized with the frenzy of the day he oppofed the court, and went into all the extravagance of the enemies of it; the parliament made him one of their committee for the counties of Suffolk and Norfolk. He was one of the reprefentatives for Stockbridge in Hants, in the ever memorable long parlia-ment.

The faction put his name amongft the king's judges, and he was culpable enough to conftantly attend as one of the commiffioners in the high court of juftice, except in the Painted Chamber on the 10th, 12th, 15th, 18th, 20th 25th, and 29th. He was in Weftminfter Hall every day, gave his affent to the infamous fentence, but re-fufed to fign and feal the warrant.

The parliament in gratitude to him, put his name in the council of ftate in 1649 and 1650, which appears all the employment or advantages he derived from his bafe compliances; his for-tune was too large to make him fubfervient to the party.

At the reftoration he furrendered himfelf to a ferjeant at arms; but was excepted for life and eftate in the claufe of the bill of indemnity.

October 10, 1660, he was arraigned at the Seffions
Houfe in the Old Bailey; and on the 16th was
tried: when called upon, he faid, " My lord, in
" 1648 we were under a force, under the tyranny
" of an army; they were our mafters; for a ma-
" licious and traitorous heart I had not.   I do ab-
" folutely deny figning the warrant for fummon-
" ing the court, and alfo for execution of the
" king; at the time of fealing I had that cou-
" rage and boldnefs, that I protefted againft
" it."

The council faying, " we do not queftion him
" for that, but fitting in the high court of juf-
" tice, and that upon the day of fentence; do
" you deny that?" he replied, " my lord, I
" cannot fay pofitively;" but fays the council,
" if you deny the matter of fact, it muft be
" proved," he faid, " I cannot fay pofitively,
" but it may be I might."   " Either fay po-
" fitively you did" re-joined the council, " or
" elfe let the witneffes be called."

He then faid, " truly my lord, I think I did,
" but my after actions—The Lord Chief Baron
ftopping him faid, " Mr. Heveningham, that
" fhall be confidered."   The council however
interpofed, and told his lordfhip 'that, " to fit
" upon the day of fentence was high treafon in
" itfelf, and is an evidence of compaffing and
" imagining the king's death."

Finding that he could not avail himfelf of his
plea, he told the judge, " I fhall lay hold of the
" declaration.   I came in upon the declaration;

" I pray your lordſhip to intercede for me to
" the king, and both houſes of parliament; I
" pray the mercy of this court."

The jury returning a verdict of " Guilty,"
and the council aſking him if he had any thing
more to ſay why ſentence ſhould not be paſſed
upon him, he replied, " My lords, I have nothing
" more to ſay, than I have ſaid formerly, only I
" plead the benefit of the proclamation, and caſt
" myſelf upon the mercy of our moſt gracious
" ſovereign, and deſire your lordſhips to be me-
" diators on my behalf."

The Lord Chief Baron addreſſing him, ſaid,
" by the act of indemnity of which you claim
" the benefit, and we ought to take notice of it,
" we are to proceed to judgment, but no execu-
" tion of the judgment is to be, until another
" act of parliament by the conſent of the king,
" it ſhall be ordered ; and therefore I need not
" ſpeak any more of that, or any exhortations to
" prepare yourſelf for death ; our work is only to
" give judgment ;" which was accordingly done.

This gentleman was not executed, and his majeſty compaſſionating a family which had for its
loyalty been often diſtinguiſhed, and from whom
had deſcended ſo many knights; reſtored to his ſon
the ancient eſtate and ſeat of Heveningham, who
was,

William Heveningham of Heveningham, Eſq.;
he married Mary, daughter of John, Earl of
Dover, by whom he had Sir William Heveningham; and Abigail, married to John Newton, Eſq.

fon and heir of Sir John Newton of Barro Court, in Gloucefterfhire, Bart.

The family became extinct, I think, in the grand fon of the regicide, Henry Heveningham of Heveningham, Efq. lieutenant of the band of gentlemen penfioners, who married Frances, daughter of William, Lord Willoughby of Parham, widow of Sir John Harper of Swarkefton in Derbyfhire, Knt. and alfo widow and relict of Henry, Earl of Bellamont of the kingdom of Ireland. Mr. Gough, in his additions to Suffolk in the Britannia, fays, that there is a tradition that the family were never fortunate after the concern of one of them in King Charles I.'s death. Heveningham is now the feat of the Vannecks, and is one of the fineft in the county of Suffolk.

The Life of JOHN HEWSON, *Efq.*

JOHN HEWSON, Efq. was a foldier of fortune, and rofe from the loweft fituation, having originally, it is thought, been a cobler; at the time of the death of King Charles I. he was a colonel.

Such a man was a fit inftrument for the bafe purpofes he was defigned for; and being named one of the commiffioners, he fat in that moft hateful tribunal every day, except January the 13th, and he figned the warrant to complete the wickednefs.

He joined in every form of government, and was knighted, and made one of Oliver the protector's lords; his chief fort lay in a military line, though he alfo acted often in a civil one. Amongft Oliver's lords I have given farther particulars of this adventurer, who was fortunate in efcaping from the kingdom at the reftoration, which he furvived but a little time, dying at Amfterdam in 1662; had he not fled, nothing could have faved him, as he had been peculiarly bufy in the black deed.

We do not wonder at men who had rofe from fuch mean beginnings, without education or connections, and unufed to reflect upon confequences, doing what their fuperior officers urge; but that gentlemen of rank, of fortune, who have long been protected by a regular government, like the perfon laft named, is wonderful.

This man had nothing to lofe; he could not be

degraded by a lower fphere, than that from which he had emerged; and, except for crimes, he could not go into greater contempt; but even as a foldier of fortune he would have found infinite advantage to have ftopped fhort in his career, for then, by that wife lenity the king fhewed, he would have enjoyed the fruits of his valour, though he had fo often fought in a wrong caufe.

I cannot but fubjoin an extract from a letter of Henry Cromwell to fecretary Thurloe, dated December 19, 1655; which fhews how troublefome and worthlefs Hewfon was, as well as his fons; and becaufe it places that very good man, Henry Cromwell, in one of his moft amiable points of view. After faying that he had endeavoured to carry himfelf with moderation to all, he was not a little furprifed at Colonel Hewfon's having fent a complaint againft him to his highnefs the protector, which every fober perfon knew to be untrue, and that he had owned that he took it upon the information of others. He fays, " I muft " needs confefs I am not a little amazed hereat, " and have noethinge to quiett my fpiritt, but " through grace, the integritie of my owne harte " in my actions. As a man I could fitt downe " under my difcouragements, (which are not a " few); but my confidence is in the Lord, whoe " will in due time bringe forth the hidden things " of darknefs to light, and will make manifeft the " moft fecrett defignes of men. If Colonel Hew- " fon muft be believed (with his three anabaptift

VOL. I. Z

" fons) I muſt be made a liar, if not worſe;
" what hath made all the ſober godly people in
" Ireland afraide of that intereſt, and groane
" under their oppreſſion; ſome of the incloſed
" will make it appear, as alſo that I ame not
" without ane intereſt in godly men, whoe not
" believe of me, as Colonel Hewſon would ſug-
" geſt. The bearer will tell you of any actings
" heer, and what my camp and councells have
" bin, and whither they have tended. I have
" nothing in my ey of ſelfe: its the honour of
" God, the ſafety of his highneſs, good of ſober
" people I aime at. Let his highneſs doe with
" me as he pleaſe, ſend me into a Welch cottage,
" if it be for his ſervice. If the bearer doe not
" meet with ill company by the way (though
" judged their friend having been courted and con-
" gratulated) I doe not at all fear his relation of
" things heer, wherewith he is thoroughly ac-
" quainted. I deſire you will gett ſpeedy acceſs
" to his highneſs, before he getts to Wallingford
" Houſe."

A century and a half has fixed the character
of Henry Cromwell in the juſteſt eſtimation,
the exact oppoſite to Hewſon's. What became
of his family is unknown; the poſterity of theſe
men ſo highly guilty having ever been aſhamed of
owning from whom they deſcend.

The Life of ROGER HILL, *Esq.*

ROGER HILL, Efq. was a gentleman defcended from a very ancient family in the county of Somerfet, probably of thofe of Pitmifter. He was returned a member of the long parliament for the borough of Bridport, in Dorfetfhire, as he had been for that of Taunton in the preceding one; and upon the commencement of the civil war, the parliament appointed him one of their committee in his own county of Somerfet.

He was too good a lawyer, and if not too honeft a man, to accept the office of one of his majefty's judges, or to take any part in that national misfortune, the king's death.

Oliver made him one of his judges, after calling him to the coif, though he is faid to have been a barrifter of but little practice and of fmall eftate; it is to be remarked, that he was only called gentleman in the return of the writ, appointing him a member of parliament.

It is certain, however, that if he did not poffefs much paternal property, he acquired no inconfiderable portion of wealth; for he purchafed the Bifhop of Winchefter's manor of Taunton-Dean, the beft, it is fuppofed, in England; and if the lives had been fuffered to run out, would have produced, it was thought, 12,000l. per annum; but that I think too incredible for belief. He was a commiffioner of Haberdafhers' Hall.

The reftoration muft have been to him a very mortifying event, levelling him again to, at leaft, his original fituation.

We have a letter from him to Thurloe, the fecretary, dated Bury, April 11, 1655, relative to the unfortunate perfons to be tried for an attempt to reftore the exiled king. His conduct feems beneath the dignity of a judge, being rather that of an informer: this gives us a very mean opinion of his worth.

The Life of CORNELIUS HOLLAND, Esq.

CORNELIUS HOLLAND, Esq. was a native of Colchester, in the county of Essex: his father was so unfortunate as to die in the Fleet, where he had been imprisoned for debt. He was originally nothing more than a servant to Sir Henry Vane, where, it is not improbable, he might imbibe those pernicious principles that brought him to a very general disgrace; for leaving his master, he passed into the service of the Prince of Wales; in an office, however, very humble in the houshold, but he rose to be comptroller; and he obtained such favour in the court, by procuring some monopolies, a custom then too prevalent, that by it he became a person of very considerable property. He likewise had an office in the Green-cloth, where he behaved so ill, that he was deprived of it.

The moment the court were in want of his assistance, he deserted it, refusing to contribute to the expences of the Scotch war in 1639: and procuring a seat in the long parliament, upon a vacancy, for New Windsor, he constantly persisted in the most violent courses, being entirely guided by the opinion of his old master, Sir Henry Vane.

In the year 1646 he was named a commissioner, on the part of England, in the treaty for the conservation of peace with Scotland; and as a deserter from the court and person of his sovereign, and in compenſation for the loſſes he had ſuffered on that account, the parliament was extremely laviſh to him, both before and after the king's death, in which he took particular pleaſure, we may ſuppoſe, by his conſtant attendance upon that iniquitous proceeding; for having been named one of the commiſſioners, he ſat every day in Weſtminſter Hall, aſſiſted in giving judgement: nor was he abſent from the Painted Chamber but upon the twelfth of January; his name, however, is not to the warrant for execution.

Upon the eſtabliſhment of the commonwealth, he was made one of the council of ſtate in 1649, and again in 1650.

Few, from ſo ſmall a beginning, obtained ſuch conſiderable grants as Mr. Holland; he ſuperceded the Counteſs of Dorſet in the care and management of the houſehold of the children of the late king: this poſt he held three or four years.

He had likewiſe a grant of paſtures belonging to the crown in Buckinghamſhire, at a place called Creſslow, in the vale of Ayleſbury, for twenty-one years, worth to him, ſays Lord Hollis, *de claro*, ſome fifteen or ſixteen hundred pounds a year; others, worth from one thouſand eight hundred pounds, to two thouſand pounds; and this only at the trivial rent of twenty pounds a year, which he got diſcounted.

He reſided in Somerſet Houſe for ſome time with his family; and he was keeper of Richmond Palace, which he uſed as a country retreat. He was commiſſary for the garriſons at Whitehall and the Mewes, and had an office in the Mint.

He, no doubt, hated Cromwell, who muſt have had a particular contempt for him; yet having too much to loſe, he ſubmitted to his government. In 1655 he was one of the commiſſioners for the county of Berks, appointed to put in execution the orders of his highneſs and the council, for ſecuring the peace of the commonwealth. He, no doubt, rejoiced in the return of the long parliament: the council of officers in October 1659 put him, with others who were in the army, in truſt to govern the public affairs, until ſome more permanent means could be deviſed.

At the reſtoration he was excepted abſolutely, both as to life and eſtate; and we may ſuppoſe that had he been taken, he would have expiated his treaſonable ingratitude by a public execution.

Happily for himſelf, he effected his eſcape; the manner was thus: going to his native place, Colcheſter, that he might get privately away the firſt opportunity, the major of the town being informed that a ſuſpected perſon was lodged at one of the inns, and it being ſuppoſed that he was Major-general Lambert, the houſe was ſearched at four o'clock in the morning, and his horſe ſeized; but he having left it, to receive a ſum of money owing to him by a merchant of that place, who was to ſet out the next morning for London, and having intelligence of what had happened at the inn, was by the favour of his friend conveyed out of the town, effected his eſcape, and ſoon after got an opportunity to leave the kingdom; when he joined his fellow exiles at Laufanne, in Switzerland, where he ended his days in univerfal contempt.

He muft have amaffed a vaft fortune, for he gave with one of his daughters, at her marriage, five thoufand pounds; and ae he had ten children, had he given them each the fame, it would prove that he muft, at leaft, have been worth fifty thoufand pounds, a fum of great magnitude in the laft century. It is probable that had he remained loyal and true to his fovereign, he never would have acquired fo much; it is more, that he would have partook in thofe misfortunes that he was fo greatly acceffary in bringing upon his royal mafter; but in the end he would have been rewarded and efteemed, honoured of all good men: but as it was, he was forfaken by all, but his companions in misfortunes, who fecretly muft deteft him, as worfe than themfelves. The fplendour in which he had lived at home would make the poverty he was doomed to, in a foreign land, ftill more irkfome. The mifery and difgrace he had entailed upon his progeny muft, to fo ambitious and avaricious a man, have been a greater evil; but the ftings of a guilty confcience, the worft of all that he could endure.

The Life of Sir THOMAS HONYWOOD, *Knt.*

SIR Thomas Honywood, Knt. was of the family of Charing, in Kent, who, though extremely attached to the parliament intereſt, could not be prevailed upon to commit ſo violent an outrage againſt ſociety as to aſſiſt in deſtroying the king.

This did not injure him, even in the eyes of his own party; he became highly valued, and truſted by the protector Oliver, who created him a lord of his upper houſe, amongſt whom his Life has been given by me, in the *Cromwell Memoirs*; I ſhall therefore only add here, that he ſurvived the reſtoration, and died at a very advanced age, leaving a family.

I cannot but here remark, that as he was a brother-in-law to Sir Henry Vane, it was greatly to his honour that he did not yield to the powerful ſolicitations which muſt have been uſed to make him forfeit every principle of loyalty, of juſtice, and mercy.

The Life of THOMAS HORTON, *Efq.*

THOMAS HORTON, Efq. was of the meaneft extraction, being originally a fervant and falconer
to Sir Arthur Hefelrigge, and, " from a recruit,
" fairly perched to a regiment of horfe." He
greatly diftinguifhed himfelf in South Wales, in
May, 1648, where, at the head of three thoufand
horfe and foot, he defeated the royalifts commanded by Major-general Langhorne, though
nearly as ftrong again in forces; and, to crown
the victory, he took the major-general prifoner,
with twenty-fix captains, and an hundred and
fifty other officers, and three thoufand Welch,
obtaining alfo many colours and arms.

This was fo important a victory, that the parliament ordered a thankfgiving for it; and they
rewarded thofe who brought the intelligence, giving Colonel Bethel 150l., Captain Mercer 100l.,
and Captain Wogan received an order to have
his arrears audited. As a farther proof of their
gratitude, they voted, that the land they had before given to Major-general Langhorne, when he
fought in their caufe, fhould, now he had borne
arms againft them, with other lands, to the
amount of one thoufand pounds a year, belonging
to loyalifts, fhould be fold, and the money arifing
from the fale diftributed to the colonel, his officers, and foldiers.

He was put in the commiffion of the high

court of juftice, and fat every day, except on January the 8th, 10th, 12th, 13th, 18th, 20th, 22d, and 23d, in the Painted Chamber ; but he attended every day in Weftminfter Hall, and he fet his hand and feal to the warrant for putting his fovereign to death.

His regiment, in 1649, was drawn by lot to go into Ireland, and on that occafion they fhewed their diflike to him, petitioning the parliament that they would permit Colonel Marten, or whomfoever elfe the houfe fhould be pleafed to fix upon, to be their commander in chief, and that they would pay him ; for which they received the thanks of the houfe ; though it certainly was highly inexpedient to have encouraged the foldiers to make their election of thofe under whom they might chufe to ferve. Soon after, they evinced how little fuch profeffions are to be relied upon ; for Cromwell being named to the command of the Irifh army, and appointed lord lieutenant of that kingdom, thefe men refufed to go with him, and foon after difbanded themfelves. This is the laft circumftance that I have feen in which this regicide had any concern ; only it is evident that he was dead before the reftoration, when his name was inferted in the claufe of the act of indemnity, excepting him as one who was to be adjudged as a traitor, and his lands forfeited to the crown. His origin was mean, his rife rapid, his career fhort, and his memory infamous.

The Life of JOHN HUTCHINSON, *Efq.*

JOHN HUTCHINSON, Efq. was eldeſt ſon of Sir Thomas Hutchinſon, of Outhorpe, or Obethorpe, in Nottinghamſhire, Knt. Sir Thomas was one of the repreſentatives in the long parliament, for the county of Nottingham, and both father and ſon were of the parliament-committee for it.

This gentleman drew his ſword in the intereſt of the parliament, and entered very deeply into their deſigns from the commencement of the civil war, and roſe from a cornet to be a colonel. The parliament entruſted him with the important poſt of being governor of Nottingham Caſtle; and in 1643, he wrote to his employers, that the Earl of Newcaſtle had offered him ten thouſand pounds to appoint him governor of it under the king, and make it hereditary in his family, and alſo to create him a baron, if he would ſurrender it to him for the uſe of his majeſty; all which he had refuſed.

In the following year, he attacked a part of the king's garriſon of Newark, ſlew Captain Thimbleby, and took fifty priſoners; and the next day, captured more of the loyaliſts, in which number were twenty gentlemen and officers, with ſixty of their horſes and furniture.

He was not ſo fortunate in the year 1645, for a troop of horſe from the ſame place, having ſtormed a fort upon Trent Bridge, near his garrifon, became mafters of it, and put about forty of them to the fword.

At this time there exifted fome differences between the governor and the committee of the county; and it being fo great and important a fituation which he held, it was referred to a committee of both kingdoms to take care for the fafety of the place.

He was then become a member of the houfe of commons, I prefume for the county, upon the death of his father. A little time after, he had another engagement with the royal troops, and obtaining the advantage, took fixty horfe and forty-eight prifoners, fome officers and arms.

As one of the army he was extremely folicitous to deftroy the king, and being appointed one of the commiffioners of the high court of juftice, he was both publicly and privately active in the ruin of his unhappy fovereign, being one of the committee to carry it on, and he fat every day in the Painted Chamber, and in Weftminfter Hall, except on the 17th and 25th days of January, and figned the warrant for execution.

The parliament, under the control of the army, named him one of the council of ftate in both 1649 and 1650, but he never more was trufted; a mutual jealoufy taking place, he hated Cromwell, and that great man defpifed him; he was deprived of his government of Nottingham Caftle; and at length it was ordered to be demolifhed by its laft governor, Captain Poulton, though it had been repaired at a very great ex-

pence, and rebuilt in a very beautiful manner:
it is obfervable, that a great part had been taken
down, and the iron, and other materials, fold by
King Charles I. juft before the civil war.

He was now reduced to the ftate of a private
gentleman, from which the protector would not
permit him to again emerge; for when, in 1656,
he wifhed to be returned for the county of Nottingham, he was fo oppofed by the government,
that he loft his election.

When the republican government was reftored,
he again took his place in the long parliament
that re-affembled; and, to the great furprize of
all, extremely preffed the houfe to proceed againft
Sir Henry Vane, for not removing into the country, according to their order, though he was, it
was known, fo indifpofed, as not to be able without great danger of his life; but at this time he
had made his peace, through General Monk, with
King Charles II. though it is wonderful by what
means, for he had then no government, no important caftle to deliver up; he was not therefore put
in the exceptive claufe in the bill of indemnity as
one of the king's judges, which faved himfelf and
his family from public difgrace: but he was too
obnoxious to retain his feat in the convention parliament, or to go at large; he was therefore fent
prifoner to Deal Caftle, in Kent, where he died, and
his remains were fent down to Outhorpe, and buried in the vault he had long before prepared when
he rebuilt the church. In his religious principles
he fet out as a rigid prefbyterian; he afterwards

became a ftaunch independent, and probably he died in the communion of the church of England.

By his pardon he was enabled to leave his feat and manor of Outhorpe, and the manor of Salterford in the Foreft, with his acquired property, to his fon, Charles Hutchinfon, Efq.; but had he acted with a true patriotifm, when he faw the government likely to be deftroyed by the fword, by liftening to Lord Newcaftle's propofition, he might have entailed upon his family a moft diftinguifhed rank and a confequence, that, once loft, was never to be regained.

The family fold their large feat and eftate of Outhorpe about thirty years fince, when they removed to Woodhall Park, in Hatfield, Herts, which came to them by marriage with the heirefs of the Botelers; but the Rev. Julius Hutchefon, of Bowes, near Southgate, in Middlefex, about two or three years ago difpofed it to the Marquis of Salifbury, who has pulled down the old manfion, though the repairing of it had coft that gentleman from three to four thoufand pounds. This information the author received fince he wrote the life of this regicide, and alfo, that this lineal defcendant of his is in poffeffion of a MS. written by the widow of the guilty Mr. Hutchinfon, relative to the important times in which fhe lived: it was hoped that it would have been lent, to copy what muft have been highly gratifying to both the public, and the writer of thefe volumes; but he was not fortunate enough to obtain the perufal of it.

The Life of RICHARD INGOLDESBY, *Efq.*

RICHARD INGOLDESBY, Efq. was of a very genteel and ancient extraction in Lincolnfhire; a relation to the great character Cromwell, and went
all the lengths that the army had propofed to
themfelves.

He was appointed one of the king's judges, but
never fat any day except, as he faid, cafually as
he went to fpeak with fome that were there, in
the Painted Chamber, where they met to fign the
warrant of execution, and that then Cromwell
took his hand, and forced him, by guiding the
pen whilft he wrote his name; but he forgot to
fay that his feal was alfo forced from him, and
ufed.

He followed Oliver in all his fortunes, and was
made by him one of the lords of the upper houfe:
at the deftruction of the Cromwellian intereft, to
which he was very faithful, he cordially united in
the reftoration of monarchy, to which he feemed
ever attached after Oliver's diffolution of the long
parliament; and purfuing and feizing General

Lambert, the head of the republicans, it was fo
effential a fervice, that he defervedly obtained
the royal pardon, and he was permitted to enjoy
the ample eftate he had raifed out of the diftrac-
tions of his country; which, as generally happens to ill-acquired wealth, his fon and heir dif-

fipated, and died a penfioner in the Charter-houfe.

It was fingular that his regiment fent up to parliament, previous to the king's trial, a petition in the moft determined language againft the fovereign; fo well had he tutored them; but in fuch times as thefe were, it was laudable to purchafe the moft obnoxious characters. See more of this gentleman and his family in the Cromwell Memoirs.

The Life of HENRY IRETON, Esq.

HENRY IRETON, Esq. was defcended from a good family in Nottinghamfhire; he married a daughter of the celebrated Oliver Cromwell, and was one of the firft perfons in the parliament army, for whofe intereft he alike ufed his pen, or his fword; he has been juftly called the Caffius of the party; and he was a man that had fo great an averfion to the royal power, and fuch an un-daunted temper, that no danger could awe him; and he was by far the moft to be dreaded of the whole of the oppofers of King Charles I.

 He was the bufieft of any in this infamous mur-der of his fovereign; at whofe mock trial he was abfent only on the 12th, 17th, 18th, 24th, and 25th days, in the Painted Chamber, and he figned the warrant for execution.

He died in 1651, whilft lord deputy of Ireland, of the fatigues occafioned by his attending the fiege of Limerick: this, with never changing his cloaths, made him fo liable to be infected with the plague, that it co-operated to deftroy him.

Ireton was a man dear to the republicans, but extremely hateful to all others; he was a fangui-nary, violent man, who feemed to have wrenched from his frame every fentiment of humanity and tendernefs.

Had he furvived, Cromwell would have had

more difficulty to have brought him into his ambitious fchemes, than any other. He was the
father of that very eccentric character, Mrs. Ben-
difh : for the hiftories of both, I muft refer my
reader to the Cromwell Memoirs.

The Life of JOHN JONES, Esq.

JOHN JONES, Esq. was a brother-in-law to Cromwell, having married one of his sisters; he was undoubtedly a soldier of fortune, though he had a small property of his own, which he inherited from his ancestors. He was entirely in the commonwealth interest, which he constantly pursued, and no circumstance of life perhaps was more pleasing to him, than that in which he sat as a judge upon his sovereign.

He attended each day of the mock trial, except on the 10th, 13th, and 18th, in the Painted Chamber, and on the 22d in Westminster Hall, and he signed the warrant for destroying the devoted monarch.

Overawed by Oliver's superior genius, he acted entirely as he was directed by him, and became one of his lords; he joined the army in destroying the power of Richard, vainly flattering himself that he should be able, with his associates, to carry on the affairs of the nation in the way of a republic; but the people at length, tired of the confusion and disorder occasioned by the destruction of the legal government, with joy returned to where only they could remain in safety.

He paid the forfeiture of his crimes, being one of the regicides that was executed at the restoration, as an expiation for the blood of a sovereign, whom it was his duty to have defended, and not affifted in deftroying.

This unfortunate man was only raifed by his alliance with Cromwell to any fort of confequence; in himfelf he had neither fortune to command, nor a mind to force the attention of mankind, being a very weak, enthufiaftic fanatic. He was executed at Charing-crofs, October 16, 1660. In the Cromwell Memoirs a more particular account is given of him.

The Life of JOHN LAMBERT, *Esq.*

JOHN LAMBERT, Efq. was one of the moſt conſpicuous characters during the interregnum, and in point of military knowledge, equal perhaps to Fairfax, and inferior only to Cromwell.

He declined taking any part in the immediate deſtruction of the prince, whom his arms had greatly contributed to ruin.

Oliver could not win him over to his intereſt, though he ſtudied with the greateſt care ; and after his death he practiſed the ſame arts againſt Fleetwood, which Oliver had towards Fairfax, and with the ſame ſucceſs.

But the nation was extremely averſe to the continuance of the confuſion the want of a regular government had occaſioned, and he was in the end ſent to the Tower, from whence eſcaping, he flew to arms, but ſubmitted without reſiſtance to Ingoldſby, who had been ſent after him ; he was excepted out of the act of indemnity ; and died a priſoner in Guernſey.

Had he bounded his ambition, he would undoubtedly have preceded Monk in obtaining the ducal honours ; but his aim was the ſovereignty ; his whole policy had been to have the title and power of protector.

See more of him in the Cromwell Memoirs.

The Life of FRANCIS LASSELS, Esq.

FRANCIS LASSELS, Esq. was of a very ancient family in Yorkshire; he resided at Stank near Northallerton in that county, for which he was a committee-man both to the parliament, and the protector Oliver.

He went into the parliament army, and became a colonel; and in September 1648, he, and Colonel Bethel were sent to assist at the siege of Scarborough, because three hundred of the Walloons had been sent thither by the Prince of Wales, and they soon took the castle and town, with many prisoners.

He was intirely in the interest of the army, who procured his name to be put in the commission to try the king, and he sat in the Painted Chamber on January the 8th, 10th, 13th, 17th, 18th, 19th, 20th, 22d, 23d, and 25th, and in Westminster Hall the 20th and 22d; but he did not attend on the day when sentence was passed, nor signed the warrant, so that he was in no danger at the restoration, and was returned a member in the convention parliament, though a known republican.

He was probably in himself a very private gentleman, fit for no other employment than the part he took in the army, for his name never occurs but as a committee-man for his own county ever after; perhaps he had retired thither, and chose to reside upon his own paternal estate,

without interefting himfelf farther in government affairs, from which he was fo diftant. He
married Frances, daughter of Sir William St.
Quintin, created a baronet by King Charles I.

The Life of JOHN LENTHAL, Esq.

JOHN LENTHAL, Esq. was of Oxfordshire, the well-known speaker of the house of commons in the long parliament.

The junto who usurped the government could not in decency do less than put his name in the bill for constituting the high court of justice, because they pretended to act under the authority of that very parliament, at which he was the head; but as far as he did go with them, he had too much prudence to do what he knew no law permitted, and what every law forbade.

He survived the restoration and was then in the utmost disgrace; he died soon after with the greatest penitence for the sanction he had given to fraud, force, usurpation, and rapine.

His history is also given in the Cromwell Memoirs.

The Life of ROBERT LILBURNE, Esq.

ROBERT LILBURNE, Esq. was of very ancient and genteel family in Yorkshire: he early went into the parliament army, where, by the patronage of Cromwell he rose to be a colonel; and as his brother the well-known John Lilburne, of factious memory, had been fined for his conduct in the Star Chamber, it gave him a prodigious hatred to the court, and even the person of his majesty.

The regiment he commanded was supposed to be the most mutinous of any in the army, yet they agreed in 1647 to go, if called upon, into Ireland; he with Ireton, Okey, Rich, and Harrison, were soon after appointed to draw up some heads of advice to be presented to the general, by the council of war; stating that, " they acknowledged and promised due obedience to the " general, and requested he would remind the " parliament to consider, and resolve those things " which had been presented to them from the " army, and desiring that as soon as the necessary " great affairs should be done, that a period " might be set to the parliament.".

He defeated Sir Richard Tempest in Lancashire in the year 1648, where each party shewed great valour; he took six hundred of the horse, and three hundred others, and of the prisoners many were knights and gentlemen; a signal victory, when his own force was but six hundred in all; but, it is not to be supposed, that a wellcontefted engagement could be without his lofing fome, as Whitlock writes.

Finding however, that the Scots were entering England to join Langdale, he prudently drew nearer to Lambert's forces, and throughout the war he fhewed great bravery and conduct.

Under the immediate direction of Cromwell he fat as one of the king's judges, and attended in the Painted Chamber on the 15th, 17th, 19th, 23d, 25th, and 27th day of January; and all the days in Weftminfter Hall; and figned the warrant to carry into execution the full completion of the horrid bufinefs.

He attacked the loyal and truly great Earl of Derby in 1651 with three regiments, and defeated his lordfhip at Wiggan in Lancafhire; and fo completely, that of one thoufand five hundred men that he brought into the field, he hardly had thirty, when he efcaped to King Charles II. at Worcefter; th engagement lafted about an hour.

He was in 1653 appointed commander in chief in Scotland, which kingdom he greatly affifted in bringing to abfolute fubmiffion to the Englifh parliament; marching to the very extremity of the highlands, and was every where victorious; he remained there until 1654, and was as true to Cromwell, as he had been to the parliament, and perhaps much more pleafed in ferving the latter, than the former.

The protector not only continued him one of the committee of his divifion in Yorkfhire, and of the city of York, but gave him very great authority there under Lambert, the major-general; and when that gentleman fell into some discontent, and was superseded, that important office was conferred upon him, and he was well adapted for such an odious undertaking, for he packed juries, and was as assiduous in privately ruining the royalists as he had been openly in the field. When he had seized Lord Bellasyse at York in 1655, he wrote to Secretary Thurloe, to know his highness' farther pleasure about him; " for as I remember," says he, " that he was one " pricked down, I intreat your speedy answer " herein, and I shall be glad to know what you " do in general with such *kind of cattle.*" His conduct was particularly severe, especially against the *scandalous ministers,* by which we are to understand the orthodox loyal clergy.

Lord Fauconberg tells Henry Cromwell, the lord deputy of Ireland, in a letter dated April 20, 1658, that " Colonel Lilburne is at home a mal- " content, because General Monk has changed " some of his officers."

Upon the ruin of the protectorial power, he was one of the officers of the army, who went to the speaker Lenthal at the rolls, to acquaint him, that they would restore the parliament, and that they were devoted, as they expressed it, to the *good old cause*; but immediately after he joined the army interest, and was one of the council of officers who were to govern, until some other means were settled.

At the reftoration he was excepted abfolutely as to life and eftate, though he had furrendered himfelf; he was tried at the Seffions Houfe in the Old Bailey, October 16, 1660, and pleaded not guilty; but the facts of fitting the laft day, and figning the warrant for putting the king to death being proved, he was convicted; and being afked what he had to fay why fentence fhould not be paffed, he replied, " I fhall refer myfelf without " farther trouble to the court; my lord, I beg " the benefit of the proclamation."

Government which was wifely merciful, remitted the fentence, and fent him to the Ifle of St. Nicholas, near Plymouth, where he died in Auguft 1665, aged 52; happily his father was living at the time of his trial, fo that his children inherited Tuickley in the bifhoprick of Durham, their grandfather's eftate, and probably others in Yorkfhire.

This gentleman had two other brothers at leaft; John, one of them, the plague to King Charles I. the commonwealth, and Oliver the protector, was a lieutenant-colonel; another was Colonel Henry Lilburne, who left the parliament intereft, and was killed at Tinmouth fighting for King Charles I. dying with great refolution and gallantry, when deferted by all his men, " chufing " rather to fall honourably in that loyal action, " than to live longer under the tyranny and op- " preffion of the fectaries," of which his brother John became the champion. Captain Thomas Lilburne was in the fervice of the protector in

Scotland, and perhaps was another brother, if not, a near relation.

What a complicated misfortune was the civil war to this family, and what a heart-rending grief muſt it have been to their father; even Robert the regicide had little ſatisfaction in his northern tyranny whilſt it laſted, and which would make the laſt ſolitary years of his life paſs with many a ſorrowful, retroſpective ſigh.

The Life of PHILIP Lord LISLE.

PHILIP LORD LISLE was the eldeſt ſon and heir of Robert Sidney, Earl of Leiceſter, who oppoſed the government of King Charles I. He conſtantly joined in all the different ones that ſucceeded that monarch's death; but he was never the perſonal enemy, if ſuch a diſtinction is accurate, to the king; and therefore never joined the army, nor the junto of the parliament, in their violent actions againſt the life of that ill-fated monarch. As one of the protector Oliver's lords, his hiſtory appears in the Cromwell Memoirs: I ſhall, therefore, only remark, that he died in peace and honour in 1697-8.

END OF VOL. I.

CPSIA information can be obtained at www.ICGtesting.com
Printed in the USA
LVOW051359180312

273547LV00003B/21/P